My first wish is that you may really enjoy this book and my next wish is that you may remember where you borrowed it

GEORGE CHARLES WOLF

THE PHILOSOPHY OF MAN

THE PHILOSOPHY OF MAN

CHAPTER I

LIFE

PROLOGUE

Man, we observe, is a *living* being, a being endowed with life. At the very outset of our philosophical study of man, we shall endeavor to determine precisely what we mean when we say that a being *lives.* In our introductory and general view of reality, as presented in the philosophy of being,[1] we discovered that a limited being is necessarily composed of the act of existing (*esse*) and limiting essence. Moreover, we acquired an understanding of substance and accidents as the principles which underlie the manifold activities of a limited subject. We found, furthermore, that a corporeal substance must be a composite of substantial form (the specifying factor of the essence) and matter, which in some way is the individuating and limiting principle. It follows that man — since he is a being which is limited, multiplied within the species, and constantly changing — must be the subject of potential-actual composition in the three orders of existence, essence, and activity.

This same triple composition is found in all corporeal substances, even in those that are non-living. Man, however, is a *living* substance. Accordingly, the problem that arises at the beginning of our philosophical study of man is this: What do we understand when we say that man *lives?* Are the activities mani-

[1] See: Henri Renard, *The Philosophy of Being,* second edition (Milwaukee: Bruce, 1946) pp. 46–77.

fested by a living being — man, animal, or plant — merely a more perfect type of transient action? Do the operations of a living being, and in particular those of man, constitute its life? What is the first intrinsic principle from which the vital operations of a living being proceed? What is the metaphysical basis for the difference between the most general types of living beings, and to what type does man belong? These are some of the initial inquiries that must be made in a philosophy of man, and their solution is the aim and purpose of this chapter.

Division: There will be three questions. The first is concerned with the operations of living beings, the second with living beings themselves; the third question will be an inquiry into the general types of living beings.

Question I

OPERATIONS OF LIVING BEINGS

This question is divided into three articles in which we shall examine: (1) the immanence which characterizes the operations of living beings; (2) two general types of immanent action; (3) apparent immanent action.

ARTICLE I: The Operations Proper to Living Beings Are Immanent

Since the nature of a being is known through its operations,[2] it will be necessary, for the purpose of distinguishing living from non-living beings, to observe the general character of the operations

[2] Cf. *In III Sententiarum,* 35, 1, 1, ad 1^{m}.) ". . . since nothing acts except in so far as it is in act, the mode of action in every agent follows from its mode of existence." (*S. Th.,* I, 89, 1, *c.*) Cf. *Contra Gentes,* II, 79.

The Philosophy of Man

By HENRI RENARD, S.J.
CREIGHTON UNIVERSITY

Second Edition
Revised and Enlarged

By MARTIN O. VASKE, S.J.
MARQUETTE UNIVERSITY

THE BRUCE PUBLISHING COMPANY
MILWAUKEE

IMPRIMI POTEST:

LEO J. BURNS, S.J.
Praep. Prov. Wisconsinensis

NIHIL OBSTAT:

JOHN A. SCHULIEN,
Censor librorum

IMPRIMATUR:

✠ ALBERT G. MEYER,
Archiepiscopus Milwauchiensis
Dec. 13, 1955

(Fourth printing — 1956)

FOREWORD

THE PHILOSOPHY OF MAN is a textbook intended for use in a three-hour credit course in the curriculum of American colleges. Its aim is to present a synthesis of St. Thomas' philosophical reflections on man and thereby to lay a firm foundation for a science of morals.

In presenting such a synthesis, one may expect to encounter pedagogical difficulties of considerable magnitude. Some of these difficulties could be lessened, perhaps, by recasting the Angelic Doctor's thought in a modern setting, by rearranging his arguments according to the needs of a strictly philosophical order, and by isolating his philosophy from its theological context. But such a procedure would involve grave risks of mistaking his purpose, of weakening his doctrine, and even of misrepresenting his thought. One need only recall what M. Gilson has written on this subject — in his admirable work, *Le Thomisme* — to realize the hazards of presenting the philosophical content of St. Thomas' theological works in an order not their own.

Accordingly, the present revised edition of THE PHILOSOPHY OF MAN continues to follow in the main the order of the treatise *de homine* of the *Summa Theologica*. To make the book of greater service to the college student, explanations of certain difficult sections have been expanded, abstruse points relegated to the footnotes, and comprehensive summaries added at the end of each chapter.

It is suggested that the first three chapters be covered rapidly on first presentation, then taken at length and in detail by way of review at the end of the course. Some teachers may prefer to begin with Chapter III after presenting the first article (on immanent operation) of the first question of Chapter I. This can be done without serious difficulty. Where necessary to effect a saving of class time, we suggest that the chapter on habits be omitted, especially if these are taught at length in the Ethics courses.

This little book was written to continue the exposition of the philosophy of St. Thomas begun with the publication of *The Philosophy of Being* and now supplemented by *The Philosophy of God* and *The Philosophy of Morality*. The series, far from being intended as a substitute for the writings of the Angelic Doctor, is meant to be an aid to American youth in their endeavor to understand his profound existential thought. In order to prepare the student to read the works of St. Thomas directly, many classic passages from his principal works have been incorporated into the body of the text. It is believed and fervently hoped that through this direct and intimate contact with one of the greatest thinkers of all time many young minds may be brought to contemplate and to love Truth.

H. R.
M. V.

INTRODUCTION

The Philosophy of Man is a metaphysical study of man. It is not concerned with biological problems; it does not examine those experimental questions which come within the scope of the science of psychology. Rather, our philosophical treatise will study man as man, that is, man as a rational being.

To make such a study possible, the experimental method, which limits itself to quantitative measurements of the sensible material elements in psychic activity, cannot suffice. It is true that we must always begin with data obtained through sense operations, for all natural knowledge in man has its roots in experience. The philosopher, however, seeks a knowledge that goes beyond the mere sensible manifestations of the real. By means of a reflection upon his intellectual insights into the data of sense, the philosopher is able to arrive at a profound understanding of existing reality. Such a mode of inquiry, when directed toward man, will be an intellectual endeavor to obtain a true knowledge, not only of human nature, but also of what is needed to understand the existing nature, the rational supposit, the person.

The central problems of the philosophy of man lie, not on the essential, but on the existential level; and, consequently, any solution which fails to rise to this same level is necessarily inadequate and incomplete. The problem of man's unity, for example, is fundamentally an existential problem; for a being has unity as it has "to be." Moreover, it is because man's act of existing (*esse*) is the act of living (*vivere*) that the existent man, despite his manifold immanent operations, is a perfect unit. Man's soul, we shall discover, is a subsisting form; although informing matter, it has existence independently of matter. Knowledge, we shall find, is an immanent operation in which the knower is the known;

knowledge is intentional existence. All these momentous truths are existential solutions to fundamental problems that arise in our study of man.

Accordingly, a philosophy of man must make use of metaphysical methods and metaphysical principles, not only in the discovery of its findings, but also in organizing its conclusions into a unified body of knowledge. The result will be an ordered progression of absolutely certain knowledge formulated by way of judgment (*via iudicii*); not a mere summary of principles and conclusions derived by way of discovery (*via inventionis*), which would lack the stature of true science or wisdom.

Indeed, it would seem that the true philosophic method proceeds by way of judgment supported and accompanied by the way of discovery. The process of philosophizing is not an initial discovery of reality. In teaching students of college age, we may suppose that they have acquired at least a confused knowledge of life, of the soul, of knowledge itself. Hence, we are not teaching in a complete intellectual vacuum; we are not attempting to communicate knowledge to intellects that are still *tabulae rasae*. Rather, as teachers of philosophy, our chief function is to help the student to clarify and organize his knowledge, to build upon the knowledge already possessed, and to link this knowledge to first principles. Indeed, the student has not philosophized in the strict sense of the term until he has seen the absolutely necessary nexus of the conclusions acquired by way of discovery with the first principles which are absolutely true. For this process, the way of discovery cannot suffice; the way of judgment—the way of resolution to first principles, even to metaphysical first principles—is needed.[1]

In beginning our study of man by facing and solving the problem of man's existential unity, we are enabled to avoid at the

[1] ". . . human reasoning, according to the way of inquiry and discovery, proceeds from certain things absolutely understood — namely, the first principles; and, again, in the way of judgment, returns by resolution to the first principles, in the light of which it examines what it has discovered." (*Summa Theologica*, I, 79, 8, *c*.)

outset the pitfalls of a Cartesian dualism, from which in modern times two pure but erroneous positions on the nature of man have taken their source: Idealism and Materialism. For, when we lose sight of the truth that man's unity results from the oneness of the act of existing (*esse*), which is "to live" (*vivere*), the natural outcome of our study will be an excessive stressing of the distinction between human operations, and, in the last analysis, an excessive emphasis of the distinction between the essential principles in man. In the end, the student becomes so impressed by the distinctions and, we might almost say, the opposition among the diverse kinds of vital operations as to fail to realize the import of man's existential unity. This mode of procedure can readily engender in many a student's mind an exaggerated dualism, which may eventually find its resolution in some form of Subjectivism or Materialism. The history of philosophy after Descartes gives eloquent witness to resolutions of this kind.

It seems to us, therefore, that the order adopted by the more recent writers of textbooks on the philosophy of man is not an improvement over the procedure of St. Thomas. Indeed, taking the modern mind as it is, such an order of presentation may prove a definite danger. By beginning the discussion with separate sections on the vegetative, sensitive, and intellectual operations, the fundamental problem of unity is often relegated to the very end. Consequently, in the last classes of the course, the student is expected to revise all his notions of distinction among parts which heretofore had seemed the major topic of the treatise. Moreover, owing to lack of time, the important discussion on the nature of the soul and its union with the body must often be omitted or at best hurriedly studied.

We have elected to follow the order set by St. Thomas because it seems metaphysically true and pedagogically sound. Consequently, after a general discussion of the operations of living beings and of life, we shall begin at once with the problem of the unity of man.

CONTENTS

proper to living beings. The philosopher must search for a common element in the activities found only in living beings. He discovers this common element in the fact that their operations are *immanent.* This statement must be explained.

Preliminary Notion of Immanent Operation: Non-living beings, we observe, move only when moved by another. Living beings, on the contrary, move themselves; they are the causes of their own local movement, or, at least, of their own vegetative changes[3] — nutrition, growth, and reproduction. When such a being is no longer capable of causing its own motion, it is no longer considered to live.

> . . . We can gather to what things "to live" (*vivere*) belongs, and to what it does not, from such things as manifestly possess life (*vivere*). Now "to live" manifestly belongs to animals. . . . We must, therefore, distinguish living from non-living things by comparing them to that by reason of which animals are said to live; and this it is in which life is manifested first and remains last. We say then that an animal begins to live when it begins to have *motion* (*motus*) *of itself* [italics added]; and as long as such motion appears in it, so long is it considered to live. When it no longer has any motion of itself, but is moved only by another, then its life is said to fail, and the animal to be dead. Whereby it is clear that those beings are properly called living that move themselves by some kind of motion.[4]

More Precise Notion: It is obvious that the notion of vital operation obtained in this first consideration is derived from the *material* self-motion of corporeal living beings. This preliminary notion must be refined and made more exact so as to include: (1) the sensory operations, which, as we shall discover, are somewhat immaterial, and (2) the intellective operations, which are strictly immaterial, that is to say, spiritual. In this precise sense, we

---

[3] The vegetative operations — nutrition, augmentation, and generation — will be discussed in detail at a later stage in this course.

[4] *S. Th.*, I, 18, 1, *c.*

understand immanent operations to be those "whose principles are within the operator, and in virtue of which [principles] the operator moves itself to operation."[5]

> . . . For this is the first reason why some beings are said to live, namely because they are perceived to have within themselves something that moves them in some way; whence, the name "life" has come to be applied to all beings that have within themselves the principle of their own operation; whence, too, some beings are said to live because they have intellection or sensation or volition, and not merely because they move locally or grow.[6]

The operation, therefore, which distinguishes living beings from those that are non-living is self-operation, whether it be material, partly immaterial, or spiritual. Accordingly, a living being is one that has within itself the principle of its own operation.[7]

Transient and Immanent Action Compared: A limited being is not its end; rather, it is in potency to its end and acts to attain this end. Only by action of some sort can it achieve its full development, its full actualization. Now action is of two general kinds: the transient action which was studied in the philosophy of being,[8] and the immanent operation of living beings considered in this chapter. When we compare these two types of action, we note several important points of difference:

a) Transient action—for example, the action of heating—is in the *patient;* an extrinsic agent acts upon a distinct patient. The vital activity of a living being, on the other hand, is intrinsic to the *agent;* the action is not "received" in a distinct patient.

---

[5] *S. Th.,* I, 18, 2, ad 2^m.

[6] *De Veritate,* IV, 8.

[7] It should be noted that our consideration is concerned primarily with the self-operation of living beings that are limited. Such operations can truly be termed self-*motion,* since there is a real passage from potency to act, in as much as the limited nature is perfected by its own operation. On the other hand, in God operation is one with the Divine act of being and consequently does not imply a motion or change.

[8] Cf. *The Philosophy of Being,* pp. 137–140.

Rather, the vital operation remains "in" the agent, that is to say, it begins and terminates in the agent, and for that reason this type of action is aptly called *im*manent.[9]

b) Transient action is the predicament "action" (motion as from an agent). Immanent action is a *quality*.

c) Transient action is the act, the perfection, of a being in *potency;* it implies the passing of a patient from potency to act. Immanent action is the act, the perfection, of a being *in act;* it is the act, the perfection, of the agent, not of a distinct patient.[10]

Living Beings Are Supposits: Transient action, we have seen, implies more than one supposit: agent and patient. Immanent action, on the contrary, is action within a single supposit; in this type of action, a complete, distinct, individual substance (a supposit) perfects itself by its own operation. Although such a being may have many distinct parts (and many activities), these parts act primarily and directly for the good of the whole, the existing substantial unit; the finality of the various parts (and activities) is primarily the perfection or good of the whole, not of the parts alone. Since the living being *acts* as a substantial unit, we know that it *is* a substantial unit (a supposit), for as a thing is so does it act (*agere sequitur esse*).

In brief: those beings are living which act immanently; and since immanent action necessarily is action within a supposit which

---

[9] ". . . action is twofold. Actions of one kind pass to external matter, as to heat or to cut, while actions of the other kind remain in the agent, as to understand, to sense, and to will. The difference between them is this, that the former action is the perfection, not of the agent that moves, but of the thing moved; whereas the latter action is the perfection of the agent." (*S. Th.*, I, 18, 3, ad 1^{m}.) Another text considers the principle of operation. "In things which are moved or perform some action there is this difference: that some have the principle of their motion or operation within themselves; but others have this principle outside themselves." (*De Ver.*, XXIV, 1, *c.*)

[10] ". . . an action of this kind [immanent action] is the act [perfection] of the agent; and, although motion is an act of the imperfect, that is, of what is in potency, this kind of action is an act of the perfect, that is to say, *of what is in act* [italics added]. . . ." (*S. Th.*, I, 18, 3, ad 1^{m}.)

it perfects, living beings must be supposits; that is to say, a living being must be a perfect existential unit.[11]

ARTICLE II: Two General Types of Immanent Action

Act of the Perfect: Immanent actions are of two general types. The first, the *act of the perfect,* comprises the sensitive and intellectual functions. The act of knowledge, for example, is strictly immanent, in no way transient; it is the operation of a knowing power which is in act to place the operation called knowledge. Consequently, in the very act of knowing, there is no passing of the faculty of knowledge from potency to act, for a being is changeable only in so far as it is in potency. Rather, the operation flows ("emanates") from the faculty, which is "perfect"[12] in the sense that it is in act.

Act of the Imperfect: Vegetative functions are a less perfect type of immanent action and hold a midway position between the perfection of the act of a perfect being (sensitive and intellective operations) and the imperfection of transient action, thus partaking somehow in the nature of both. The vegetative operations bear a certain resemblance to transient action, for the perfection of one part of the vegetative unit is communicated to another part which did not previously possess it. The quantitative (integral) parts of the organism — roots, trunk, leaves, for example — are distinct one from another. One part in act causes another part to pass from potency to act; thus there is a certain transience in vegetative activity. On the other hand, since the entire being is a strict unit, that is to say, a supposit, the vegetative operation begins and terminates in the agent. The operation must, there-

[11] A mechanical unit, for example, an automobile, in a certain sense moves itself, but it is not a perfect unit, a supposit. Consequently, it is not a living being and its "self-motion" is but a series of transient actions. Although a corporeal *living* being may have many quantitative parts, it is an existential unit, a supposit existing by one substantial "to be."

[12] "To sense and to understand are a certain type of motion in so far as motion is said to be the act of a perfect [being]." (*S. Th.,* II–II, 179, 1, ad 3^{m}.)

fore, be called an immanent operation. This type of immanent action Aquinas calls the *act of an imperfect being.*

> . . . Those beings are properly called living that move themselves by some kind of movement (*motus*), whether it be movement properly so called, as the act of the imperfect, that is, of a thing which exists in potency, is called movement; or movement in a more general sense, as when said of the act of the perfect, as understanding and sensing are called movement. . . .[13]

ARTICLE III: Apparent Immanent Action

There are certain corporeal beings which seem to move themselves and yet cannot be called living; their activity is only apparently immanent. Smoke, for example, will rise of itself; a stone will fall naturally to the ground. Evidently, such motions cannot be called the operations of a living being. What, then, distinguishes them from the truly immanent actions found in other corporeal beings, as, for example, the vegetative processes in plants or the local movement of animals? To answer this question it is necessary to distinguish two types of local movement.

Local Motion and Locomotion: A vital act not only begins in the agent, but must somehow terminate in the same supposit. Now local motion, of itself — even when caused by the nature itself, that is to say, when it begins from within — does not terminate in the same supposit. In itself, therefore, local motion is not an immanent but a transient operation. Only that type of local motion proceeding from a sentient being which we call *loco*motion denotes that the subject of the motion is living. The reason is that local movement of this kind presupposes some sort of *knowledge* and *desire,* some type of awareness. These are obviously immanent actions. On the other hand, local motion in inanimate beings, even when proceeding in some way from the nature itself — as in the case of the rising smoke and the falling stone — does not pre-

[13] *S. Th.,* I, 18, 1, *c.*

suppose an immanent operation in the nature preceding and directing the motion. Such local motion in non-living beings flows immediately from the determination of their nature to their end. Hence, St. Thomas insists that although these natures really "move of themselves (*moventur seipsis*), they are not moved by themselves (*a seipsis*),"[14] that is to say, they do not move locally through immanent actions preceding and accompanying this local motion.

Activity With "Static" Finality: Another reason may be given why the local motion of non-sentient bodily beings cannot be called immanent or self-perfecting operation. It is the perfection of these bodies to be at rest (or, at least, to be in a state of equilibrium); it is their nature to move only in order to seek rest. Their nature is not an intrinsic principle of constant, dynamic action which is perfective of the nature. Rather, these beings are inclined to move only when displaced from their natural conditions or from their proper place.[15] This type of tendency or inclination we shall call "static" finality.

Activity With "Dynamic" Finality: The true immanent action of living corporeal beings, on the contrary, is a constant activity. Their nature is an inclination, not to a state of rest, but to a fuller development and actualization by self-perfective action that does not cease. Indeed, cessation from these operations does not perfect

[14] "*Eorum autem quorum principium motus et operis in ipsis est, quaedam talia sunt quod ipsa seipsa movent, sicut animalia; quaedam autem quae non movent seipsa, quamvis in seipsis sui motus aliquod principium habent, sicut gravia et levia: non enim seipsa movent, cum non possint distingui in duas partes, quarum una sit movens et alia mota sicut in animalibus invenitur; quamvis motus eorum consequatur aliquod principium in seipsis, scilicet formam; quam quia a generante habent dicuntur a generante moveri per se. . . . sed a removente prohibens per accidens; et haec moventur seipsis, sed non a seipsis.*" (*De Ver.*, XXIV, 1.)

[15] ". . . to bodies whether light or heavy, movement does not belong except in so far as they are displaced from their natural conditions, and are out of their proper place; for when they are in the place that is proper and natural to them, they are at rest. . . . Furthermore, heavy and light bodies are moved by an extrinsic mover, either generating them and giving them form, or removing obstacles from their way. . . . They do not therefore move themselves as do living bodies." (*S. Th.*, I, 18, 1, ad 2^{m}.) Cf. *De Ver.*, XXIV, 1, 1. Modern physical theory would explain such occurrences in terms of gravitational forces whose action is reduceable to some kind of transient, not immanent, action.

the living nature; rather, cessation implies that this nature is no longer in existence, that it no longer lives.[16] The inclination of a living corporeal nature to an end to be attained by constant vital motion we shall term "dynamic" finality.

Question II

LIVING BEINGS

This question is divided into three articles in which we shall discover that: (1) for living beings to exist is to live; (2) the existence of living beings is life; (3) living being is an analogous notion.

ARTICLE I: For the Living, "To Be" Is To Live

Problem: Living beings are those which operate immanently; they are the principles, the agents, of their own operations. Now an agent acts in so far as it is in act. Living beings, since they are true agents with respect to their own vital operations, must, therefore, be *in act* to act immanently. The philosopher, in his inquiry into the nature of living beings, desires to know what is the first, intrinsic, *actual* principle that enables a living being to operate immanently.[17] He wants to ascertain what is the root factor in a living being by which it is in act as a vital agent. This first, intrinsic,[18] actual principle in a living being, from which its immanent action proceeds, cannot be:

[16] ". . . plants and other living things move with vital movement, in accordance with the disposition of their nature, but not by approaching thereto, or by receding from it, for in so far as they recede from such movements, so far do they recede from their natural disposition." (*S. Th.*, I, 18, 1, ad 2^{m}.)

[17] It should be noted at this juncture that philosophers will give diverse answers to this question depending on their philosophy of being. An essentialist philosophy will find this first radical principle in the essential order. An existential philosophy worthy of the name must go beyond a consideration of the essence and look to the absolutely first order of existence for a satisfactory explanation of the operations of living beings.

[18] We are not concerned with an inquiry into the absolutely first *extrinsic* principle of operation of living beings. From *The Philosophy of Being* we know that

a) An *accident,* for an accident is "that to which is due a 'to be' in another"; an accident is not a first principle. We must, therefore, look to the substantial order to discover the primary principle of vital operation. Hence, to say that to live is but to act immanently is, obviously, a superficial answer to a profound existential problem.

b) The first principle of vital activity cannot be *matter,* for matter is a *potential* principle in the essential order; moreover, if matter were the first principle of immanent action, all corporeal beings would exercise the operations of life.

c) This principle cannot be *substantial form,* which, although an actual principle in the essential order, is a potential principle in the order of existence.

Solution: By a process of exclusion, we find that we must rise to the existential order for the complete solution of our problem. Now in that order, the actual principle is "to be" (*esse*). We conclude that the first, intrinsic, actual principle by virtue of which a living being operates immanently is the existential act, "to be."[19] Accordingly, in the most radical sense, "to live" is not immanent operation.[20] Rather, to live is to exist so perfectly that

God is the first principle and last end of all reality outside Himself. Living creatures, however, are true principles of their own operation. See: *The Philosophy of Being,* pp. 133–136.

[19] We do not deny the causality of the substantial form as the essential principle of the operations of a living being. The substantial form is the intrinsic cause of the limitation of existence to a definite type of being, and in this case to a type of *living* being. We must, however, keep in mind that the actuality even of form results from the existential act, "to be." Nevertheless, in our study of man, we shall direct most of our consideration, not to the act of existing, but to man's substantial form, the soul. The reason is that to us, "to be" is not directly intelligible beyond the fact that it actuates the essence, making it exist. Hence, having established the fundamental truth that "to live" is the "to be" of a living being, we shall proceed by a study of the substantial form, the soul, in order to understand what the living rational animal we call man really is. None the less, in our study of man's form, we must not lose sight of this basic existential truth: a being lives, not because of something superimposed or engrafted upon its nature, but because of its existential actuation, its "to be" (*esse*). For a living being, to exist is to live.

[20] This statement is not true of the divine "To Live." For, since God is the pure act of existence, in Him "to be" and to act are identical.

the nature is enabled to perform the operations termed immanent. In brief: the "to live" of a living being is the substantial "to be."[21]

> . . . For since an animal is said to be a living being because it has a soul whereby it has "to be," as it were by its proper form, it follows that "to live" is nothing but a particular kind of "to be" resulting from a particular kind of form.[22]

Not every "to be," however, is a "to live"; but every "to live" is a "to be"—a "to be" so perfect that the existing nature[23] can enact immanent operations. "To live," therefore, is not a power distinct from and superadded to an existing being; rather, it is that type of "to be" which a being must have in order to move itself to immanent action.[24]

Argument: A being acts in so far as it is in act. The operations of any being, therefore, are due fundamentally to this, that it exists—that it is or has a "to be"—since the act of being is "to be." Any being, then, which performs the operations of life (any living being) does so precisely because it is in act, because it has a "to be."

But the act (perfection) of a living being is "to live."

Therefore, "to live" is the "to be" of a living being.

Predication: "To live" must be predicated not only of living creatures but of God as well. We must remember, however, that creatures are not their own "to live," since they are not their own "to be." God, on the contrary, since He is His own "To Be," is His own "To Live."[25] "To live," therefore, is *directly* predicated of God, *indirectly* of creatures.

---

21 "*. . . vivere viventis est esse . . .*" (*De Ver.*, IV, 8); "*vivere autem viventium est ipsum esse eorum . . .*" (*Summa Contra Gentes*, I, 98); "*. . . vivere dicitur esse viventium . . .*" (*S. Th.*, II–II, 179, 1, ad 1m).

22 *C. G.*, I, 98.

23 Nature here designates the essence considered as the principle of operation.

24 "*Illud vivere dicemus quod habet res prout est movens seipsam ad operationem aliquam.*" (*De Ver.*, IV, 8.)

25 "*Deus autem est suum esse. Est igitur suum vivere et sua vita.*" (*C. G.*, I, 98.)

ARTICLE II: For the Living, Existence Is Life

Primary Meaning of "Life": "To be" is the act, the perfection of being;[26] it is the concrete actuation of the essence. Now the act of existing is not an abstraction, but a reality attained in the existential judgment. "Existence," however, is an abstract conception; in this knowledge we attain the act of existing, the "to be" (*esse*), as if it were an essence, a "whatness," a form. This defect in our conceptual knowledge of existence results from the natural limitation of the human intellect, which can properly conceive only corporeal essences, not "to be." Consequently, in its effort to reach a more complete understanding of "to be," the human intellect is forced to express its knowledge of this supreme perfection as if it were an abstract quiddity or essence. Hence, we ordinarily speak not of "to be," but of *existence.*

The same holds true as regards our notion of life. Just as "existence" signifies abstractly the concrete "to be" (*esse*), so does "life" signify abstractly the concrete "to live."[27] Moreover, since "to live" is identical with the "to be" of living beings, it follows that *life* is nothing else than the "to be" of a living being[28] conceived abstractly, as if it were an essence or form.

Hence, life is not a form or essence; yet we must admit that, owing to the weakness of the human intellect, we are forced to conceive it as if it were a form or essence, precisely because our concept of "life" is the result of an abstraction from the concrete "to live."

St. Thomas further points out that life and "to live" are not related as essence and "to be." Rather, their relation is the same

---

[26] See: *The Philosophy of Being*, p. 48.

[27] "*Vita enim viventis est ipsum vivere in quadam abstractione significatum; sicut cursus non est secundum rem aliud quam currere. . . .*" (*C. G.*, I, 98.)

[28] "*. . . vita dicitur dupliciter. Uno modo ipsum esse viventis. . . . Alio modo, dicitur vita ipsa operatio viventis. . . .*" (*S. Th.*, I–II, 3, 2, ad 1^{m}.)

as that between race (*cursus*) and "to run," of which the former signifies the act of running in the abstract, the latter in the concrete. Accordingly, we cannot argue that since "to live" is "to be," life is essence.[29]

From this discussion we conclude that in the most profound meaning of the term *life is the "to be" of a living being conceived abstractly.*

Predication: We are now in a position to solve the problem concerning the mode in which we predicate "life" of God and living creatures. Like "to be," *life* is said of God *directly;* God *is* life. Of living creatures, on the contrary, life can be affirmed only *indirectly;* living creatures *have* life. The reason for this should now be obvious. In God "to live," which is "to be," is identical with the Divine Essence. The contrary holds true as regards living creatures. Since they are limited, they are composed of essence and "to be." They are not their own existence; rather, they *have* existence distinct from their essence. Since the existence of a living being is life, living creatures *have* life, that is to say, life is predicated of them indirectly.

Secondary Meanings of "Life": 1. The term "life" is used perhaps most frequently to signify the operations[30] of living beings, as when we say that a certain person is "full of life."

2. Sometimes the term is used to name a substance or substances from which vital operations proceed, as in the statement, "There may be life on Mars." Obviously, such an affirmation does not refer primarily to the immanent operations that would manifest the substance[31] that lives; rather, it refers first and foremost to the substance itself which is the principle of vital action and which is manifested as living by some external appearance.

---

[29] "*. . . vita non hoc modo se habet ad vivere, sicut essentia ad esse; sed sicut cursus ad currere, quorum unum significat actum in abstracto, aliud in concreto. Unde non sequitur, si vivere sit esse, quod vita sit essentia.*" (*S. Th.*, I, 54, 1 ad 2m.)

[30] Cf. *ibid.*, I–II, 3, 2, ad 1m.

[31] Since substance is the first object of knowledge, concrete operations without a subject would be unintelligible.

> . . . Our intellect, which knows the essence of a thing as its proper object, derives its knowledge from sense, of which the proper objects are external accidents. Hence, from external appearances we come to the knowledge of the essence of things. . . . The same must be said of life. The name is taken from a certain external appearance, namely, self-movement, yet not precisely to signify this, but rather *a substance to which self-movement and the application of itself to any kind of operation belong naturally* [italics added]. To live, accordingly, is nothing else than to exist in such a nature; and this it is that life signifies though abstractly. . . . Sometimes, however, life is used less properly for the operations from which its name is taken, and thus the Philosopher says that to live is principally to sense or to understand. . . .[32]

3. At times the term "life" is used to express an habitual manner of action, as when we speak of the "contemplative and active life," a "virtuous life," or a "self-indulgent life." In these instances, the term "life" stands for the complexus of immanent operations proceeding from a rational agent which by repeated actions has acquired definite habits of action either good or evil.

4. Sometimes the term "life" is used to signify vegetative operations, as when we say that man has "existence, *life,* sensation, and understanding."

It will be clear from this discussion that the term "life," like the term "being," is capable of various significations. Needless to say, this diversity of meanings has been the source of much confusion among philosophers in their efforts to solve the problem of life.

ARTICLE III: "Living Being" — an Analogous Notion

The Notion: Being (*ens*) cannot be defined as "to be" (*esse*), nor as essence alone; rather, being is that which *is,* that whose act (perfection) is "to be." Since the "to be" of a *living* being is "to

[32] *S. Th.,* I, 18, 2, *c.*

live," we may say that a living being (*vivens*) is that whose act is "to live."[33] When the term "being" is used as a subject, it signifies no definite essence, no definite "to be," no definite relation of essence to "to be." By a special mode of "abstraction"[34] our intellect forms a notion (*ratio*) of essence (any essence) indeterminately related to "to be." Such a notion indeterminately embraces all reality and is, therefore, termed a transcendental notion. When, however, "being" is actually said of a definite subject, the relation of essence to "to be" is made definite by a more explicit apprehension of the essence. This is to say that when we actually affirm "being" of a concrete, existing subject, the term stands for a definite, individual essence — there are no indefinite essences — with a definite relation to a definite "to be." We may express this same truth with greater stress on the existential factor by saying that the term "being," when referred to an individual existent, signifies a definite "to be" proportioned to a definite essence: by a relation of identity in the case of God; by a relation of real distinction in limited beings.

In like manner, the notion "living being" is formed by "abstracting" from all definite determination of the relation of essence to a "to be" which is a "to live." The resulting notion, which is quasi-transcendental — since it indefinitely embraces all living beings — is that of *essence indeterminately related to "to live"*; or, if one wishes to emphasize the existential element, the notion is that of "to live" proportioned to essence.

Predication: In predicating "living being" of a concrete, individual existent, we must make definite the relation of the essence to "to live." There are always two factors involved in such an affirmation: (1) essence related to (2) "to live," but the relation between these two factors varies in every living being, and hence must vary in every affirmation. For no two living beings are entirely the same; yet no two living beings are entirely different.

[33] We should recall that "to live" is a more perfect type of "to be."

[34] We are concerned here with the "abstraction" of *ens transcendentale*, not of *ens commune*. See: *The Philosophy of Being*, p. 89 *et seq*. Cf. p. 182 of this work.

We express this similarity by affirming that an essence is related to "to live"; we express the difference by making definite the relation existing between the two terms, essence and "to live." In God, for example, the relation is that of identity; God is a living being whose Essence is identified with His "To Live." In creatures there is a real distinction between the terms of the relation: they are not "to live"; they merely possess it. The analogous predication of "living being"—by the analogy of proportionality—may be shown by a diagram as follows:

God is a living being	To live (Life) is to Divine Essence	real identity
	as	
Angel is a living being	to live (life) is to angelic essence (pure form)	real distinction
	as	
Man is a living being	to live (life) is to human essence (spiritual form and matter, etc.)	real distinction

We conclude that *living being* is an analogous notion. It signifies that whose act is "to live." It can be directly predicated of all living beings by an analogy of proportionality.[35]

[35] The following diagram may prove helpful in pointing out the relation between "to live," life, and living being.

Concrete Act	*Abstract Conception*	*Analogous Notion*
"to be"	existence	"being"
"to live"	life (in the most profound sense)	"living being"

Question III

GENERAL TYPES OF LIVING BEINGS

This question is divided into two articles of which the first will formulate the general principle for the division of beings into their most generic types; the second article will be an application of this principle to the world of living things.

ARTICLE I: Metaphysical Foundation for Distinction of Living Beings

There are different types of immanent action more or less perfect. Since the mode of operation manifests the mode of being, we conclude that there are different types of living beings, different modes of living, that is, of participating in "to live" (*vivere*). In a noteworthy article of the *Summa Theologica,*[36] St. Thomas gives us a metaphysician's panoramic view of the world of living beings, beginning with the lowest forms — plants — and rising even to the supreme living being, whose very essence is "to live" — God. By indicating the causal factors implied in the various types of immanent actions, the Angelic Doctor distinguishes living beings into their broadest types: vegetative, sensitive, and intellectual.

General Principle: ". . . A thing is said to live in so far as it operates of itself and not as moved by another [is independent of a mover]. Hence the more perfectly this [self-operation and independence from a mover] is found in anything, the more perfect is life in that being."[37] The deduction about God is immediate: since God is Pure Act (the First Mover Unmoved), He is in no way dependent on another for His self-operation. It follows that life ("to live") is most perfect in God.

---

[36] *S. Th.,* I, 18, 3. This discussion is a paraphrase of the article of St. Thomas.
[37] *Loc. cit.*

Limited beings, on the other hand, since they are not pure existential act, must somehow be moved in order to move themselves, that is, in order to cause their own immanent operations. Now dependence on an extrinsic mover varies fundamentally in as much as all or only some of the causal factors of action depend on the extrinsic cause. The more perfectly the living being is independent of the extrinsic mover as regards these elements of action, the more perfectly will such a being participate in the perfection of living.

Causal Factors of Action: In any action, including immanent operations, there are three causal factors, some or all of which may be determined by the vital agent itself or by an extrinsic mover. These elements are: (*a*) the *end,* which moves the agent by being desired, (*b*) the *form* or definite direction which the action takes, and (*c*) the actual carrying out or *execution* (efficient causality) of the action.[38] The more perfectly and completely these factors are determined by the operating subject itself, the more perfect the operation will be, and, accordingly, the more perfect will be the being from which the action proceeds.

ARTICLE II: Application of the Principle to Living Things

Plants: There are living beings which move themselves only with respect to the *execution* (efficient causality) of their actions. The form of the action and the end of the action are determined for them by the nature of the being. These are the plants.

Animals: There are living beings which move themselves not only as regards the execution of their action but even as regards the *specification* (formal causality) of their action. These are the animals. The form which determines their action is acquired by their own operation, through their own sense knowledge. They do not, however, move themselves as regards the end (finality) of

[38] The material cause is not considered here, because it is not a perfecting but rather a limiting element in an action.

their action. Thus a hungry dog is determined to pursue the hare which comes within its field of vision. No matter how perfect their action may be, brute animals cannot propose to themselves the end of their operation, for this end has been implanted in them by nature; and by natural instinct they are moved necessarily to an action through the form acquired by the senses.

Men: Finally, there are living beings which move themselves as regards all three factors of operation: execution, specification, and even as to the immediate *finality* of their actions. These are the rational animals (men), which have the power of proposing to themselves proximate ends[39] to which they freely move themselves. Consequently, their actions are essentially more perfect than the actions of brute animals; and, since the mode of vital operation manifests the mode of living ("to live"), men are specifically distinct from the brute.

A fundamental limitation, however, characterizes man. Although man is able to determine his particular, immediate ends, he is unable to determine his last end. His intellect is necessarily moved to know being and in the light of being to form the first principles which it must accept. His will is necessarily determined to the last end, happiness, which it cannot but desire. This necessary determination of man's nature to the last end manifests his dependence upon an extrinsic intellectual cause, that is, upon a Being whose nature is its end, whose action is its very nature. God, therefore, is in no way dependent on another for His immanent operation, and, consequently, He is the most perfect living being.

We conclude that there are three specifically distinct modes of participating in the act of living: vegetative, sensitive, and intellectual. Man, we shall see, is a highly complex living being and manifests all three modes of living.

---

[39] We shall show later, in the treatise on freedom, that the proposing of an end can only be done by an intellect, whose province it is to know the end and the means to the end, and to order a means to the end. Cf. *De Ver.*, XXIV, 1, *c.*

SUMMARY

Question I

OPERATIONS OF LIVING BEINGS

To understand the nature of living beings we must observe the operations that belong to living beings precisely as living.

Article I: *The Operations Proper to Living Beings Are Immanent*

1. The operations proper to living beings *begin and terminate* in the operator. Accordingly, those beings are living that are the principle of their own operation.

2. Unlike transient actions, immanent operations are the *act* of a being *in act;* they are the perfection of the *agent,* not of a distinct patient. They belong to the predicament "quality."

3. Since the operations of living beings are immanent, living beings must be perfect existential units, that is, *supposits.*

Article II: *Two General Types of Immanent Action*

1. Act of the *Perfect:* Sensitive and intellective operations directly imply no passage from potency to act. They are the operations of a being (or faculty) already in act.

2. Act of the *Imperfect:* Vegetative operations have a certain transience, for the perfection of one part is communicated to another. Yet the operation begins and terminates within the vegetative supposit and is therefore immanent.

Article III: *Apparent Immanent Action*

1. Local motion *of itself* does not manifest a being as living, for it does not terminate in the same supposit and therefore is a type of transient action. *Loco*motion, however, since it presupposes some kind of knowledge and appetite, which are strictly immanent operations, is a sign that the being from which it proceeds is living.

2. Moreover, those beings which manifest apparent immanent action move only *to seek rest,* not in order to perfect themselves by constant activity as do the living.

Question II

LIVING BEINGS

Article I: *For the Living, "To Be" Is To Live*

1. Since a being acts in so far as it is in act, the *absolutely first* intrinsic principle of immanent operation in a living being is the

existential act, "to be." "To live," therefore, is a "to be" so perfect it enables the nature to act immanently.

2. "To live" must be predicated *indirectly* of living creatures, *directly* of God, since the former *have* "to be"; God, however, *is* "To Be."

Article II: *For the Living, Existence Is Life*

1. In the *primary* and most profound sense, "life" is the "to be" of a living being conceived abstractly. It is the existence of a living being.

2. There are many *secondary meanings* of the term "life": (*a*) vital operations, (*b*) living substances, (*c*) habitual manner of action, (*d*) vegetative operations.

Article III: *"Living Being" — an Analogous Notion*

1. The *notion* indeterminately embraces all living beings, for it abstracts from all definite determination of the relation of essence to "to live" (to be).

2. In *predicating* "living being" of concrete, individual existents, the relation of essence to "to live" is made definite by a more explicit apprehension of the essence. Such a predication is *analogous* by analogy of *proportionality* in which the two factors are essence and "to live."

Question III

GENERAL TYPES OF LIVING BEINGS

Article I: *Metaphysical Foundation for Distinction of Living Beings*

1. *Principle:* The more perfectly self-motion (and independence from a mover) is found in anything, the more perfect is life in that being.

2. *Causal factors of action:* This self-movement may occur as regards: (*a*) execution (efficient cause), (*b*) specification (form), (*c*) finality (end) of action.

Article II: *Application of the Principle to Living Things*

1. *Plants* move themselves only as regards the execution of action. The form and end of the action are determined for them by their nature.

2. *Animals* move themselves as regards execution and specification. The form which determines their action is acquired by their own operation through sense knowledge. They do not, however, determine the ends of their actions.

3. *Man* moves himself as regards the execution, specification, and immediate finality (end) of his action. He does not, however, determine his last end.

Thus, plants, animals, and man are essentially distinct.

CHAPTER II

THE UNITY OF MAN

PROLOGUE

Man, we observe, is a *living* being of a high order. We have seen that immanence characterizes the operations of living beings; these beings are the agents of their own activity. We have also shown that the first, intrinsic, actual principle of immanent operations — the first (existential) principle of life in a living being — is the substantial "to be." Since that which has a substantial "to be" is a perfect existential unit, it follows that living beings must be supposits. All this has been established in the opening chapter.

In the present discussion, we shall first make some brief and general observations concerning the various operations[1] discovered in the complex living being who is the object of our study. We shall find that, at the lowest level, man possesses material operations in common with the lowest type of living beings, the plants; consequently, man is a corporeal substance, a body. On the other hand, at the highest level, we shall discover operations in man (understanding and willing) that transcend the individuating influence of matter. Obviously, a being that is the source of such

[1] Although our philosophical study of man must center on the intellectual operations which are proper to man as man, nevertheless, it will be necessary to examine the sentient and vegetative operations, since in man the intellectual operations are in some way dependent on these lower functions. The *detailed* study of the vegetative and sensory operations, however, is best left to the biological sciences, which possess the experimental methods and techniques needed for the study of man on that particular level. Certainly, these operations should not constitute a major portion of the subject matter of a philosophical inquiry into the nature of man.

perfect activities cannot be a purely material being; yet, both these (understanding and willing) and the material operations on the vegetative and sensitive plane are attributed to one and the same supposit—man. How can this be done? This difficulty is made even more impressive when we find that the first (essential) principle of these operations, the soul, is subsistent, that is to say, the soul in no way depends upon matter for its act of existing, for its "to be."

Is man, therefore, two complete beings, two supposits—a body which is the source of material operations, and a distinct spiritual soul, the source of thought and volition? Or is man one? This is the last and the crucial question of the chapter, and we shall attempt to show that man, despite his many and diverse operations, is a perfect existential unit existing by one substantial "to be," though his nature is obviously dual, a composite of matter and spiritual form.

Division: This chapter, accordingly, will contain three questions in which we shall discuss: (1) the various immanent operations of man, in general; (2) the nature of the human soul, which is the first (essential) actual principle of these operations; (3) the union of soul and body.

Question I

IMMANENT OPERATIONS OF MAN (IN GENERAL)

This question is divided into three articles in which we shall briefly examine: (1) the vegetative, (2) cognitive, and (3) appetitive operations of man.

ARTICLE I: Vegetative Operations

In common with the plants, man exercises certain operations which are not found in non-living corporeal beings. Indeed, we are able to distinguish between these two types of beings by the presence or absence of these immanent operations:

a) *Nutrition* is an immanent operation by which a corporeal living being assimilates food into its own substance, keeps the body in a state of good repair, and replenishes depleted energies.

b) *Augmentation* (growth) is the activity by which a living body attains its due quantitative development. This process is not a mere additive function in which many homogeneous parts are assembled and receive a certain spatial unification; rather, it is a vital operation in which a corporeal living being changes what is for the most part non-living material into its own living self so as to reach its full quantitative perfection.

c) *Generation* (reproduction) is the vital operation by which a living corporeal being gives rise to new individuals of the same specific perfection. It is primarily an activity in which a living bodily substance perfects itself or a part of itself so that a new living being can be produced.

ARTICLE II: Cognitive Operations of Man (Knowledge)

Human Knowledge Implies a Becoming, an Immaterial Reception of Form: Besides participating in the vegetative functions, man enjoys the higher operations which we call knowledge; he is capable of sensing and understanding. These operations imply that the knower somehow is conformed to the known, that he receives the form of the known, that he *becomes* the known.

This type of becoming (of reception of form) must be carefully distinguished from the becoming of material transient action, in which a form is received "with matter" (*cum materia*), that is to say, *materially* and *subjectively,* thus limiting the form to one subject. Water, for example, when heated, receives the form heat; the water is assimilated to the heating agent according to form *and matter*. Its heat is distinct from that of the fire and belongs to the water alone, which has subjectively received this form.

The same type of change occurs when my hand is heated. In this case, however, besides the physical heating process, there is an awareness, a sensation of a warm *object*. The mere heating of the hand, although necessary for a sensation of warmth, is not the sensation itself; otherwise, all heated subjects would feel heat.[2] Rather, simultaneously with the heating process another change takes place, in which the knowing subject is assimilated to the heating agent according to form but *not according to matter*. This is more obvious, perhaps, in the case of a color sensation, for example, the sensation of a red wall. In this instance, the sense of sight assimilates (receives the form) the redness without assimilating the paint. In both of the examples given, the knower has received the form of the object "without matter" (*sine materia*), that is to say, *immaterially* and *objectively*. While remaining itself, the knowing subject has received a perfection, a form, beyond itself; it has become—and hence *is*—the object in an immaterial way.

Immateriality the Root of Knowledge: Knowers differ from non-knowers inasmuch as the knowers can "become" other things in knowledge; their form is less restricted,[3] less limited than the form of the non-knowers. Now that which limits form is matter. Knowing beings, therefore (whether sentient or intellectual), have a form which is less limited by matter than the forms of non-cognitive agents. This is to say that the forms of knowers are more or less perfectly independent of matter, immaterial. We must further conclude that since immateriality is the root of knowledge, the greater the freedom from matter, the more perfect the knowledge.

Sense Knowledge: In man we observe two kinds of knowledge. The first, which man has in common with the brute animals, is

---

[2] Cf. *S. Th.*, I, 84, 2, *c*.
[3] Cf. *ibid.*, 14, 1, *c*.

called sense knowledge. This type of knowledge is *individual* and particular, not universal as is the concept in intellectual knowledge. The reason is that human knowledge implies the acquiring, the reception of form (the forming of a likeness). Now whatever is received is received according to the conditions of the recipient. Since our sense knowledge is obviously individual and particular, the sensible object must be received in the knowing subject without matter *but with the individual conditions of matter,* for matter is the principle of individuation. Consequently, the operation of sensing and the immediate subject from which it proceeds must be somewhat *material* in nature. Such knowledge is limited to an experience of individual, corporeal objects.

Intellectual Knowledge: Our intellectual knowledge, on the other hand, although dependent on sense knowledge for its data, can reach even to the essences of things. This knowledge is not a mere experience of individual, sensible qualities; rather, it is a knowledge in which the absolute or *universal* nature can be attained. Thus the nature conceived can be affirmed truly of all the individuals that participate in the nature, although each has its own individual, material differences.

Strict Immateriality of Intellectual Knowledge: As we reflect upon the universality of intellectual knowledge, we come to realize the radical difference between intellectual and sense cognition in terms of independence from matter. The proper object of human intellectual knowledge is the corporeal essence, whose individuation is due to matter. If, then, man's intellect attains the *universal* nature common to corporeal substances of the same species, the knowledge process must imply a removal of individual representative elements present in the sensory knowledge of these corporeal objects. Since the individuality of sense knowledge is due to limitation by matter, a cognitive operation that does away completely with this individuating influence (and presents the object according to the specifying or formal element common to all the individuals of a class) must be a strictly immaterial operation. Such an operation is spiritual and must proceed from a principle entirely independent of matter in its existence. In sense knowledge, on the other hand, we know that some remnants, some vestiges of material influence remain, for sense knowledge is of the individual and particular, not of the universal.

In brief: the senses receive the form of the corporeal object without matter but *with* the individuating conditions of matter; the intellect receives the form even *without* the individuating conditions of matter. Hence, sense cognition is somewhat material, while intellectual knowledge is strictly immaterial.

ARTICLE III: Appetitive Operations

Besides the vegetative and cognitive operations, we observe in man tendencies or inclinations to the good consequent upon knowledge. We are not concerned here with the natural appetite of man, which is the necessary tendency of human nature to its last end, happiness. Rather, we wish to examine briefly such operations as liking, loving, desiring, choosing, enjoying—all of which are directed in some manner toward that which has been cognized as good. We shall call actions of this type *appetitive* operations.

Two Types of Appetite: It seems fairly obvious that we can consciously tend only to a good that is known. It is also quite evident that the appetite will need to be proportioned to the knowledge, so that on different levels of knowledge there must be distinct appetites. Only in a metaphorical sense do we hunger for justice; in the strict sense, hunger is an inclination on the sensory level consequent upon *sense* knowledge of a material, sensible good. The "hunger" for justice, on the other hand, is truly an appetitive operation but is consequent upon *intellectual* knowledge of a suprasensible good. Appetitive operations of this type can attain to immaterial good and because of a higher end can even have for their object some material things for which there is a positive dislike on the level of sensory appetite. We may, for example, will to take a bitter medicine, in order to regain our health. Appetitive operations of this kind have for their principle the intellectual appetite, the will. They are a further manifestation of man's superiority over the world of brute animals and plants.

Question II

NATURE OF THE HUMAN SOUL,[4] FIRST (ESSENTIAL) PRINCIPLE OF IMMANENT OPERATION

The operations of man, which we have briefly examined in the preceding question, proceed from an intrinsic actual principle, for an agent acts in so far as it is in act. In the first chapter, we pointed out that the first intrinsic principle which enables a living being to operate immanently is the substantial "to be," which is the actual principle in the existential or absolutely first order.[5] Since only essences, and not the "to be," are properly conceivable by the human intellect, it is necessary to carry our investigation into the *essential* order.[6] We now seek to know the nature of the

[4] Why do we not at this point treat of the nature of the body? Why do we rise immediately to a study of the soul? The reason is — as we may recall from the philosophy of being — that matter of itself is pure potency; its specific perfection is from the form which in man we call the soul. The body of man is not that of an animal, is not a tree or a stone; it is a human body precisely because of the actuation of matter by the soul. In order to understand man's body we must acquire a knowledge of the nature of man's soul.

[5] Only by rising to this order can we hope to give an explanation that is really worthy of a philosophical inquiry into the principles of vital operation. Explanations that do not rise to this level are at best essentialist explanations which necessarily fail to grasp the profundity of the Angelic Doctor's existential solution to the problem of life. The same may be said of those explanations of knowledge and of the unity of man which prescind from the existential order.

[6] The "to live," which is the "to be" of a living being, is determined and limited by the nature or essence. It comes to the nature through the act, the form, of that nature. *"Forma dat esse."* We shall call the act or form of human nature the *soul.* The soul is the active principle of life in man. It is that principle by which and because of which man has three modes of life (living) — vegetative, sensitive, and rational.

"first (essential) principle of life," of vital operations in man. We shall call it the *animating* principle or "soul" (*anima*),[7] a principle which *in*animate bodies do not possess, since their forms are of lower perfection. There are other more immediate principles of vital operation in man, for example, the sight, the intellect, the will; and we know from a previous reflection that the absolutely first intrinsic principle — a principle necessarily in the existential order — is the substantial "to be." In this question, however, we shall be concerned with the first *essential* principle of vital operation in man.

Division: This question is divided into five articles: (1) the soul is not a body; (2) the soul is simple, (3) spiritual, (4) incorruptible, (5) created.

ARTICLE I: The Soul Is Not a Body;[8] It is the Act of the Body

Although at present we are not able to give a strict definition of the soul — that will be the result of our search — we may state that we are seeking a clearer knowledge of the first intrinsic principle (in the order of nature or essence) of human life, that is to say, of vital operations in man. This first principle of life we shall call the animating principle or human soul.

The Angelic Doctor argues that the *first* principle of vital operation cannot be a body (a composite of matter and form) or a bodily organ, such as the heart or brain. For, if bodies were first principles of life by their very essence,[9] that is, precisely

[7] There seems to be a prejudice in some quarters against the ancient Anglo-Saxon term "soul." Various terms can be substituted: vital principle, animating principle, principle of life, intrinsic source of immanent operation, psyche, etc. Although these terms smack less of "medievalism," they are but synonyms for the same term — soul, which signifies the essential actual principle of a corporeal being capable of immanent operations.

[8] *S. Th.*, I, 75, 1.

[9] Essential definitions are convertible. Thus, every man is a rational animal, and every rational animal is a man.

as bodies, all bodies would be principles of life, of vital operation, and, consequently, all bodies would be living beings. The fact is that many of them are not living, for example, stones, the air, minerals. Therefore, the first principle of life, of vital operation, in man is not a body.

> It is manifest that not every principle of vital operation is a soul, for then the eye would be a soul, since it is a principle of vision. . . . But it is the first [essential] principle of life [vital operation] which we call the soul. Now, though a body may in a certain sense be a principle of life, as the heart is a principle of life in an animal, yet no body can be the first principle of life, for to be a living thing (*vivens*) does not belong to a body as a body; otherwise every body would be a living thing (*vivens*), or a principle of life.[10]

We may further conclude that if a body is a living being rather than non-living, this is true not because it is a body, but because it is a definite or special type of bodily being. The fact that it is this definite type of body (a living body) must be due to something intrinsic to the bodily being, to a specifying principle, which we shall call the *act* (perfection) of the body, since it gives the body a perfection which the latter of itself—in so far as it is a body—does not possess. *This act of the body we call the soul.*

> . . . It belongs to a body to be a living thing, or even a principle of life, inasmuch as it is such (*tale*) a body. Now that it is actually such a body it owes to some principle which is called its act. Therefore the soul, which is the first principle of life, is not a body but the act of a body. . . .[11]

ARTICLE II: The Soul Is Simple[12]

The soul is the act of the body. What is it in itself? Is it a composite being; that is, is it composed of distinct parts, or must

[10] *S. Th.,* I, 75, 1, *c.*
[11] *Loc. cit.*
[12] *S. Th.,* I, 75, 5.

we attribute to the soul the perfection called simplicity?

Simplicity: The notion of simplicity is so fundamental and primary that it cannot be strictly defined. Such a notion, however, can be clarified by a descriptive definition or by a denial of its opposite. When we affirm that something is simple, we implicitly deny that it is composed of parts,[13] and, since there are many kinds of parts (or principles), there must be many types of simplicity. Accordingly, when we say that the human soul is simple, it will be necessary to explain what precise type of composition we are excluding from the soul, whether it be a composition of essential[14] parts, of quantitative parts, the composition of essence and "to be," or that of substance and accidents. Obviously, since the human soul is a limited reality, we do not intend to exclude composition in the existential order, that of essence and "to be." Nor do we deny that the soul can be actuated in the order of activity. Accordingly, the substance of the soul must be distinct from its accidents (faculties and operations). All that we wish to show at this point is that the soul (1) has no essential parts—is not composed of matter and form[15]—and that (2) it has no quantitative parts.[16] We need not discuss integral parts, since they are a species of quantitative parts.

Simplicity Implies a Great Perfection: The notion of simplicity, which is obtained by denying composition, denotes much more than a mere negation of parts. It designates a positive perfection, "a definite *disposition* because of which a being need not be made of parts."[17] Like unity, which is not a mere denial of division, but

---

13 "*Simplex significat dispositionem secundum quam aliquid aliqualiter se habet, quia videlicet non est ex pluribus constitutum.*" (*In XI Met.*, lect. 7.)

14 By essential parts we mean the two principles of corporeal essence, that is, matter and form.

15 At the time of St. Thomas, some theologians were of the opinion that the soul as well as the angelic forms were composed of form and "spiritual" matter. This fact explains the reason for and the place of article five in the seventy-fifth question.

16 Quantitative parts are extended parts, that is, parts outside of parts.

17 *In XI Met.*, lect. 7.

first connotes a subject, simplicity demands the reality of being as a foundation for the negation of parts. Since the composition of parts implies limitation, simplicity indicates a very great perfection; and, as St. Thomas explains, in the same kind or genus of being, the more noble or perfect a thing is, the more simple it must be.[18] The human soul, we maintain, although it is composite in the existential order, has neither essential nor quantitative parts.

The Soul Has No Essential Parts: That which is composed of essential parts — matter and form — must be a body. But the soul of man is not a body, as has been explained in the preceding article. Therefore, the human soul is not composed of essential parts, but is essentially simple.[19]

St. Thomas proposes an argument based on the manner in which the intellectual soul receives the forms of things in intellectual knowledge. We must bear in mind, in order to understand this proof, that knowledge in man presupposes that the knowing subject, while remaining itself, in some way "becomes" the object, by receiving the perfection (the form) of the object known. Now whatever is received, is received according to the condition of the recipient. If the recipient is a composite of form and individuating matter, whatever it receives must be received as individuated by matter. If, on the other hand, the recipient is devoid of matter, it will receive forms without the individuating influence of matter, that is, absolutely, as universals. Now the intellectual soul receives the intelligible forms of things absolutely, that is,

---

[18] *"In quolibet genere tanto aliquid est nobilius, quanto simplicius."* (*C. G.*, I, 28, 5.) We must not misconstrue this statement, and imagine that under any circumstances it is always more perfect to be more simple. This holds true only of beings that are in the same order. (Cf. *In IV Sent.*, d. 11, q. 2, a. 1, ad 1^m.)

[19] St. Thomas proposes an argument for the essential simplicity of the soul based on the soul's role as form of the body. The argument states that a form, as form, must be an actual principle, which, obviously is not composite itself. If the adversary admits that the soul has for its subject prime matter directly, he must admit that the soul is essential act and therefore simple. If the opponent wishes to say that the soul itself is a composite of matter and form, St. Thomas will grant him the supposition, but he insists that by *soul* he means that part which is the actual principle. Cf. *S. Th.*, I, 75, 5, *c*.

as freed from the individuating influence of matter. For man in his intellectual knowledge knows things according to their essences, and not according to their individual material conditions as do the senses. Consequently, the intellectual soul, since it receives these forms without the conditions of matter, must exist *without matter in its constitution;* in other words, the human soul has no essential parts.[20]

> It is clear that whatever is received into something is received according to the condition of the recipient. Now a thing is known in as far as its form is in the knower. But the intellectual soul knows a thing in its nature absolutely; for instance, it knows a stone absolutely as stone; and therefore the form of stone, according to its proper formal notion (*ratio*), is in the soul absolutely. Therefore, the intellectual soul is an absolute form, not something composed of matter and form. For if the intellectual soul were composed of matter and form, the forms of things would be received into it as individuals, and so it would know only the individual, as happens in the sensitive powers which receive forms in corporeal organs, since matter is the principle by which forms are individuated. It follows, therefore, that the intellectual soul, and every intellectual substance which has knowledge of forms absolutely, is exempt from composition of matter and form.[21]

The Soul Has No Quantitative Parts: By quantitative parts we mean extended parts, occupying space in three dimensions so that one part is outside another. Now a being is extended and has quantitative parts by reason of matter. Moreover, that which has matter as a constituent principle of its essence is a body. But the soul, as we have shown, is not a body. Therefore, the soul does not have quantitative parts.[22]

---

[20] It is interesting to note that this proof is offered by St. Thomas not as a demonstration of the spirituality of the soul, but of its simplicity. The argument does not proceed from operation but rather from "reception."

[21] *S. Th.*, I, 75, 5, *c.*

[22] This argument proves that the human soul is not quantitative *per se,* that is, according to its nature; for only a body is by its nature the subject of quantity. Nor is the human soul quantitative *per accidens,* that is, by reason of its subject; for if the human soul were quantitative by reason of the body of which it is the form,

ARTICLE III: The Human Soul Is Spiritual[23]

Spirituality: Owing to a fundamental error in the philosophy of Descartes, there has been considerable confusion in the minds of modern philosophers concerning spirituality and simplicity. As early as the seventeenth century, Bossuet warns his readers[24] that when St. Thomas Aquinas speaks of the spiritual, he does not mean merely that which is unextended and indivisible because it is not matter, but rather, that which is strictly immaterial, whose "to be" is independent of matter. A form, such as the first principle of immanent operation in a dog, is not matter. It is not divisible, and consequently is a *simple* form.[25] But it is by no means spiritual. The reason is that the form of the dog depends on matter for its "to be"; such a form cannot exist unless united to matter. Hence, although it *is not matter,* it is a *material* form and therefore corruptible. Descartes erred by confusing and identifying spirituality with simplicity, thereby concluding that whatever is material must be extended (have parts outside of parts) because it is not spiritual. For Descartes, matter is extension and the simple is necessarily spiritual.

---

then by dividing a living man we should be able to multiply individual men, which is obviously contrary to fact.

St. Thomas thought that the souls of the lowest animals and of plants were extended by reason of the body of which they are the act, and, consequently, that the souls of such living beings are sometimes divided, as occurs in the grafting of plants and the division of earthworms. Such changes, we believe, may be better explained as the eduction of a new form by mere separation, since in beings of this sort the whole is virtually contained in the relatively few parts, which are nearly homogeneous in structure and have a minimum of specialized function. Such parts are equivalently or virtually the whole and need only to be separated to be and to function as existential units or living wholes; mere separation educes a new living form from the potency of matter.

[23] *S. Th.,* I, 75, 2.

[24] *"Saint Thomas . . . ne croit pas que l'âme soit spirituelle précisement . . . pour être, indivisible. Spirituel, c'est immatériel. Et St. Thomas appelle immatériel ce qui non seulement n'est pas matière, mais qui de soi est indépendant de la matière."* (Bossuet, *De La Connaissance de Dieu et de Soi-Même,* c. V.)

[25] Obviously, this form itself is not a composite of matter and form; the dog is that.

Spirituality Presupposes Simplicity: The simplicity which we discussed in the preceding article does not necessarily imply spirituality. Such simplicity merely excludes parts (essential and quantitative), whereas spirituality not only supposes essential and quantitative simplicity, but, over and above, denotes existence independent of matter. Not every simple reality is spiritual, but every spiritual thing must be simple. A spiritual form, besides being essentially and quantitatively simple, exists independently of matter. Accordingly, we may define spirituality as *existential independence from matter;* to be spiritual is *to be* (to exist) independently of matter.

Grades of Immateriality: Spirituality is the highest type of immateriality. Since God is pure existential act, the farthest removed from matter, He is pure immateriality. From a metaphysician's point of view, all reality may be arranged in a scale with Pure Act at the highest point and pure potency (prime matter) at the lowermost. Between these extremes are various modes or degrees of participating in the immateriality of God; all creatures, even bodies, since they participate in "to be," participate in pure immateriality; their form is not matter but a participation in Pure Act.

The diverse grades of the immateriality of creatures are manifested by the varying perfection of the operations which these creatures place. At the lowest level of the scale is the world of *inanimate* beings, whose forms are so immersed in matter that their sole operation is that of resistance and attraction.

Manifesting a more perfect operation are the ***plants,*** which are able to move themselves as regards the execution of their own vegetative actions. They are able to change other bodies into themselves through the process of assimilation; they "receive" the forms of other things *"with the matter."* Consequently, theirs is a greater freedom from the limitation of matter, and hence a greater participation in immateriality.

Surpassing the plants in perfection, the brute *animal* world is manifested by operations on the sensory level, in which there is far greater freedom from the limiting influx of matter. For, animals through sense knowledge "become" other corporeal things; they receive the forms of other things "*without* the matter," though always *with the individual conditions of matter.*[26] Thus they approach more closely the immateriality of pure existential act than do the plants.

Above the realm of brute animals is the world of rational beings, of *men,* who — in the cognitive operation proper to them (intellection) — acquire the forms of things *without* matter and even *without the individual conditions of matter.* Here we find strict immateriality in the order of operation, and consequently we must find it also in the order of existence. The form of man, although informing matter, is manifested by its strictly immaterial operation of universal knowledge as existing independently of matter. Such independence from matter we shall call *spirituality* or immateriality in the *strict sense.* The immateriality of brute animals, which enables them to become other corporeal things in sensory knowledge, we shall call immateriality in the *wide sense.*

Independence From Matter: One thing is *existentially* independent from another if it is able *to be,* that is, to exist without the other. This means that the other in no way enters as a causal element into the "to be" or becoming of the first being. For that which proceeds from a cause is dependent on that cause. To clarify the precise point to be demonstrated, it will be helpful to

---

[26] Although there is a qualified independence from matter in sensation in so far as the knowing subject is the object intentionally, yet sensation must be called unqualifiedly a material operation. The reason is that the operation of sensation is caused by a composite (conjunct) of form and matter, of sense faculty and sense organ. ". . . sensation and the attendant operations of the sensitive soul are obviously accompanied by bodily change; and thus, in the action of seeing, the pupil of the eye is changed by the likeness (*species*) of color; and it is the same with the other sense operations. Thus it is evident that the sensitive soul has no operation of its own by itself (*per se*), and that all its operations belong to the composite. It follows from this that since the souls of brute animals have no operation by themselves (*per se*), they are not subsistent [spiritual]. For in the same way does every being have 'to be' and operation." (*S. Th.,* I, 75, 3, *c.*)

discuss briefly the various kinds of independence and dependence as regards matter.

1. *In the Order of Existence:*

a) A form is *dependent* on matter in the order of existence if it is educed from the potency of matter. Such a form can cease to exist. This is true of any material form whether that of inanimate beings, plants, or brute animals.

b) A form is *independent* of matter in the order of existence if it can exist without matter, even when, as in the case of the soul of man, it is conjoined to matter which it actuates. Such a form has its own "to be"; it cannot be educed from the potency of matter, nor is it corruptible, that is, reduceable to the potency of matter. A form of this kind is strictly immaterial, spiritual. Such, we claim, is the soul of man.

2. *In the Order of Operation:*

a) A substantial form is *dependent* upon matter in the order of operation when the principle of the operation is a composite of matter and form, so that matter is a co-principle of action. Such dependence upon matter is observable in the operations of vegetative and sentient beings. Even the sentient operations of man are dependent on matter as a co-principle of operation.

b) A form is *independent* of matter in the order of action when the principle of the operation is solely the form, even though this form is united to the body as its act. Unlike the operation of sensation, matter does not enter in as a co-principle of action. We propose to establish that such is the case in the action called understanding (*intelligere*). Nevertheless, as we shall see, the objective data for the act of understanding in man is provided by the senses.[27]

---

[27] Because the human soul is not a pure spirit but rather the act of the body, it naturally depends upon sense knowledge (phantasms) for its objective data. This, of course, in no way implies that matter is a co-principle of intellectual knowledge, or that matter is an efficient cause of the immanent act of understanding. Some philosophers have called this dependence on sensory data in the order of object an extrinsic dependence.

Relations Between Operation and Existence: We can know what a thing is through what it does; as a thing acts, so it is. "For nothing can operate except a being which is in act; consequently, a being operates according as it is."[28] From this it follows that: (*a*) A form which is the principle of operation independent of matter — that is, whose operation does not require matter as a co-principle — must be free from matter as to its act of existing, for its "to be." Such a form is a *subsisting* form, a spiritual form. (*b*) On the other hand, a form which depends in all its operations upon matter as a co-principle must also depend upon matter to exist; it is *existentially* dependent on matter. Such a form is not subsisting, not spiritual.

Subsistence and Spirituality: A subsisting being is one which exists of itself (*per se*) and consequently does not depend upon another intrinsic principle for its existence. A dog, a plant, a man are subsistents; color, size, shape are not. The *form* of a dog, however, because it depends upon another principle — upon matter — for its act of existing, is not a subsistent. The soul of man, we shall prove, does not depend on another intrinsic principle for its existence; it has "to be" independently of matter. The human soul, therefore, is subsistent. Now, since spirituality signifies existential independence from matter, it follows that a form which subsists, that is, a form which is (existentially) independent from matter, is necessarily spiritual.[29]

In a celebrated article[30] on the nature of the soul, the Angelic Doctor first proves that the human soul is *incorporeal,* that it has no composition of matter and form. He then demonstrates that man's intellectual operation proceeds from this incorporeal principle alone, and not at the same time from a material co-principle. This is to say that the human soul is independent from matter in

[28] *S. Th.,* I, 75, 2, *c.*

[29] Thus a dog is a subsisting being, but is not spiritual; nor is its substantial form a subsistent form. Accordingly, the form of the dog is not spiritual.

[30] *S. Th.,* I, 75, 2.

its intellectual operation. From this he argues that the soul is independent of matter in its existence, that it is a ***subsisting form,*** hence spiritual. This order we shall follow in our demonstration.

Demonstration

1. The Human Soul Is Incorporeal: In reading the argument of St. Thomas, one should keep in mind that human knowledge presupposes the reception of a representative form of the object to be known. This representative form is the term of a motion, of a passage from potency to act on the part of the knowing principle. Now, no corporeal principle while remaining itself can acquire any material form, for it already possesses a determinate form in its own nature.[31] Thus a body (a corporeal being of a determinate form) can materially become another body, but in doing so it no longer remains itself. Now the human soul, while remaining itself, can receive through intellectual knowledge the forms or natures of *all* corporeal things, of all bodies.[32] Consequently, the human soul, the principle of intellection, cannot have a definite corporeal form in its own nature impeding the knowledge of all bodies. This is to say that the human soul is incorporeal.

> . . . It must be allowed that the principle of intellectual operation which we call the soul of man is a principle both incorporeal and subsistent. For it is clear that by means of the intellect man can

[31] That which is receptive of certain perfections must be in potency to those perfections; it cannot at the same time be in act as regards the perfection to be received. To illustrate this point, St. Thomas gives the example of the sick man's tongue, which is filled with a bitter humor and consequently can taste nothing else. A healthy tongue, on the other hand, since it has no actual taste in itself, can respond to all things in the range of taste from those that are sweet to those that are sour. A healthy ear, since it has no sound of itself, can hear all sounds that fall within its range. On the other hand, the organs by which we perceive temperature have their own temperature, and hence can respond only to the stimuli of bodies that are of a different temperature. So also the tongue, when it is infected by a bitter humor, cannot respond to the taste stimuli of bodies of a different taste; it is no longer receptive of a new form, for it is already in act with regard to taste.

[32] The soul understands what a body, a corporeal thing, is; for it can form a definition of corporeal being as such.

> know the natures of all corporeal things (*corporum*). Now whatever can know certain things cannot have any of them in its own nature; because that which would be in it naturally would impede the knowledge of other things. Thus we observe that a sick man's tongue, which is infected by a . . . bitter humor, cannot sense anything sweet, and everything seems bitter to it. Therefore, if the intellectual principle contained within itself the nature of any body, it would be unable to know all bodies. Now every body has its own determinate nature. Therefore it is impossible for the intellectual principle to be a body.[33]

This argument may be briefly stated in the following *syllogism:* That which has a definite corporeal nature (form) cannot receive any other corporeal nature (form) and remain itself. But the principle of intellectual operation, which we call the soul of man, can receive through knowledge the natures of *all* bodily things.[34] Therefore the soul of man cannot have the nature of any body; that is to say, the human soul is something incorporeal.

The *minor* has already been explained. Since the soul understands the nature (definition) of body as such, it is capable of knowing all bodies. The *major* rests on the principle that "the recipient must be free from [or stripped of] the nature of the thing received."[35] For whatever is in potency (receptive) cannot simultaneously be in act as regards the perfection to be received.[36]

---

[33] *S. Th.,* I, 75, 2, *c.*

[34] We say "can receive" advisedly; that is, we speak of knowledge to be obtained in the future. We do not deny that a subject may know its own nature immediately, as angels do.

[35] ". . . *recipiens debet esse denudatum a natura recepti, sicut pupilla caret colore.*" (*Quaestio Unica de Anima,* art. XIV.) The same principle, but limited to the order of knowledge, is expressed by St. Thomas (commenting on Aristotle) as follows: "*Intus apparens enim prohibebit extraneum et obstruet.*" (*In III De Anima,* lect. 7, no. 680.)

[36] "Whatever is in potency to something and is receptive as regards a perfection, lacks that to which it is in potency and in respect of which it is receptive; as is true of the pupil of the eye, which is potential and receptive with reference to colors, and thus lacks every color. In like manner, our intellect's mode of understanding intelligibles is such that it is first in potency to its intelligible objects and receptive with reference to them, just as the senses are as regards sensible objects. Therefore, the intellect lacks all those natures (*res*) the understanding of which is its natural tendency. Accordingly, since our intellect's natural inclination is to understand all sensible and bodily things, it must lack every bodily nature, just as the

The soul, therefore, since it can receive the perfection of all bodies, is truly incorporeal.

2. The Human Soul Is a Subsistent Form: To discover whether a form is existentially independent of matter, that is, whether it is subsistent, we must examine the operations that proceed from that form. The reason is that the mode of operation manifests the mode of existing; for a being acts in so far as it is in act, and the first act of any being is "to be." Now the operation to be examined is the act by which man understands bodily beings, whether successively as this or that body, or under the generic conception of body. Such an operation cannot be dependent upon a corporeal organ as an instrument. For the determinate corporeal nature of the organ would be a hindrance in the acquiring of the forms of all corporeal beings.

Let us propose an example to clarify this principle. If the intellectual principle operated dependently upon the organ of sight, it would attain only the knowledge of colored bodies. Thus, the bodies that manifest themselves only under the aspect of sound, taste, odor, touch could never be known. Being limited to the knowledge of one type of body, the soul would not be able to form the definition of body as such; it would never know the nature of body, and consequently could not know all bodies. We conclude that the principle of human intellection, since it can know all bodies and even the nature of bodies, must operate independently of the body. Now, as a being operates, so it is. Accordingly, the principle of intellectual operation exists independently of the body, of matter, as a co-principle. In other words, the human soul is a subsistent form; it is spiritual.

---

sense of sight lacks all colors. For if this sense possessed some color, this color would render impossible the seeing of other colors, just as a feverish tongue, which has some bitter humor in it, cannot receive a sweet taste. So also the intellect, if it had a determinate nature connatural to it, would be impeded from the knowledge of other natures. . . . From this we conclude, not that the intellect lacks a determinate nature, but that it has this nature alone, that it is potential (*possibilis*) as regards all things." (*In III De Anima,* lect. 7, no. 680.)

> . . . It is impossible for it [the intellectual principle] to understand by means of a bodily organ, since the determinate nature of that bodily organ would impede knowledge of all bodies; as when a certain determinate color is not only in the pupil of the eye, but also in a glass vase, the liquid in the vase seems to be of that same color.
>
> Therefore, the intellectual principle which we call the mind or the intellect has an operation of itself (*per se*) in which the body does not share. Now nothing can operate of itself (*per se*) except that which subsists of itself (*per se*). For nothing can operate but what is in act; wherefore a thing operates according as it is. . . . We must conclude, therefore, that the human soul . . . is something incorporeal and subsistent.[37]

In *syllogistic* form, this argument may be presented as follows: Whatever can operate independently of matter must exist independently of matter. But the intellectual soul can operate independently of matter. Therefore the intellectual soul must exist independently of matter, that is to say, it is spiritual.

The *major* premise is an application of the general principle that the mode of operation is dependent upon the mode of existing, since a being operates in so far as it is in act. In the order of discovery, we observe the operations of a nature in order to rise to a knowledge of its mode of existing. The *minor* is based on the established truth that the intellectual soul can know all bodies. Hence, there can be no material co-principle causing its operation. For such a material co-principle would impede the soul's knowledge of all bodies.[38]

---

[37] *S. Th.*, I, 75, 2, *c*.

[38] "It is evident that the principle by which man understands is a form that has 'to be' in itself (*in se*) and is not merely a principle by which something is. For the act of understanding (*intelligere*) is not performed by a bodily organ; for there could be no corporeal organ that would be receptive of all sensible natures, especially since the recipient must be divested of the nature of the received, just as the pupil of the eye lacks color. Every bodily organ, however, has some sensible nature; but the intellect by which we understand knows all sensible natures. Consequently, it is impossible that its operation, which is to understand, be exercised through a bodily organ. From this it is obvious that the intellect has an operation

Summary of Both Arguments: The close relation between the two arguments presented above will become apparent when they are formulated as a single proof. The fundamental truth that underlies both arguments is this: If the soul had matter in its make-up, or if it depended upon a distinct material principle in order to understand, *it could never know the natures of all corporeal beings*. In such a supposition, the soul, at best, would be limited to the knowledge of one type of bodies, that is to say, it would know in accordance with the determination resulting either from a constitutive formal element or from the material co-principle of knowledge.[39] Now the soul of man is capable of knowing the natures of all bodies. Consequently: (1) the intellectual principle, the soul, cannot itself have any bodily form or nature; it must be incorporeal; (2) in this knowledge, the soul cannot depend on a bodily organ. The intellectual operation, therefore, is independent of matter. Since action is proportioned to existence, it follows that the human soul must exist independently of matter; it is a subsistent form. Since a subsistent form is spiritual, the human soul must be spiritual.

---

of itself (*per se*), in which the body does not share. Now a thing operates according as it is; for those beings which have 'to be' *per se* operate *per se;* but those beings which do not have 'to be' *per se* do not have operation *per se*. . . . Accordingly, it is evident that the intellective principle by which man understands has a 'to be' more perfect than that of the body, and independent of the body." (*Quaestio Unica de Anima,* art. XIV.)

39 To illustrate these two determining factors of knowledge, St. Thomas offers the examples: (1) of a sick man's tongue filled with a bilious humor, to which everything — even honey — seems bitter (for it can acquire no other humor, being already filled with bile); (2) of the colored vase, which, because of its determinate color causes all liquids contained therein to appear of the same color. Underlying these examples is a fundamental metaphysical principle that, in order to acquire a perfection, the recipient must be in potency as regards that perfection. This principle is valid even in the realm of knowledge; for in order to produce the immanent act of knowledge, the knowing subject must be actuated by receiving a representative form of the object; the knower must "become" the known intentionally (representatively). Consequently, the knower, before the act of knowing, must be in potency, that is, it must lack the perfection (the representative form) which it is about to receive. It cannot possess the form or nature which it will acquire, since nothing can receive what it already has. Should it already possess that nature or form, it can know nothing, or, at best, it can know only according to the determination it already possesses.

Argument From Universality of Intellectual Knowledge: Another argument for the spirituality of the human soul is more commonly proposed. This proof is based upon a reflection on the universality of intellectual knowledge as contrasted with the individuality of sense knowledge. Through the visual sense, for example, we apprehend something as this white thing. In intellectual knowledge, on the other hand, we apprehend this "white" as *man, dog, cat,* and the like; we apprehend the absolute nature of that which is presented to the sense as white; we understand the *nature* which the known object has in common with other beings of the same class. Moreover, we can even conceive "whiteness" as a sensible quality of the individual existing thing, which can be found in other existents as well. We see, therefore, that in intellectual knowledge we apprehend things without their individual differences. Now matter is the principle of individuation. Hence, this operation must proceed from a principle which is independent of matter.

> Because the human soul knows the universal natures of things, it perceives that the intelligible species [representative form of the object] by which we understand is immaterial. Otherwise [that is, if the species were material], it would be individuated, and consequently could not lead us to the knowledge of the universal essence. Now from the fact that the intelligible species is immaterial philosophers concluded that the intellect is independent of matter.[40]

The mode of action corresponds to the mode of the agent's form. The operation which follows upon the actuation of the intellect by the eduction of a spiritual representative form (intelligible species) of the object must, accordingly, be a spiritual operation. Moreover, "since only what exists can act, every being is ordered to operation and action as it is ordered to 'to be.'"[41] It follows that the soul, which is the first (essential) principle of

---

[40] *De Ver.*, X, 8.

[41] *"Cum enim agere non possit nisi quod est, unumquodque hoc modo se habet ad operandum vel agendum quo modo se habet ad esse."* (*De Pot.*, III, 9.)

the spiritual operation of intellection, must have a "to be" independently of matter; that is to say, the human soul is spiritual.[42]

ARTICLE IV: The Soul of Man Is Incorruptible (Immortal)[43]

Incorruptibility and Immortality: The words *incorruptible* and *immortal* are often used as synonyms. To be faithful to the terminology of St. Thomas, however, we must reserve the term *immortality* for the incorruptibility of living things, the ever-enduring conservation of a "to be" which is a "to live." Incorruptibility, on the other hand, is a more general term and is applicable to any being that cannot undergo substantial change.

Types of Incorruptibility: The schoolmen distinguish between *essential, natural,* and *gratuitous* immortality. God alone is essentially immortal, since only His essence is "to be." Consequently, He necessarily exists. Natural immortality belongs to any finite spiritual substance. Gratuitous immortality is a gift of God to a corporeal being, which of its own nature tends to corrupt. Since this type of immortality — which was bestowed on the first parents of the human race — is known only through Revelation, we shall not treat of it in our philosophical discussion of this question. We are not concerned here with either gratuitous or essential

---

[42] It is interesting to note that (to my knowledge) St. Thomas uses this argumentation only once to prove directly the spirituality of the soul. On the other hand, he proposes it several times to establish that the soul is not composed of matter and form, that it is a simple form. Now the fact that a principle of being is a simple form does not make it necessarily spiritual. It has been suggested that St. Thomas in such texts is not merely proving the simplicity of the soul, since this simplicity is quite evident from earlier discussions. He is refuting, rather, the doctrine of such doctors as St. Bonaventure, who, while admitting the spirituality of the soul, thought that it was composed of form and *spiritual* matter. This explains why, after showing in the first article of the seventy-fifth question that the soul is not a body, and after proving in the second article that the soul is spiritual, St. Thomas proposes the following problem in the fifth article: Is the soul composed of matter and form, that is to say, Is the soul composed of *spiritual* matter and form?

[43] *S. Th.,* I, 75, 6.

immortality; our inquiry is whether the human soul is immortal by its very nature.

Corruption: Since immortality is opposed to corruption of a living being, it will be necessary, in order to establish that the soul is immortal, to prove that it cannot undergo corruption. Now corruption of living beings is called death; it is the necessary outcome of the natural tendency of corporeal things to non-being. To explain our meaning, we shall distinguish between two types of corruption according to the diversity of its cause. The first is that which results from the inclination that a nature has to break up of itself (*per se*); the second is that which comes about accidentally (*per accidens*) on account of the corruption of another being or principle of being on which the nature depends for existence.

Natural (Per Se) Corruption: Whenever a being is composed of act and potency in the order of essence, that is, of matter and form, such a being will naturally corrupt, provided the requisite conditions and dispositions are present. The reason is simply this: Matter, since it is of itself pure potency, can acquire any material form. Although actuated by a definite form, which places the resulting nature in a definite species, matter remains in potency to all other material forms. Consequently, all that is required for corruption of a being whose essence is a composite of matter and form is the action of an agent capable of producing the dispositions necessary for the eduction of a new form. The eduction of a new substantial form from the potency of matter is simultaneous with the reduction of the old form to potentiality; and, since along with the form there comes a proportionate "to be," a new being will exist at the term of the change. In other words, the corruption of one corporeal being is the generation of another (or others).

Any being, therefore, whose essence (nature) is composed of matter and form is naturally corruptible; it will corrupt when the conditions necessary for a substantial change are present. On the other hand, a being whose nature (essence) is simple is not naturally corruptible. Consequently, ***the soul of man is not naturally corruptible because it is essentially simple.***

Accidental (Per Accidens) Corruption: Whenever a form ceases to exist because of the destruction of a being in which this form inheres and exists, we may say that this form is corrupted *accidentally*. Such is the case with accidental forms whose subject is being destroyed. Thus the whiteness of paper is corrupted when the paper is burned. In this instance, the accidental form, color, does not corrupt naturally of itself, but by reason of the corruption of the substance, the subject in which it inheres. Something similar is true of all material substantial forms, which are educed from the potency of matter, and depend upon matter for their "to be" (as well as for their coming to be). Although such forms are simple, as for example the substantial form of a dog, they are not immortal, for they ***can be reduced to the potency of matter.*** These forms are said to corrupt when the corporeal being of which they are the substantial form corrupts; thus these forms are corrupted accidentally. Here again our conclusion regarding the soul of man is evident: ***The soul of man cannot be corrupted accidentally because it is subsistent.***

> . . . We must assert that the human soul, which we call the intellectual principle, is incorruptible. For a thing may be corrupted in two ways: in itself and accidentally. Now it is impossible for any subsistent being to be generated or corrupted accidentally, that is, by the generation or corruption of something else. For generation and corruption belong to a thing in the same way that "to be" belongs to it, which is acquired by generation and lost by corruption. Therefore, whatever has "to be" in itself (*per se*) cannot be generated or corrupted except in itself; while things which do not subsist, such as accidents and material forms, acquire "to be" or lose it (*dicuntur fieri et corrumpi*) through the generation or corruption of composites. Now it was shown above that the souls of brutes

> are not self-subsistent, whereas the human soul is, so that the souls of brutes are corrupted when their bodies are corrupted, while the human soul could not be corrupted unless it were corrupted in itself (*per se*).
>
> This is impossible, not only as regards the human soul, but also as regards anything subsistent that is form alone. For it is clear that what belongs to a thing by virtue of the thing itself (*secundum se*) is inseparable from it. But the "to be" by virtue of itself belongs to form, which is an act. And thus matter acquires actual existence (*esse in actu*) according as it acquires form, while corruption occurs in it (*accidit in ea corruptio*) in so far as the form is separated from it. But it is impossible for a form to be separated from itself; and therefore it is impossible for a subsistent form to cease to exist.[44]

This argument may be summarized in the following *syllogism:* Whatever cannot be corrupted of itself or by reason of another, upon which it depends, is immortal. But the human soul cannot be corrupted either of itself (*per se*) or by reason of another (*per accidens*), on which it depends. Therefore, the human soul is immortal.

The *major* premise is the definition of immortal being. The *minor* is easily explained. The human soul is not corruptible of itself because it is a simple form and has no essential or quantitative parts. It is not corruptible because of another (the composite), for it is subsistent; it cannot be reduced to the potency of matter.

"To Be" Is Inseparable From Subsisting Form: In demonstrating that the human soul is incorruptible *per se,* St. Thomas in the text just quoted enunciates a principle which may prove difficult to understand: "That which belongs to a thing by virtue of itself is inseparable from that thing." He then applies this principle to the human soul: ". . . But the 'to be' [of a subsisting form] belongs by virtue of itself to the form and this form is an act." The conclusion follows with necessity: The "to be" of a subsisting form is inseparable from it; that is to say, the subsisting form must continue to exist; it cannot corrupt.

44 *S. Th.,* I, 75, 6, *c;* cf. *C. G.,* II, 55; also *Quaestio Unica de Anima,* art. XIV.

The principle stated in the major premise has often been misunderstood. It becomes clear, however, in the application made in the minor. The act of existing, as regards the corporeal essence, man, whose form is subsistent, does not belong primarily to the composite. On the contrary, the "to be" of man *by virtue of itself* belongs rather to the form. This act of existing, which is the "to be" of the form, is communicated by the form to the matter. The form, therefore, is fully and directly actuated; for, since in itself the soul is an act (perfection), once actuated in the order of existence there remains in it no existential potency. Hence, no new "to be" can be acquired. The subsisting form, therefore, is incorruptible.

On the other hand, the act of existing of a composite whose form is not subsistent belongs by virtue of itself neither to the form nor to the matter. Rather, the existential act belongs primarily to the composite essence. Matter, however, which is the potential principle of that essence, is in potency to other forms and is not fully actuated; nor is the essence fully actuated by the "to be." Hence, when the matter acquires another form (and another existence), the first material form is reduced to the potency of matter — it "corrupts" — and together with it the corporeal being is corrupted, as another corporeal being begins to exist. We see, therefore, that a non-subsistent form is "corruptible" in the sense that it is reduceable to the potency of matter. Only a subsisting form, consequently, is truly incorruptible. It is not educed from the potency of matter; it exists independently of matter; consequently, it cannot be reduced to the potentiality of matter.[45]

Argument From Natural Desire: St. Thomas also offers an

---

[45] A parallel text, concerned with angelic forms, may help to clarify this argument. ". . . incorporeal substances, because they themselves are subsisting forms . . . do not admit the privation of this act [existence], since 'to be' follows upon form. . . . Hence, in the form itself there is no potency to non-existence; and so such substances are immutable and invariable as regards their 'to be.'" (*S. Th.*, I, 9, 2, *c.*)

argument — he calls it a sign — for immortality based on man's natural desire for never-ending existence. It should be noted that this is not an argument from "consciousness"[46] — a human nature is a human nature whether conscious or not — but an argument based on an analysis of human nature. Because this nature through the intellect in some way apprehends existence absolutely and for all times, it necessarily desires always to exist, without temporal qualifications. Now this fundamental appetite is intelligible only in so far as it flows from an inclination of nature, from a natural tendency to continue always to exist. Moreover, the term of such a natural desire must be attainable, otherwise human nature would be a tendency to an unattainable end, a contradiction. Hence, the soul must be immortal.

> A sign of this [immortality] may be gathered from the fact that everything naturally desires to exist after its own manner. Now in things that have knowledge, desire ensues upon knowledge. The senses, however, do not know existence (*esse*) except under the conditions of here and now, whereas the intellect apprehends existence absolutely and for all time; so that everything that has an intellect naturally desires always to exist. But a natural desire cannot be in vain. Therefore every intellectual substance is incorruptible.[47]

The argument may be expressed in the following *syllogism:* The term of a natural desire is attainable, otherwise the nature is a contradiction. But in every intellectual substance never-ending existence is the term of the natural desire. Therefore, never-ending existence is attainable by every intellectual substance. It follows that man's soul, which is an intellectual substance, must be immortal.

---

[46] Arguments based on "consciousness" must be used with caution in philosophy. Individual internal experiences *of themselves* cannot warrant the formulation of universal principles that are applicable to human nature as such. Only by a philosophical analysis and reflection on these experiences can we make an induction leading to a law extending to all rational beings.

[47] *S. Th.,* I, 75, 6, *c.*

ARTICLE V: The Human Soul Is Created

The question, "Whence the soul?" is readily answered once we have established that the human soul is a spiritual, subsisting form independent of matter for its existence (and consequently also for its coming into existence). Because the soul is not a material form, matter has no potency for it, and, consequently, no extrinsic agent however powerful could educe the soul from the potency of matter. Accordingly, since the human soul cannot be educed from matter as from a pre-existing subject, it has no strict becoming (*fieri*); its coming into existence is dependent upon an extrinsic cause alone. Such a coming into existence is *to-be-created*. Now God alone can create,[48] for He alone is pure act in the existential order. Consequently, the human soul must be created immediately by Him.

> . . . The rational soul cannot come into existence (*fieri*) except by creation, which, however, is not true of other forms. The reason is that, since to-come-to-be (*fieri*) is the way to existing (*esse*), it belongs to a thing to come into existence as it belongs to it to be. . . . Properly speaking, it does not belong to any non-subsisting form to-come-to-be, but such are said to come into existence by the fact that the subsisting composites come into existence. On the other hand, the rational soul is a subsistent form . . . and so "to be" and to-come-to-be belong properly to it. And since it cannot come-to-be out of pre-existing matter — whether corporeal, which would render it a corporeal being, or spiritual [matter], which would involve the transmutation of one spiritual substance into another — we must conclude that it cannot come-to-be except by creation.[49]

[48] In the philosophy of God, the truth that only God can create is carefully examined. See: Henri Renard, *The Philosophy of God* (Milwaukee: Bruce, 1951), p. 195.

[49] *S. Th.*, I, 90, 2, *c*. Another pertinent text is the following: ". . . since the intellectual soul has an operation independent of the body, it is subsistent, as was proved above; and so to-be and to-come-to-be are proper to it. Moreover, since it is an immaterial substance, it cannot be caused through generation, but only through creation by God. Therefore, to hold that the intellectual soul is caused by the begetter is nothing else than to hold the soul to be non-subsistent, and to perish with the body." (*S. Th.*, I, 118, 2, *c*.)

This argument may be expressed in the following *syllogism:* As a thing operates, so does it exist and come into existence. But the soul of man operates and exists independently of matter. Therefore, it comes into existence independently of matter. But such a mode of coming into existence is to-be-created. The human soul, therefore, is created.

Question III

UNION OF SOUL AND BODY

Introduction

Problem: Throughout this course of study we are trying to give a philosophical answer to the question, "What is man?" It appears that man is a corporeal being (a body), as is manifest from his sentient and vegetative[50] operations, which proceed from matter as a co-principle. But, as we have seen in the preceding question, the being which we call man is also the source of operations that transcend the influence of matter; he is the source of the spiritual operation of intellection. Is man, therefore, a spiritual being and the body an illusion? Is he "mind" and not matter? Or is he really two things — body and soul, "mind and matter" — united in some way? If the latter is true, what sort of union exists between the soul and the body, between the principle of spiritual operations and the principle of material activity? Is this union a mere accidental union, a dynamic union, perhaps, in which the more perfect being — the soul or "mind" — directs the less perfect being, the body, as a rider directs his mount? Or is the union of body and soul a substantial union, so that man, though obviously dual and composite in many ways,

[50] The biochemical activities discernible in man are not distinct from the vegetative functions.

is a perfect existential unit? These are the questions that the philosopher must answer in order to give a satisfactory solution to the fundamental problem in any philosophy of man, the problem of man's unity; and according to the solution of this pivotal problem, a philosophy of man will stand or fall. We may roughly divide the principal positions that philosophers have taken with regard to this problem into three broad groups: (*a*) monistic views of the nature of man, (*b*) exaggerated dualism, and (*c*) the moderate dualism of the realist tradition.

1. Monistic Positions: A monistic position, whether that of Materialism or that of Idealism, is fundamentally an evasion of the "mind-body" problem. Such views of human nature, in their extreme and pure forms, admit only one element in man, either "matter" or "mind."

For the *materialist,* intellection is but a more perfect and more complex form of sensation; vegetative activities are reduced to chemical processes; in brief, the operations of man from the most perfect to the least perfect are explained as functions of "matter." In such a view of man, the problem of the union between spiritual soul and body simply does not exist.

The strict *idealist,* on the other hand, owing to a subjectivist explanation of knowledge, is locked up in a universe of his own "mind." In the extreme forms of Idealism, knowledge and reality are held to be convertible; the real is the contents of the "mind." The existence of the body is either denied (spiritualism), or it is claimed that the body has no intelligible role in human nature. Consequently, Idealism has no problem concerning the unity of man.

From this over-simplified treatment of the two extreme but pure philosophical positions concerning the nature of man, it becomes evident that Materialism and Idealism fail to come to grips with the central problem of the philosophy of man.

2. Exaggerated Dualism: Of those philosophers who have faced and have attempted to solve the problem of the union of body and spiritual soul in man, many have fallen into serious errors resulting from a fundamental Manicheism,[51] which declares that matter is evil and that its union with the soul is very weak and imperfect, if not altogether unnatural. Those philosophers whose doctrine is tainted by this error insist that the soul would be more perfect were it free from the bondage of the body. They consider the soul to be a form very much like a pure spirit, an angel rather than a form *of* matter,[52] which necessarily implies limitation by matter. In such a conception of man, union of soul and body is harmful to the soul, and, because harmful, it must be an imperfect union. The consequence is that man is not really a composite of body and soul; rather, he is a soul, a pure spirit — an angel, if you wish — which is imprisoned in, and burdened with, a body of flesh.

We, on the contrary, are confident that the union of the soul with the body is neither harmful to the soul nor imperfect. In point of fact, the union of body and intellectual soul is necessary for the perfection of man even as regards his intellectual operations. Although the intellectual soul depends in no way on matter for performing the immanent operation of understanding, nevertheless it needs sensory data from which it derives its intelligible representations. Its knowledge, which is primarily that of the corporeal world, is acquired through the instrumentality of the senses. Sensation, however, which is a partly material operation, depends on bodily organs. It follows that the intellectual soul needs the body in order to perfect itself even as an intellectual principle. We conclude that the body is for the good of the soul; indeed,

[51] Manicheism was founded by Mani, a Persian who lived in the latter half of the third century. We are best informed of this movement by St. Augustine, who was for a time an adherent of it.

[52] "Although the intellectual soul, like the angel, has no matter from which it is produced, yet it is the form *of* a certain matter, in which it is unlike an angel. Therefore, according to the division of matter, there are many souls of one species; while it is quite impossible for many angels to be of one species." (*S. Th.*, I, 76, 2, ad 1^m^.)

the body is very precious to the soul, for without it no human operation, not even the specifically human operation of intellection, could naturally occur.

Two fundamental misconceptions underlie most forms of exaggerated dualism, whether it be the ancient dualism of Plato or its more modern Cartesian offspring. The first error is the conclusion that since the soul is a subsisting substance, the soul is man and man is a soul.[53] The second error confuses the nature of the human soul with that of angelic forms. According to the adherents of this doctrine, the human soul, since it is intellectual and incorruptible and has for its end perfect happiness, must be the same type of being, the same species, as a pure spirit—an angel.[54]

In refuting the first error (man is a soul), St. Thomas points out that the sentient operations (as well as intellectual activities) are attributed to the supposit, man. These sentient operations cannot be the operations of a spiritual principle alone, such as the soul of man, but necessarily demand a subject composed of matter and form, of body and soul. The reason is that these operations are accompanied by bodily changes which manifest a dependence on matter.[55] Since these sensitive operations must be attributed to the supposit, man, we conclude that man is not the soul, but rather a *composite of soul and body.*[56]

---

[53] Cf. *S. Th.*, I, 75, 4.

[54] Cf. *ibid.*, 7, *c.*

[55] ". . . sensation and the attendant operations of the sensitive soul are evidently accompanied by change in the body, as in the act of vision, the pupil of the eye is affected by the likeness of color. The same is manifest with regard to the other senses. Hence, it is clear that the sensitive soul has no *per se* operation of its own, and that every operation of the sensitive soul belongs to the composite." (*Ibid.*, 3, *c.*)

[56] This thouht is clearly expressed by E. Gilson in *The Spirit of Medieval Philosophy* (New York: Scribner's, 1940), p. 185: ". . . what is there to prevent us from going further and identifying the intellect with the man? Precisely the fact that men have other operations besides the intellectual. Even if we wanted to identify the man with his soul, we should be faced with a difficulty of the same kind. Such an identification would be possible in the doctrine of Plato or in that of St. Augustine, because for these philosophers, sensation is an operation proper to the soul and one in which the body plays no part. And that, moreover, is why we

Regarding the second error (the soul is an angelic form), we need only to recall the principle that a perfection which is multiplied (and therefore limited) must be received in a limiting potency. There are many men; consequently, the essential perfection of man, his form, must be limited by an essential potency, matter. Angels, on the other hand, are pure forms without relation to and limitation by matter. Consequently, there can be no multiplication of angels within the species. Since men, however, are multiplied within the species, the formal element of man, the soul, cannot be of the same species as an angel; rather, the human soul has a relation to matter; it is limited by matter.

> . . . In incorporeal substances it is plain that there cannot be diversity of number without diversity of species. . . . For a separate form cannot be understood otherwise than as one of a single species. Thus, supposing a separate whiteness to exist, it could only be one, for one whiteness does not differ from another except as in this or that subject. But diversity of species is always accompanied by diversity of nature.[57]

The soul of man, therefore, is not a pure form; it is a form not only *in* matter, but made to inform matter, to coexist with matter. It is true that the human soul is a spiritual form, that it is intellectual and consequently can reach even to things divine. But these it cannot know naturally except through a knowledge of the world of material things. For man is not a soul; he is a composite of spiritual soul and body. "We are dealing no longer with a pure intelligence, but with a principle of intellection which requires a body to achieve its proper operation; and hence the human soul represents, in comparison with the angel, an inferior grade of intellectuality."[58]

---

have seen them defining man as a soul using a body. But since we refuse to disassociate the unity of man into two accidentally united halves, we are bound to admit that the substantial form we have described is only a part of man."

[57] *S. Th.*, I, 75, 7, *c.*

[58] E. Gilson, *Philosophy of Saint Thomas Aquinas* (St. Louis: Herder, 1929), p. 205.

The two errors discussed above (man is a soul and the soul is angelic) cause insuperable difficulties in any explanation of man's unity. All attempts of an extreme dualism to explain the union between body and soul as a union of two *beings* must end in failure, whether it be the dynamic union of Plato or the pre-established harmony of Leibniz. At best, such unions are of an accidental sort and fail to explain the strict unity of the corporeal-spiritual existent that is man.

3. Moderate Dualism: Only by rising to the existential order can the philosopher hope to give an adequate explanation of the union of body and soul in the existential unit, man. We already know that St. Thomas held a dualism in the order of essence, a composition of two distinct elements — matter and spiritual soul. This essential duality, however, does not impede the existential unity of man; for man is *one supposit,* a being in act by a single substantial "to be." This existential unity of man, we shall explain, is intelligible only because the intellectual soul is the substantial form of the body.

Division: This question is divided into four articles: (1) the intellectual soul is the substantial form of the body; (2) the intellectual soul virtually contains the lower forms; (3) the presence of the soul in the body; (4) definition of the soul.

ARTICLE I: The Intellectual Soul Is the Substantial Form of the Body[59]

Problem: The human soul is not man, nor is it an angelic substance. Yet it is something spiritual; for the operation proper to the soul of man is intellectual knowledge — the knowledge of essences. This cognitive operation, which we call the act of understanding, is a spiritual act performed without a corporeal organ.[60]

[59] *S. Th.,* I, 76, 1.

[60] *Ibid.,* 75, 2, *c.* It is true, however, that in the order of *object,* the intellectual soul depends on sensory activity to present the data from which universal knowledge is abstracted.

Nevertheless, we do not attribute the act of understanding to the intellectual principle alone but to the whole man, the composite, which is also the subject of sensitive and vegetative operations. The problem now confronting us is this: Why must the operation of understanding in man be attributed to the composite?[61] Or, to present the problem more concretely: If human intellectual operation is a spiritual action and in no way includes matter in its make-up, why must I say that Socrates, the man, understands, and not that the intellectual soul of Socrates understands? The soul alone, a spiritual principle—not the body—is the reason for the perfection of the strictly immaterial activity of understanding. Consequently, it would appear that the *soul alone* understands, not the body, nor the composite of soul and body. How, then, can intellection, which is a spiritual operation, be attributed to one and the same supposit which is also the principle of the material operations of vegetation and sensation? The problem, therefore, is to discover the nature of the *union* of the intellectual soul with the body, a union so intimate as to necessitate that the operation of understanding be attributed not to the soul, but to man, the composite.

Solution: The fundamental solution is that the soul is the act, the substantial form, of the living human body; or, more precisely, the human soul—a spiritual, subsistent, but incomplete substance—is related to matter as the essential act of an essential potency. In this union, the soul, a subsisting reality, communicates substantiality together with the act of existing to the body. The resulting composite unit, man, exists by one substantial "to be." Man, therefore, is a perfect unit, a supposit; and, since actions belong to the supposit[62]—not to a part or principle, but to the complete being in act—all the operations of man must be attributed to

[61] A fundamental epistemological position is implied, viz., that the reality of the object is the source of true knowledge, of our judgments and attributions.

[62] ". . . actions belong to supposits and wholes, and, properly speaking, not to parts and forms and powers; for we do not say properly that the hand strikes, but a man with his hand. . . ." (*S. Th.*, II–II, 58, 2.)

the whole man, the person, whether they be the operations proceeding directly from the soul[63] alone (intellection and volition), or from the composite (sensitive and vegetative activities). We shall show that *the intellectual principle in man, which we call the soul, is united to the body as its substantial form.*

Definitions: The *substantial form* is (*a*) the first, intrinsic, *actual* principle of a corporeal essence. Hence, the substantial form is the first principle of action of that essence, for a being acts in so far as it is in act. Because it is the formal cause of the nature, the substantial form is also (*b*) the principle of the substantial "to be,"[64] not the efficient (effective), but the *formal*[65] principle of substantial existence. Accordingly, form and matter exist by virtue of one substantial "to be"; they are united in one substantial act of existing, and in that way they form a perfect unit. This perfect existential unit we call a *supposit.*

The *supposit* is: (*a*) "a distinct something subsisting in a nature"; that is to say, it is a complete, individual substance existing by its own substantial "to be"; the supposit is that which exists. Hence, it is (*b*) the subject *which* acts, for only that which is in act (a being) can operate. We also infer from this that the supposit is (*c*) the *subject of all attribution;* all operations must be affirmed of the supposit. The reason for this is clear: because of the oneness of the substantial "to be," which is the supreme

---

[63] The soul is the principle *by* which (*principium quo*) man knows. Man, the person, is the principle *which* (*principium quod*) understands. To man, therefore, and not to the soul, must all human operations be attributed.

[64] Let us recall that for the living being, "to be" is "to live."

[65] "To be another's substantial form, two conditions are required. One of them is that the form be the principle of substantial existence to the thing of which it is the form; and I speak not of the *effective* but of the *formal* principle, whereby a thing is and is called a being. From this follows the second condition, namely that the form and the matter are united (*conveniunt*) in one 'to be,' which is not the case with the effective principle [the efficient cause] with that to which it gives 'to be.' This is the 'to be' in which a composite substance subsists, which, although consisting of matter and form, is one because of the [one] 'to be.' " (*C. G.*, II, 68.) The distinction between formal and efficient principle is extremely important. As the mover of the body, the soul is an efficient principle, but as substantial form, the soul is the formal cause of man.

perfection of a being, all operations, even the operations of a part or principle, are an expression of the dynamism of the existence of that being. For the "to be" is the actuation, not of a part, but of the whole subject or supposit. Consequently, the whole subject, the supposit, is the subject of attribution.

1. Proof From Definition of Substantial Form: In any bodily being, the first (essential) principle of operation is the substantial form. Now the first principle of operation in a *living* body, that is, in a living corporeal being (including man), is the soul, whether the operation be merely vegetative, or also sensitive, or — as is true in the case of man — even intellectual. Therefore, the intellectual soul is the substantial form of the living human body.

> . . . That whereby primarily anything acts is a form of the thing to which the action is attributed. . . . The reason for this is that nothing acts except in so far as it is in act; and so, a thing acts by that whereby it is in act. Now it is clear that the first thing by which the body lives (*vivit*) is the soul. And although life is manifested through various operations in different grades of living beings, that whereby we primarily perform each of all these vital operations is the soul. For the soul is the first principle by which we are nourished, sense, and move ourselves locally; and likewise it is the first principle by which we understand. Therefore this principle by which primarily we understand, whether it be called the intellect or the intellectual soul, is the form of the body.[66]

It is precisely because the intellectual soul is the substantial form of the body that we must attribute to the whole rational supposit, and not only to the soul, even those operations which are strictly spiritual, that is, those activities which are placed by the soul alone, independently of any material co-principle. This consideration will be the basis for the following proof, which is substantially the same as the first.

2. Proof From Attribution of Intellection to the Supposit:[67] Sup-

[66] *S. Th.,* I, 76, 1, *c.*
[67] *Loc. cit.* The following is a paraphrase of the body of this important article.

pose we were to deny that the soul is the form of the body. We would then be confronted with an insurmountable difficulty in explaining why we attribute the operation of intellection to man, the supposit, rather than to a part, the intellectual soul. Moreover, we would be contradicting a fact of our own experience that it is we who understand, rather than a particular part or principle. Moreover, it appears that any other kind of union except that in which the soul is the substantial form of the body fails to explain this attribution and experience.

When an action is attributed to a rational supposit, it can be attributed in one of three ways: (1) by virtue of the *whole self,* e.g., a physician heals himself; (2) by virtue of a *part* of the self, e.g., a man sees with his eye; (3) through an *accidental quality,* e.g., something white (a white man) builds a house. The third way is called accidental attribution; the first two modes are types of essential attribution. We shall now apply these distinctions to the attribution of intellection to the supposit, man.

When we affrm that the man Socrates understands, we immediately exclude the third of the possibilities illustrated above. Certainly, we do not attribute the action of understanding to Socrates accidentally, for that which is affirmed of man precisely as man is affirmed of him essentially; it is obvious, for example, that Socrates does not understand in so far as he is white or tall.

Nor do we affirm that Socrates understands by virtue of his whole self (the first possibility). If this were the case, Socrates would be but a principle of understanding, a soul alone, as Plato held. This cannot stand, for we perceive that it is *we* ourselves who *sense* as well as understand. Since sensations cannot occur without bodily organs, it is obvious that the body is a part of man.

We conclude that we must attribute the act of intellection to Socrates as proceeding from a part, an essential part of Socrates. Now this essential part, which in a corporeal being is either matter or form, evidently cannot be matter, since the operation of understanding is independent of matter. Accordingly, intellection must be attributed as proceeding from the formal part of the essence. *The intellectual soul, therefore, is the substantial form of the body.*[68] It is most intimately united to the body as its essential act.

Union Proposed by Averroes: After proposing this satisfying solution, St. Thomas proceeds to explain the error of the great Arabian commentator of Aristotle, Averroes, who postulated for all men a single subsisting intellect, existing separately and communicating with the different individual men through a sort of continuation of the phantasm. The absurd consequences of this theory are that we could never attribute the act of understanding to any individual man; rather, the "separated intellect" would understand. We could never, in this supposition, state that Socrates understands; rather, he or his phantasms would be understood.

"Mover and Moved" Union Proposed by Platonists: Besides the theory of Averroes, we must reject the error of certain Platonists who thought that the intellect is united to the body merely as a mover is united to the object moved, and not as a substantial form.[69] In such a union, the act of understanding could never be attributed to the whole man; it would be the soul—not man—that understands. We do not deny, of course, that the soul is the principle of motion for the body,[70] since it is the principle of vital operation; but the union of body and soul in man is of a much more intimate nature than that of mover and moved. Such a union would be an accidental, not an existential union and would not suffice to explain the fact that we attribute intellection

[68] The point to keep in mind is that man is known to be man precisely because of his act of understanding. If he were known as man because of his act of sensing, then a sentient soul would be his substantial form.

[69] This union is exemplified by that between rider and mount, or that between pilot and ship. In both of these instances, the union is one in the order of activity alone, a dynamic union, certainly not a union in the essential or existential order.

[70] The problem of the soul moving the body offers no great difficulty in Thomistic philosophy. The reason is that in the Thomistic view body and soul are united, not as two complete beings, but as two essential principles of the same being. The soul is the first essential principle of motion.

to the same composite, man, who also vegetates and senses.

Summary of Argument: The operation of understanding — a spiritual activity — is caused by the soul alone. Nevertheless, this action is attributed to the whole man, the supposit, who also is (and perceives himself to be) the subject of corporeal operations (sensation and vegetation). But these facts are unintelligible unless the intellectual soul is united to the body as its substantial form; no other mode of union[71] can explain this attribution. We conclude that the intellectual soul must be united to the body as its substantial form.

3. Proof From Operation Proper to Man: St. Thomas offers a third argument based on the principle that the substantial form is the cause of operations proper to a nature. The specific perfection in a corporeal being is from the substantial form. The proper operation of a being manifests its specific perfection and is caused by that which gives the specific perfection to the being. Now the soul alone is the principle of the operation proper to man (the act of understanding).[72] Therefore, the soul is the cause of the specific perfection in man; it is his substantial form.

> . . . The nature of each thing is shown by its operation. Now the proper operation of man as man is to understand, for it is in this that he surpasses all animals. . . . Man must therefore derive his species from that which is the principle of this operation. But the species of each thing is derived from its proper form. It follows that the intellectual principle is the proper form of man.[73]

---

[71] It is sufficient to have refuted the explanations of unity offered by the Exaggerated Dualists. We need not consider the Materialistic or Idealistic positions, for the proponents of these views do not really face the problem we are attempting to solve. The Materialist attempts to evade the problem of man's dual nature by reducing intellection to a complex type of sense knowledge; the extreme Idealist holds a universe in which matter has no intelligible role.

[72] It is on account of this operation that man surpasses all other animals. From this fact, Aristotle concluded that the supreme happiness of man consists in an act of understanding.

[73] *S. Th.*, I, 76, 1, *c*.

ARTICLE II: The Intellectual Soul Virtually Contains the Lower Forms[74]

Only One Substantial Form: If the intellectual soul is united to the body as its substantial form, it is quite impossible for other substantial forms simultaneously to actuate matter.[75] This truth appears evident if we recall the principles learned in the philosophy of being concerning matter and form. Accordingly, "the same essential form makes man an actual being, a body, a living being, an animal, and a man."[76] Three fundamental reasons may be offered to substantiate this assertion.

In the first place, if this were not so, man would not be a perfect unit. The reason is that

> . . . nothing is absolutely one [a perfect unit] except by one form, by which a thing has "to be"; for a thing has both being and unity from the same source, and therefore things which are named according to various forms are not absolutely one, as, for instance, a white man. If, therefore, man were living by one form, the vegetative soul, and animal by another form, the sensitive soul, and man by another form, the intellectual soul, it would follow that man is not absolutely one. . . .[77]

A second reason is taken from the mode of predication. For example, we directly and essentially predicate both animal and man of the subject Peter. But if Peter were animal by one form and man by another, it would follow that only the first of these two perfections could be predicated directly (*per se*). We conclude, therefore, that Peter is animal and man by one and the same substantial form.

---

[74] *S. Th.,* I, 76, 3.

[75] According to St. Thomas, Plato held that there were several distinct souls in the body: a cognitive soul seated in the brain, a concupiscible soul in the heart, and a nutritive soul in the liver.

[76] *Ibid.,* 6, ad 1[m].

[77] *Ibid.,* 3, *c.*

A third reason is that the substantial form gives the first "to be"; it makes a thing to be *absolutely* (*simpliciter*), whereas accidental forms make a thing to be *such* (*tale*).

> Therefore, if besides the intellectual soul there pre-existed in matter another substantial form by which the subject of the soul were made an actual being, it would follow that the soul does not give the "to be" absolutely and, consequently, that it is not the substantial form. . . .[78]

Higher Form Virtually Contains Lower Forms: For the reasons given above, we must conclude that there is no other substantial form in man besides the intellectual soul. It is the intellectual soul which makes a man to be, to be a body, a living being (vegetative), a sensitive being, and human. By virtue of one and the same substantial form (which is the intellectual principle) man is able to perform the operations of animals, plants, and chemicals. Accordingly, the forms of these lower beings are present in the intellectual soul in some way. This presence is not an actual presence, for man is not actually a brute, nor a plant, nor chemicals, although he obviously manifests the activity of all these forms.[79] Nor is this presence merely potential, for it is in matter that these forms have potential presence. But since the intellectual form has the *power* or "virtue" (*virtus*) of these lower forms, we say that the intellectual soul *virtually* contains them: the human soul is capable of the operations of the lower forms. The reason is that a higher act contains the perfection of lower acts, and since an agent operates in so far as it is in act, the more perfect agent can perform the operations of the less perfect. To exemplify this principle, we may use Aristotle's example of the pentagon, which virtually contains a tetragon, or the ex-

[78] *Ibid.*, 4, *c.*

[79] To the experimentalist, man manifests the activity of chemicals in combination. To say that man *manifests* these activities is a true statement; to say that man *is* chemicals is false. For man is a rational animal with operations far surpassing in perfection the actions discerned in the chemical world. The nature of a being is manifested by its highest, not its lowest, operations.

ample of a large denomination in currency which has the buying power, the "virtue," of many smaller denominations.

> . . . There is no other substantial form in man besides the intellectual soul; and just as the soul contains virtually the sensitive and nutritive souls, so does it contain virtually (*virtute*) all inferior forms, and does alone whatever the imperfect forms do in other things. The same is to be said of the sensitive soul in brute animals, and of the nutritive soul in plants, and universally of all more perfect forms in relation to the imperfect.[80]

ARTICLE III: Presence of the Soul in the Body[81]

Problem: The soul, as we have seen, is the act of the body, the substantial form of the body. Because of the soul the body is *such* a body, a living body[82] specifically human. Where, then, is the soul? In the body, no doubt; certainly, it is not outside the body, for it is an intrinsic principle, the substantial form. But in which part of the body does the soul reside? Obviously, in the whole body, for the whole body is human. If this be true, it would seem that the soul must have parts outside of parts, extended or quantitative parts; and, since what is quantitative is material, the soul would not be spiritual, nor subsistent, nor immortal. In our solution to this problem, it will be necessary to explain the precise manner of the soul's presence in the human body. We may state in brief that the soul is indeed *in* the body, that the *whole* soul is in the *whole* body, and that the whole soul is *wholly* or entirely in each part of the body.

Solution: That the soul is in the whole body and in each single part of the body should not seem strange. The same is true of every substantial form. For ". . . the substantial form is the perfection not only of the whole, but also of each part. . . . For

---

[80] *S. Th.*, I, 76, 4, *c.*

[81] *Ibid.*, 8.

[82] In this context, the term "body" means matter as actuated by a spiritual form, so that the resulting composite is the principle of vegetative and sensitive operations. In this meaning of the term, *body* is inadequately distinct from the soul which is its form.

the act is in that of which it is the act, and, therefore, the whole soul must be in the whole body, and in each part of the body."[83]

But that the soul is entire, that is, wholly or totally present in each part of the body, may at first not be clear. Obviously, we do not mean that the soul is present in every part of the body by *totality of quantity,*[84] for quantity cannot be attributed to the soul either essentially or accidentally. The reason is that the soul is a simple form; it is not quantitative in itself, nor by reason of its subject.

Nor is the soul present totally in each part of the body by *totality of power;* that is to say, the soul, which is the principle of operation, cannot cause the same type of operation in every part of the body. "For it is not in each part of the body with regard to each of its powers; but with regard to the sight it is in the eye, and with regard to hearing it is in the ear. . . ."[85]

There is, however, a third kind of totality proper to forms. It is called by St. Thomas *totality of perfection and of essence,* and signifies the presence of form in as much as it informs matter and gives the specific perfection to the composite essence. Since every part of the human body is human, we must assert that the whole soul of man is present in every part of the body by *totality of essential perfection;* for the soul is the substantial form of the body. ". . . It is enough to say that the whole soul is in each part of the body by totality of perfection and of essence, but not by totality of power,"[86] and in no way by quantitative totality.

[83] *S. Th.,* I, 76, 8, *c.*

[84] This ". . . kind of totality does not apply to forms, except perhaps accidentally; and then only to those forms which have an indifferent relationship to a quantitative whole and its parts. Thus, whiteness, as far as its essence is concerned, is equally disposed to be in the whole surface, and in each part of the surface; and, therefore, when the surface is divided, the whiteness is accidentally divided. But a form which requires variety in the parts, such as a soul, and especially the soul of perfect animals, is not equally related to the whole and the parts. Hence it is not divided accidentally, namely through the division of quantity. Quantitative totality, therefore, cannot be attributed to the soul either essentially or accidentally." (*Loc. cit.*)

[85] *Loc. cit.*

[86] *Loc. cit.*

ARTICLE IV: Definition of the Soul

At the end of this long discussion on the nature of the soul and its manner of union with the body, we are able to offer a definition of the soul. It is the famous definition proposed by Aristotle: *The soul is the first act of a physical, organized body having life potentially.*[87] Let us explain this definition in detail.

a) The soul is the *act of a body;*[88] it is the perfecting principle informing matter so that the resulting substance is a body, is organic, and is in potency to vital operations. The soul is thus included in that of which it is the act, namely, the living body.

b) The soul is the *first* (essential) act, because it is the substantial form which gives the first "to be" (to live); second act, on the other hand, is operation, which gives a secondary "to be."

c) The phrase *of a physical body* distinguishes this kind of body from mathematical bodies and artifacts.

d) The term *organized* signifies that this kind of body has a diversity of parts dynamically unified, working together for the good of the whole being.[89]

e) The phrase *having life potentially* indicates that the body is in potency to vital operations, which will perfect it; that it is in potency to vital operations (second act) is due to the first act, the soul.

---

[87] *De Anima,* II, 115, 10 (412 a^{27}; b^{25}).

[88] "Body" is a term of many meanings. Here it means matter as actuated by a vital form so that the resulting composite is capable of vital operations.

[89] Why is the human soul united to such a highly organized body? To this question St. Thomas answers: "Since the form is not for the matter, but rather the matter for the form, we must gather from the form the reason why the matter is such as it is, and not conversely. Now the intellectual soul . . . holds in the order of nature the lowest place among intellectual substances. Inasmuch as this is true, it is not naturally endowed with the knowledge of truth, as the angels are, but has to gather knowledge from individual things by way of the senses. . . . But nature never fails anyone in what is necessary, and therefore the intellectual soul had to be endowed not only with the power of understanding, but also with the power of sensing. Now the action of the senses is not performed without a corporeal instrument. Therefore, the intellectual soul had to be united to a body which could be the fitting organ of sense." (*S. Th.,* I, 76, 5.)

The Human Soul: It should be noted that the definition given by Aristotle is a generic definition of the soul, and, consequently, it is applicable to vegetative and sentient souls as well as to the intellectual soul of man. The human soul is the first act of the *human* body; it is the subsistent, substantial form of man's body, which, although it actuates matter, is capable of operations independent of matter.

SUMMARY

Man has operations of which some are material, others somewhat immaterial, some strictly immaterial (spiritual). The last type manifest man's soul as being incorporeal and subsistent, that is, spiritual. Yet, both material and spiritual operations are attributed to one and the same supposit. This is not intelligible unless the spiritual soul is the substantial form of the human body.

QUESTION I

IMMANENT OPERATIONS OF MAN (IN GENERAL)

Article I: *Vegetative Operations*

1. Nutrition 2. Augmentation 3. Generation

Article II: *Cognitive Operations of Man (Knowledge)*

1. Knowledge is an *extension* of the being of the knower. Knowledge implies a "becoming," a receiving of the form of the known without the matter. The forms of knowers, therefore, are less limited than those of non-knowers. Since it is matter that limits form, the forms of knowers must be somewhat free from the influence of matter.

2. In sense knowledge, man "receives the form" of the known "without matter but *with* the individuating conditions of matter." Hence sense knowledge is particular. Such knowledge is limited by matter as a co-principle of knowledge.

3. In *intellectual* knowledge, man "receives the form" of the object "without matter *and without* the individuating conditions of matter," by abstracting from the individuating differences. Such knowledge is universal and cannot have matter as a co-principle; it is strictly immaterial, spiritual.

Article III: *Appetitive Operations*

1. In general, *appetite* is inclination to the good.

2. *Sense* appetite is inclination to sensible good consequent upon sense knowledge.

3. *Intellectual appetite* (will) is inclination to good consequent upon intellectual knowledge, and hence can have for its object even immaterial good.

Question II

NATURE OF THE HUMAN SOUL, FIRST (ESSENTIAL) PRINCIPLE OF IMMANENT OPERATION

Article I: *The Soul Is Not a Body; It Is the Act of the Body*

1. The soul is the first (essential) principle of vital operations. Such a principle of life cannot be a body *by its very essence,* otherwise all bodies would be principles of life, that is, living.

2. A body is a living body in as much as it is *such* a body, a specific type of body. The specific perfection is due to its act (form). Thus the soul, which is the principle of life in a living body, is the *act* of the body.

Article II: *The Soul Is Simple*

1. The soul has no *essential parts* (matter and form), because it is not a body.

2. Nor does the soul have *quantitative parts;* for a being has quantitative parts by reason of matter, because it is a body. The soul, however, is not a body.

Article III: *The Human Soul Is Spiritual*

Spirituality *presupposes* essential simplicity and moreover denotes *existential* independence from matter. Such a mode of existence will be manifested by the mode of operation.

1. The human soul is *incorporeal.* Whatever has a definite corporeal form or nature cannot receive any other corporeal form or nature and remain itself. But the human soul through intellectual knowledge can receive the natures of *all bodily* (corporeal) things. Therefore, the human soul cannot have the nature of any body; it is something incorporeal.

2. The human soul is a *subsistent* form. Whatever has operation independently of matter must have existence independently of matter, since as a thing operates so must it exist. But the intellectual soul (which can know all bodies) has operation independently of a material co-principle (that is, independently of bodily organs whose determinate nature would impede knowledge of all bodies). Therefore, the human intellectual soul has existence independently of matter; it is a subsistent form — spiritual.

Article IV: *The Soul of Man Is Incorruptible (Immortal)*

1. The soul of man is *naturally (per se)* incorruptible, that is, by reason of itself, because it is essentially simple — not a composite of matter and form.

2. The human soul cannot be corrupted *accidentally (per accidens)*, that is, by reason of another on which it might depend, because it is subsistent; it cannot be reduced to the potency of matter.

Article V: *The Human Soul Is Created*

As a thing operates, so does it exist, and so does it *come into* existence. But the human soul operates and exists independently of matter. Therefore, it comes into existence independently of matter; it is created, not educed from the potency of matter.

Question III

UNION OF SOUL AND BODY

Introduction:

The unity of man is the central problem of the philosophy of man. Both *Materialism* and *Idealism* in their extreme forms fail to face this problem, the former by reducing man to "matter," the latter by admitting only "mind" as real. Thus they are both "monistic" explanations of human nature. *Extreme Dualism* at best explains the union between body and soul as an accidental one. The *Moderate Dualism* of St. Thomas admits a duality in the essential order, but explains the unity of man as resulting from a single *existential* act.

Article I: *The Intellectual Soul Is the Substantial Form of the Body*

1. From the *definition* of substantial form. The substantial form is the first (essential) principle of operation in any bodily being. Now this first principle of operation in the human body is the soul (which is the principle even of intellection). Therefore, the intellectual soul is the substantial form of the body.

2. From the *attribution of intellection* to the supposit. The operation of understanding (a spiritual activity) is caused by the soul alone; nevertheless, this action is attributed to the whole man, the supposit, who also is the subject of material operations (sensation and vegetation). But these facts are unintelligible unless the intellectual soul is united to the body as its substantial form (no other mode of union can explain this attribution). Therefore, the intellectual soul must be united to the body as its substantial form.

3. From the *operation proper* to man. The primary (essential) principle of the proper operations that manifest the nature of a corporeal

being is its substantial form. But the intellectual soul of man is the primary principle of man's proper operation, the act of understanding. Therefore, the intellectual soul is the substantial form of man.

Article II: *The Intellectual Soul Virtually Contains the Lower Forms*

Otherwise: (*a*) man would not be a perfect existential unit; (*b*) we could not directly predicate *animal* and *man* of the same subject; (*c*) the substantial form would not give the first "to be."

Article III: *Presence of the Soul in the Body*

The human soul is: (*a*) *in* the body, for it is an intrinsic principle, the substantial form; (*b*) in the *whole* body, for the whole body is human; (*c*) wholly, that is, *totally* in each part of the body — not by totality of *quantity,* nor by totality of *power,* but by totality of *essential perfection,* since it is the substantial form of the body.

Article IV: *Definition of the Soul*

1. The soul is the first act of a physically organized body having life potentially.

2. The human soul is the subsistent, substantial form of the human body; although it informs matter, it is capable of operations independent of matter.

CHAPTER III

THE OPERATIVE POTENCIES

PROLOGUE

Man is the subject to which are attributed many and diverse operations.[1] He exercises the functions of vegetative life; he senses bodies according to their external manifestations; he understands the true and loves the good. We must now inquire whether these various operations are exercised *immediately* by the soul. We have seen that the soul is the first essential principle of operation in man; it is man's substantial form. Should we say, then, that the soul is the *immediate* principle of these various operations? Or is it necessary that the soul have operative potencies[2] through which it acts only mediately? In other words, are the faculties of the soul realities distinct from its essence? This is the first problem.

In the second place, as philosophers, we are interested in knowing the nature of these operative powers. Is there any manifestation of

[1] A corporeal supposit is composed of act and potency in the three distinct orders of existence, essence, and activity. Consequently, the corporeal supposit, man, is composed in the order of existence of an act, which is "to be," and a limiting potency, which is essence. Man's essence, in turn is composed of an essential act (the spiritual soul, which is the first principle of operation in the essential order), and an essential potency, matter, which is actuated by the spiritual soul. The human soul, in turn, is the subject of accidental perfections (the vital operations) and accidental potencies, which we call operative potencies or powers.

[2] The operative potencies are primarily capacities for acting, not for being acted upon.

action that can indicate what these faculties are, whether there are more than one in man, and, if so, why they must differ?

Finally, a third inquiry must be made: What are the causes of the operative powers? Does God create them? Are they, like other accidental forms, educed by the efficiency of an extrinsic agent, or are they produced by the soul itself?

Division: These three points will be studied in three articles of the first question. In the second question, we shall propose a classification of the various types of faculties of man; this will be followed by a brief examination of the nature and function of the vegetative powers. The sensitive and intellectual powers will be discussed in later chapters.

Question I

THE OPERATIVE POTENCIES (IN GENERAL)

This question is divided into three articles: (1) the operative potencies are really distinct from the soul; (2) diversity of operative potencies; (3) relation of operative potencies to the soul.

ARTICLE I: The Operative Potencies Are Really Distinct From the Soul

Problem: Can the soul act by its essence (*per essentiam*), that is, without the instrumentality of distinct faculties or powers? St. Thomas insists that an affirmative reply to this question is tantamount to making the human soul equal to God. And yet there have been many thinkers from Ockham to philosophers of the present day who have refused to accept the important truth that the human soul and its operative potencies are really distinct. It is quite probable that the reason for denying that the operative powers are distinct principles of action is rooted in the refusal of these thinkers to accept the fundamental distinction between essence and "to be" (*esse*). This is certainly true of the Nominalists, as well as of the Cartesians. As for the modern materialist, who calls himself a psychologist, it is questionable whether he has enough interest in the soul to make an inquiry about its faculties.

Our contention is that in order to place an action, man must possess definite principles called operative potencies, which are the immediate principles of operation, and that *these operative potencies are really distinct from the essence of the soul.* Of course, these potencies are not complete individual beings within the supposit man. Rather, the operative potencies of the human soul are accidental forms of the genus *quality;* they are properties, proper accidents of the soul. They are not complete beings, but principles of being; they are *immediate principles by which man acts.*[3]

First Argument (From the Fact That the Existing Soul Is an Act and Is in Act): In any limited being, an operation is an added perfection and implies — at least in its inchoation — some actuation of a passive potency. Suppose, for the sake of argument, that man's operative potencies are identical with the soul. Should such a soul exist, that is to say, should it be actuated by its "to be," all its operative potencies would be actuated and, consequently, all its vital operations would take place at the first moment of existence. Man, in such a supposition, would not perform successive operations throughout his life; he would always be in act to all vital operations. This last inference is obviously contrary to truth; accordingly, the proposed supposition, on which the inference rests, must be erroneous. We conclude that in man, the operative potencies, which are immediate principles of operation, are really distinct from their subject, the soul. In other words,

[3] Operative potencies — sometimes called active potencies — should be distinguished carefully from *passive* potency, which was studied in the philosophy of being. Passive potency is a capacity for receiving perfection, for being acted upon. Operative or active potency is a capacity for doing, for acting; it is always an act, a perfection.

the soul is in potency to operation through distinct operative potencies.

> . . . The soul by its essence is an act. Therefore, if the very essence of the soul were the immediate principle of operation, whatever has a soul would always have actual vital operations, just as that which has a soul is always an actually living being. For, as a form, the soul is not an act ordered to a further act. . . . Therefore, for it to be in potency to another act does not belong to it according to its essence as a form, but according to its potency (*potentia*). And thus the soul itself, as the subject of its potency, is called the first act, with a further relation to the second act [operation]. Now we observe that he who has a soul is not always in act with respect to his vital operations. . . . Therefore it follows that the essence of the soul is not its potency [its immediate principle of operation]. For nothing is in potency by reason of an act, as act.[4]

We may *summarize* this argument in the following words: If the soul, which is an (essential) act and always in act (by the substantial "to be"), were the immediate principle of operation, it would always be in act with regard to all its vital operations. But the consequent is manifestly false. Therefore, the soul is not the immediate principle of operation; that is, the soul operates through really distinct operative powers.

Second Argument (From the Proportion Between Act and Potency):

> It is impossible to admit that the [operative] potency of the soul is its essence. . . . Since potency and act divide being and every kind of being, we must refer a potency and its act to the same genus. Therefore, if the act is not in the genus of substance, that which is said to be potency in reference to that act cannot be in the genus of substance. Now the operation of the soul is not in the genus of substance, for this belongs to God alone, whose operation is His own substance. Therefore the divine power (*potentia*) which is the principle of His operation is the divine essence itself. This cannot be true either of the soul or of any creature. . . .[5]

[4] *S. Th.*, I, 77, 1, *c.*
[5] *Loc. cit.*

It will appear at once that this argument is based on the principle that act and potency must be perfectly correlative. If an act is in the accidental order, its potency must be in the accidental order; if an act is in the substantial order, its potency must be in the same order. The act of any limited principle of operation is the operation itself, which is in the order of accident; for limited beings are not their end, but are in potency to their end. Keeping these two principles in mind, we may formulate the argument in the following *syllogism:*

Act and potency are necessarily in the same genus. Now the operation of the soul is an act (perfection) in the genus of accident, not of substance. Therefore, the potency for this operation must be in the genus of accident. The soul, however, is in the genus of substance (and hence is really distinct from its accidents). Consequently, the potencies for operations — which are accidents — must be really distinct from the soul.

Difficulty: This argument, although extremely forceful, leaves itself open to a seemingly insurmountable difficulty.[6] The operative potency is an accidental form, and, therefore, considered in itself, it is an act. But an act of what? Of the substance, of course. That, however, seems impossible, since, according to our principle, act and potency must be in the same genus. Apparently, we either must maintain that substance is an accident, or postulate other accidental potencies inhering in accidental potencies without end.

It is a rather remarkable fact that St. Thomas did not seem to realize this difficulty, which strikes us as most formidable. At any rate, he offers no formal solution for it. The reason may well be that he never speaks of "powers" or "faculties," which suggest acts or perfections of the soul; rather, he speaks of "potencies," which are not the perfection of the soul — operation is that — but enable it to operate. Now, since potencies are not acts in regard

---

[6] Duns Scotus proposes this difficulty. Cf. *In II Sent.*, d. 16, q. 1 (Lugdunensis, 1639), p. 762.

to the soul, the problem we have just proposed is in truth an imaginary one, based on a false understanding of the meaning of the "potencies" of the soul.[7] Operative potencies, since they are not perfect acts,[8] do not specify or determine the soul. Consequently, they are not related to the soul as act to potency; on the contrary, they are the "potencies" of the soul for operation.

Third Argument (From the Relation of Operation to "To Be"):

> . . . Each proper act corresponds to its proper potency. Now in every creature, the essence differs from the "to be," and is compared to it as potency to act. . . . Now the act [perfection] to which the operative potency is compared is operation. But in the angel, to understand [i.e., the act of understanding] is not the same as "to be," nor is any operation in him or in any other created thing the same as "to be." Hence, the angel's essence is not his potency (*potentia*) of understanding, nor is the essence of any creature its operative potency.[9]

This difficult metaphysical argument may be expressed as follows in *syllogistic* form: For each limited act (perfection), there must be a proportionate potency; for example, proportioned to a limited "to be" is a limiting essence, a potency. But operation in a limited

---

[7] A reason for our pseudo-problem is a common empirical view of substance as a static, dead substratum, lacking all capacity for operation.

[8] One might object that the operative potencies are certainly perfections. They are forms; they are somehow acts, necessarily limited and individuated by the substance. Hence, the substance is their potency — which amounts to saying that the soul is the potency of its potencies. To answer this objection, we must distinguish between perfect and imperfect act. An *imperfect* act is a perfection not yet complete, not fully actuated. Motion, for example, is an imperfect act; it becomes perfect, that is, it reaches its full actuation at the term. In like manner, an operative potency is an imperfect act which becomes perfect through its operation. A *perfect* act, because it *specifies* a potency, must be received in a potency of the same genus; and that is why we postulate an operative potency distinct from the soul, since, as we shall see in the next article, the operation is the specificative act. Now the operative potency cannot be called a perfect act, because, like a habit, it is potency at the same time as it is act or form. It does not determine; it does not specify, and therefore there is no problem regarding the relation between the substantial soul and its accidental potencies or properties. They are simply not related as potency to act. Cf. Fr. Rozadowski, S.J., *Gregorianum,* 1935, p. 272 *et. seq.*

[9] *S. Th.,* I, 54, 3, *c.*

being is an act (perfection) distinct from "to be."[10] Therefore, there must be a potency proportioned to this act, which we shall call operative potency. But the potency proportioned to operation in a limited being cannot be essence, for essence is potency for "to be." Therefore, there must be a potency for operation distinct from the essence; this potency we call an operative potency.

The following is a variation of the same argument: If the operative potencies were not really distinct from the essence of the soul, operation would have to be identical with the "to be." But this is obviously impossible in all limited beings; God alone is His own operation. Therefore, the operative potencies must be really distinct from the essence of the soul.

ARTICLE II: Diversity of Operative Potencies[11]

Problem: We have seen that the operative potencies are really distinct from the essence of the soul, not as complete beings, but as immediate principles by which man acts. Our present question is this: does the soul perform its various operations through the instrumentality of one and only one faculty? It seems reasonable from a consideration of the corporeal-spiritual nature of man to suppose that his operative potencies must be many and varied, for as St. Thomas points out, the human soul "is on the confines of spiritual and corporeal creatures, and therefore the powers of both meet together in the soul."[12] Moreover, man needs a variety of sense faculties in order to know the various aspects of corporeal beings, which are the proper object of his intellect.

Our problem is to discover the reason which will enable us to distinguish the diverse operative potencies in man and to obtain a more perfect knowledge of their nature.

[10] Cf. *The Philosophy of Being*, pp. 70–71. A being whose operation is identical with its "to be" is pure act. In limited beings operation is second act, the perfection of a nature which is in potency since it is not "to be." Cf. *S. Th.*, I, 54, art. 1–3.
[11] *S. Th.*, I, 77, 3, *c*.
[12] *Ibid.*, 2, *c*.

Operation Specifies Operative Potency: We cannot obtain an immediate knowledge of the intrinsic nature of the operative potencies.[13] We may, however, by studying the operations[14] to which they are directed, arrive at a definite understanding of the nature of these powers. We can, for example, by carefully examining the way a wound was made, form some judgment as to the nature of the instrument which inflicted the wound — whether it was sharp, dull, or blunt. In like manner, a study of the operations of man enables us to rise to a knowledge of the nature of the operative potencies from which those activities immediately proceed. And, if two operations are discovered to be specifically distinct — for example, seeing and hearing — we know that their immediate principles are really distinct. In brief, *operations specify operative potencies.*

The basis for this principle is ultimately the due proportion between potency and act; it is act which specifies potency.

> . . . potency, in so far as it is potency, is directed to an act. Therefore, we must derive the nature of an [operative] potency from the act [operation] to which it is directed; and, consequently, the nature of an [operative] potency is diversified according as the nature of the act [operation] is diversified.[15]

This is to say that the purpose, or *end,* of an operative potency is to act; operation is its sole *raison d'être*. Now the end in a true sense determines and specifies, although it does so not intrinsically but *extrinsically*.[16] For example, the nature of an instrument is determined and specified by the purpose for which it is intended. Thus, the operation specifies the faculty extrinsically as a final cause.

---

[13] While the faculty itself cannot be known by us directly, we can, however, immediately have knowledge of the manifestations of the different operations of man.

[14] We cannot understand the nature of the operation unless we know its term or object.

[15] *S. Th.,* I, 77, 3, *c.*

[16] "Action, though subsequent in existence to power, is, nevertheless, prior to it in intention and logically, as the end is with regard to the agent. And the object, although it is extrinsic, is, nevertheless, the principle or the end of the action. . . ." (*Loc. cit.*)

Consequently, should we note in man operations which are specifically distinct — such as tasting and smelling — we shall have to postulate distinct operative potencies. This is the meaning of the principle, "operation specifies the operative potency."

Object Specifies the Operation: How then are operations diversified? To this question, St. Thomas answers that the *object* of an operation is the specifying factor of that operation.[17]

> . . . The nature of an operation is diversified according to the various natures of the objects. For every action is either of an active potency or of a passive potency. Now, the object is related to the operation of a passive power as the principle and as the moving cause; for color is the principle of vision in as much as it moves the sight. On the other hand, to the operation of an active potency the object is a term and an end, just as the object of the augmentative power (*virtus*) is perfect quantity which is the end of growth. Now, from these two things an action receives its species, namely, from its principle, or from its end or term. For the action of heating differs from the action of cooling in this, that the former proceeds from something hot, which is the active principle, to heat; while the latter proceeds from something cold, which is the active principle, to cold. Therefore, the [operative] potencies are of necessity distinguished by their actions and objects.[18]

Primarily Passive Operative Potencies: For a better understanding of this solution we must distinguish between two general types of faculties. There are some operative potencies which before acting are passive. They must be *put in act in order that they may act*. That which puts them in act is the object; sight, for example, is actuated by a colored object. This actuation, however, is effected by the colored object, not in as much as it is audible, rough or smooth, hot or cold, but under the precise aspect or formality of color. The precise way in which the colored thing is an object of

---

[17] It cannot be stressed too strongly that this diversification from the object is not in the order of *efficient* causality, but in the order of specification, that is, in the order of finality and object (formal causality).

[18] *Loc. cit.*

sight is termed *formal* object. It is clear then that the object — in the case of sight, color, or rather the colored — is not only in some way the efficient principle of the actuation of the faculty, but is also the reason for its specification. In other words, the ultimate reason for the distinction of operations, as well as for the diversification of operative potencies and their actuation, is the nature of the object. Specifically distinct *formal* objects — for example, color and sound as related to a sentient subject — will specify distinct operative potencies, in this case, the visual and the auditory senses.

The *material* object, that is to say, *what* these operative potencies can attain, will be restricted in accordance with the formal object. Thus sight can apprehend only those corporeal things which manifest themselves under the aspect (formal object) of color. Hence, a colorless corporeal thing, such as the air, cannot be apprehended by the sight: it does not fall under the material object of the sight; another sense with a distinct formal object must be employed. The formal object of the intellect, however, is being, not under a limited aspect such as color, sound, or taste, but precisely *as being*. Consequently, the material object of the intellect — that to which it can attain — is limitless; the intellect can attain to all being.

Active Powers: Besides the passive operative potencies, which need to be put in act so that they may act immanently, there are *active powers* or "virtues" (*virtutes*); such are the vegetative powers. These principles of action *are always in act,* and consequently do not need to be put into act. Hence, their object cannot be the principle of their action. The object is simply the *end* or *term* of their operation. Thus, for example, quantity is the end and term of the action of the power of growth. Although this end does not actuate the power of growth,[19] still it specifies the operation, since it determines the agent to act in a definite manner. Thus

---

[19] Obviously, this object (quantitative increase) does not act (in the order of efficient causality) upon the faculty, for it does not exist until the faculty acts.

this end, the term of action, manifests the nature of the operation and consequently the nature of the faculty.

Accidentally Distinct Operations: If, as we have seen, the object is the ultimate reason for the distinction between faculties, it would seem that we should need a faculty for every different kind of object — a special kind of sight, for instance, to see the *green* grass and another to see a *red* flag. To solve this problem, we must note that the object which specifies the operation is not the material, but the *formal* object.

The "material object" of an operation is the reality which is attained by the faculty in its operation. Let us take, for example, as material object of knowledge, a red sounding bell. If we refer this object to a sentient knower viewed precisely as sentient, we infer immediately that each of the two cognitive operations (seeing and hearing) which attain the reality is limited to a distinct, specific aspect (formal object) of the (material) object. Thus, seeing and hearing are specifically distinct sentient operations and consequently presuppose really distinct operative potencies[20] as their immediate principles.

Let us now consider as material objects of knowledge a *red* flag and *green* grass. It is evident that when these colored objects are referred to a sentient subject of knowledge, they will be both known under the same specific aspect (formal object) of color, and, therefore, they will be attained in the same specific type of

[20] We cannot, for example, *see* the sound of a bodily thing, nor can we *hear* its color; both senses attain their objects under a diverse formal aspect, and hence their operations are specifically distinct. On the other hand, the seeing of a *white* object and the seeing of a *green* object are but accidentally distinct operations, for both are apprehensions of color (or the colored). Also, whether the white object be snow, a rose, or even a man is accidental to the sense; for the senses do not attain to the essences of things. That, of course, is the role of the intellect, which has for its formal object being *as being;* that is to say, the intellect knows *what* appears white and that it *is*.

It should be noted that some "powers," for example, the power to persuade, or the ability to read, are a complexus of several operative potencies operating in a unified way. The operations of such "powers" do not have a single formal object which is specifically distinct, and hence they do not specify distinct operative potencies.

operation — vision. Hence, the operative potency of the sentient subject is the same for apprehending the red flag and green grass.

> . . . We must observe that things which are accidental do not change the species. . . . In like manner, therefore, not any variety of objects diversifies the [operative] potencies of the soul, but a difference in that to which the potency of its very nature is directed. Thus the senses of their very nature are directed to the passive quality which of itself is divided into color, sound, and the like, and therefore there is one sensitive potency with regard to color, namely sight, and another with regard to sound, namely hearing. But it is accidental to a passive quality, for instance, to something colored, to be a musician or grammarian, great or small, a man or a stone. Therefore, by reason of such differences, the potencies of the soul are not distinguished.[21]

ARTICLE III: Relations of Operative Potencies to the Soul[22]

Problem: The soul is a substantial principle; its operative potencies are accidents. However, they are not common accidents; they are properties of the soul; the human soul can never exist without them.[23] The present article is concerned with the origin of these potencies. Are they educed by the action of an extrinsic agent from the potentiality of their subject, the soul? Are they created directly by God? Or is the soul their active or efficient principle?

Not Created: These potencies do not arise by a direct creation, for the object of creation is a substance, not accidents, which inhere in existing subjects. We do not deny, of course, that the action of the First Cause in regard to the human soul extends not only to the substance of the soul but even to the properties because

---

[21] *S. Th.,* I, 77, 3, *c.*

[22] *Ibid.,* art. 5 and 6.

[23] The intellectual operative potencies have as *subject* the soul alone; the sensitive and vegetative potencies have as *subject* the composite; all have as *principle* the soul. Cf. *S. Th.,* I, 77, 5, *c.* and ad 2m. After death the vegetative and sensitive potencies remain in the separated soul only virtually, as in their principle. Cf. *S. Th.,* I, 77, 8.

of their natural connection with the soul.[24] But that is not precisely the problem at this point.

Not Educed From Soul: These potencies, since they are properties, cannot be educed by an extrinsic agent as common accidents are.[25] For, in order that a form may be educed by the action of an extrinsic agent, the subject out of which the form is educed must be in potency and not in act to the perfection educed. This, however, is not true of the soul and its properties. As properties, these potencies are necessarily connected with the essence of the soul. They are the "continuations," as it were, of that essence in its endeavor to act; in a certain sense, they are the links between substance and its activity. They are not new perfections to which the substance of the soul was in potency. Rather, they are the very perfections of the essence cut down, so to speak, to the stature of accidents to enable the substance, which cannot act immediately by its essence, to perfect itself in the order of activity.

The substance, therefore, with reference to these properties, must not be regarded primarily as a purely receptive subject in potency to them and actuated by them, but as an active principle — in a fashion, an efficient cause of them. And yet these properties are accidental forms; they are acts, perfections, and as such they would seem to actuate the substance in which they inhere.

> . . . Actuality is found in the subject of the accidental form prior to its being found in the accidental form; and, therefore, the actuality of the accidental form is caused by the actuality of the subject. So the subject, inasmuch as it is in potency, is receptive of the accidental form; but inasmuch as it is in act, it produces it. This I say of the proper and *per se* accident; for with regard to the extraneous accident, the subject is receptive only, and such an accident is caused by an extrinsic agent.[26]

---

[24] In this sense, we speak of the potencies as being "con-created."

[25] Common accidents are those that are educed from a subject by the action of an extrinsic agent. They need not be present as must be the proper accidents, such as, for example, the intellect in man.

[26] *S. Th.*, I, 77, 6.

Difficulty: This then, is the difficulty: How can the same subject be the efficient and the material cause of the same form? In other words: How can a being be simultaneously in act and in potency regarding the same perfection? Our answer is: This is possible when the acquired form or perfection is not a perfect, but an *imperfect act*—one which like motion somehow holds a midway position between perfect act and pure potency. On the one hand, the soul is the active principle of these imperfect acts; it is the agent which produces them and, therefore, the soul is a *quasi-efficient cause.* On the other hand, the soul is in potency to all possible actions, and because these potencies merely make action possible, it follows that they must inhere in the soul as in their *quasi-material* principle, since the soul still remains in potency to the operation, which is the perfect act. Thus St. Thomas writes: "The subject is . . . in a way the active cause of its proper accident. It is also as it were the material cause, inasmuch as it is receptive of the accident."[27]

Solution: The soul, accordingly, may be said to be simultaneously in act and in potency regarding its faculties, but not for the same reason. It is in act and is called the efficient cause in so far as the faculty is a proper accident or *property.* Now a property is not a new perfection superadded to the subject but a continuation of the essential perfection of its subject. It is not because the faculty is a perfection of the subject, but because it is an *imperfect* act—or rather because it is a *potency*—that the subject is its active principle. Yet, because this operative potency is an *accident,* a perfection, a form, it must inhere in its subject, which is in potency to the perfect act, operation. In that sense the subject is, as it were, the material cause of the operative potency.

Would it be true, then, to say that these potencies are produced by an action of the active principle, the soul? According to St. Thomas, this is not correct. No action of the soul is involved,

[27] *S. Th.,* I, 77, 6, ad 2^m^.

since the perfection produced is not new to the subject[28] and is not a perfect act. We should say, rather, that the soul, in so far as it is in act, is the efficient principle causing these operative potencies to flow from it "by a certain resultance."[29]

Question II

THE OPERATIVE POTENCIES (IN PARTICULAR)

This question is divided into two articles in which we shall consider: (1) the various types of operative potencies of the soul; (2) the vegetative powers. Subsequent chapters will contain a detailed discussion of the operations of the cognitive and appetitive potencies.

ARTICLE I: Various Types of Operative Potencies of the Soul[30]

Man, who is a perfect unit composed of intellectual soul and body, exercises the functions of three essential modes of living — vegetative, sensitive, and intellectual. Now that we have determined that man must possess operative potencies distinct from the soul, we shall apply the general principles formulated in the preceding question, and try to establish the number as well as the nature of the various faculties which man needs in the exercise of his three essential modes of living.

For the sake of greater clarity and order, we may classify the faculties of man in two ways. The first is according to the essential modes of living; that is, it takes account of the manner in which

---

[28] The nature of causal efficiency in the production of the faculties is very much like that of the production of the act of a perfect being (*actus perfecti*). In both cases the effect inheres in the agent. The difference lies in that the act of a perfect being is a perfect act, whereas the faculty is not.

[29] *S. Th.*, I, 77, 7, ad 3^m^.

[30] The following is an analysis of *S. Th.*, I, 78, 1.

the various immanent operations of man transcend more or less perfectly the transient action of mere inanimate bodily beings. The second classification is obtained by considering the object of the operations; for the object, as we have noted, manifests to us the nature of the faculty.

Classification According to Perfection of Operation: If we classify the faculties of man according as their operations transcend more or less perfectly the mere transient action of non-living corporeal beings, we discover three distinct types of operative potencies: the intellectual, the sensitive, and the vegetative.

1. Intellectual Potencies: No corporeal organ enters directly into the production of the operations of this type of operative potency.

2. Sensitive Potencies: A corporeal organ is necessary, but no material quality is required for the activities of these faculties.

3. Vegetative Potencies or Powers: Like the action of inanimate bodies, the operations of the vegetative mode of living require a corporeal organ as well as material qualities. There is, however, an important difference between the two types of activity. The vegetative function surpasses in perfection the operations of corporeal natures in as much as the principle of operation is intrinsic, while the contrary is true for non-living bodies. The latter are moved, and, having been moved, they move another body; but they do not move themselves.

Classification According to Object of Operation: If we classify the operative potencies according to the object of operation, we can distinguish five types of faculties: vegetative, sensitive-apprehensive, intellectual-apprehensive, sensitive-appetitive, and intellectual-appetitive. The reason for this classification is this: the more universal the object to which the operation of a faculty extends, the higher must be the perfection of that same faculty. In applying this principle we find that:

1. In certain operations, the object of operation is limited to *a single body*. The immediate principles of these operations are the

vegetative powers; they act only on the body to which the soul is united as its form.

2. In other operations, the object includes *all sensible bodies.* These activities emanate from the sensitive potencies.

3. In still other operations, the object is being, *all being.* These operations proceed from the intellectual faculties.

Apprehensive and Appetitive Potencies: Regarding the second and third classes a further distinction is necessary. Since the object here is extrinsic to the living subject, it can be related to the subject in a twofold manner: it can be known and it can be loved; that is, it can be united to the subject in knowledge by means of the *apprehensive* faculty, or it can be desired and sought by means of the *appetitive* faculty. Moreover, since the object is less universal in the order of sense than in the intellectual operations, we shall find two distinct types of apprehensive potencies: (1) *sensory-apprehensive* and (2) *intellectual-apprehensive;* and two types of appetitive potencies: (1) *sensory-appetitive* and (2) *intellectual-appetitive.*

Accordingly, there are in man five general types of operative potencies: the vegetative, the sensory-apprehensive, the sensory-appetitive, the intellectual-apprehensive, and the intellectual-appetitive.[31]

In studying these various faculties through their operations, we shall follow this order: (1) vegetative powers, (2) knowledge in general, (3) sensation, (4) intellection, (5) appetite in general, (6) sense appetite, and (7) intellectual appetite, the will.

ARTICLE II: The Vegetative Powers[32]

Man has certain operations in common with the world of plants: growth, nutrition, and reproduction. Since these operations are

[31] St. Thomas, as well as Aristotle, proposes another type of faculty, the locomotive powers. The findings of modern experimental science would seem to indicate that the locomotive powers are a sort of "by-product" or "resultant," if we may use such terms, of the sense appetite.

[32] *S. Th.,* I, 78, 2.

specifically distinct, they must proceed from really distinct powers.[33]

> . . . The vegetative part [of the soul] has three powers. For the vegetative part . . . has for its object the body itself, living by the soul; and for this body a triple operation of the soul is required: one whereby it acquires "to be," and to this is directed the generative power; another whereby the living body acquires its due quantity, and to this is directed the augmentative power; a third whereby the body of a living thing is preserved in its being (*esse*) and its due quantity, and to this is directed the nutritive power.[34]

Functions of the Vegetative Powers: The *nutritive* power is a power (*virtus*) by means of which a living corporeal being assimilates food into its own substance. A living body uses up energy and discards some of its material elements (catabolism). The restoring of these parts and the replenishing of depleted energies (anabolism) is the function of the nutritive power. Included in this function is the healing process in which injured parts are repaired and sometimes even replaced by the activity of the organism itself. Thus, for example, a wound in the skin will be covered with scar tissue produced by the organism's own action.

The *augmentative* power, or power of growth, is that by which a living body reaches its due size and the structural differentiation needed for performing specialized functions. Thus the operation of the augmentative power differs from that of the nutritive power, which is primarily directed to maintaining and conserving the organism.

The *generative* or reproductive power is that by which a corporeal living being produces another being of the same specific nature. This process may vary greatly in complexity: from the relatively simple reproduction by fission of the amoeba to the complicated

---

[33] In discussing the vegetative functions, we prefer to use the term "power" rather than "operative potency," which connotes a certain passivity. The reason is that the vegetative powers are not, like the sensory and intellectual faculties, partly passive.

[34] *S. Th.*, I, 78, 2, *c*.

bisexual reproduction of the higher animals. In human generation, moreover, the form which is the term of generation is a subsisting form, and for that reason is created, not educed from the potency of matter.

Many of the problems that are concerned with the vegetative operations could form the subject of further investigation but cannot be discussed at length here. It may, however, be worth while to mention several of these problems:

a) When food is assimilated into the substance of a living body, it is clear that the substantial form of the food (or of the ultimate components in the food) is reduced to the potency of matter. But which matter? Since no new form is educed from that matter, it would seem that the substantial form of the food is reduced to the matter of the assimilator. Would then the living being increase in matter? At most, we should speak of an increase of quantity, but not of matter.

b) Again, are the vegetative potencies accidental forms united to corporeal organs? What would be the organs which the nutritive and augmentative powers actuate? Are these powers localized?

c) Furthermore, why are the vegetative powers not partly passive, like the sensitive and intellectual potencies? Are they always in act? It is noteworthy that St. Thomas in speaking of the vegetative powers generally uses the word ***virtus*** or ***vires,*** that is, power or force, to indicate that they are already in act to operate and that they are not acted upon in the same sense as are the other faculties.

Differences in Perfection of the Vegetative Powers: Of the three vegetative powers, the nutritive and augmentative have their effect in the body of which the soul is the substantial form. The generative power, on the other hand, has its effect in another body; for nothing can generate itself. Since the effect of the generative power is not in the same body, its operation extends to extrinsic things, thus approaching somewhat the perfection of the operation of sense knowledge, in which the knowing subject has a certain extension of its being to other bodily things. Accordingly, of the three vegetative powers, the generative has the greatest perfection, even approaching to the dignity of the sensitive soul.[35] "Furthermore, the generative power is served by the augmentative and nutritive powers; and the augmentative power by the nutritive."[36]

Vegetative Operations and the Philosophy of Man: It will not be necessary here to examine the vegetative life from the anatomical and physiological point of view. Lengthy discussions of such things as cells, circulatory system, digestive system, nervous system, and reproductive systems are, no doubt, of considerable value. Such matters, however, more properly belong to a course in biology or physiology and are better studied there. In the philosophy of man, we are interested first and foremost in discussing the nature of man *as such*. Now man is man not precisely because of the vegetative functions of his nature, but because of his rational operations. For this reason, the chapters which are concerned with the rational life should form by far the greater part of a philosophy of man. Accordingly, we prefer to limit ourselves to the barest essentials in the treatment of the vegetative functions.

We do not deny, of course, that the particular dispositions of a particular body *here and now* will have a great influence on a particular soul. This is true not only because man is a strict unit, but especially because matter is the principle of individuation. But this particular influence of a particular body upon a particular soul is a topic which belongs not precisely to the philosopher, who contemplates universal truths, but rather to the experimentalist, who deals with individual facts.

---

[35] St. Thomas never fails to indicate the order in the hierarchy of beings. "For that which is highest in an inferior nature approaches to that which is lowest in the higher nature. . . ." (*S. Th.,* I, 78, 2, *c.*)

[36] *Ibid.*

SUMMARY

Question I

THE OPERATIVE POTENCIES (IN GENERAL)

Article I: *The Operative Potencies Are Really Distinct From the Soul*

1. If the existing soul, which is an (essential) *act* and *always in act* (by the substantial "to be"), were the immediate principle of operation, it would *always be in act* with regard to all its vital operations. But this is manifestly false. Therefore, the soul is not the immediate principle of operation; i.e., the soul operates through really distinct operative potencies.

2. Act and potency must be *perfectly correlative,* that is, in the same genus. Now the operation of the soul is an act (perfection) in the genus of accident, not of substance. Therefore, the potency for this operation must be in the genus of accident. The soul, however, is in the genus of substance. Consequently, it is really distinct from the operative potencies, which are accidents.

3. If the operative potencies were not really distinct from the essence of the soul, *operation would be identical with "to be."* But this is impossible in all limited beings; God alone is His own operation. Therefore, the operative potencies must be really distinct from the essence of the soul.

Article II: *Diversity of Operative Potencies*

1. Operations *specify* operative potencies; specifically distinct operations require for their immediate principle *really distinct* operative potencies.

2. The *object* specifies the operation. The *material* object is that which is attained by the faculty in its operation; the *formal* object is the aspect under which the faculty attains the material object.

a) Primarily *passive* operative potencies are put into act by the efficient and formal causal influx of the object.

b) *Active* powers are always in act. The object of their action is merely the end or term of action.

3. Operations that are merely *accidentally* distinct do not require diverse, that is, really distinct, operative potencies as their immediate principle.

Article III: *Relations of Operative Potencies to the Soul*

1. The operative potencies are not common but *proper accidents;* they are properties of the soul.

2. They are *not created* in the soul, nor are they educed from the soul.

3. The soul is their *quasi-efficient* cause, for the operative potencies are *proper* accidents, properties of the soul. Since they are proper *accidents,* they inhere in the soul as in their *quasi-material* principle.

Question II

THE OPERATIVE POTENCIES (IN PARTICULAR)

Article I: *Various Types of Operative Potencies of the Soul*

1. Classification according as their operations *surpass* the perfection of transient action:

a) Intellectual potencies; no corporeal organ is required.

b) Sensitive potencies; corporeal organ needed but no material quality.

c) Vegetative potencies; corporeal organ and material qualities are needed.

2. Classification according to *object* of operation:

a) Limited to a single body — the vegetative powers.

b) All sensible bodies — the sensory potencies (apprehensive and appetitive).

c) All being — the intellectual potencies (apprehensive and appetitive).

Article II: *The Vegetative Powers*

1. The *nutritive* power, by which a living corporeal being assimilates food into its own substances, renews its energies, and repairs injuries.

2. The *augmentative* power, the power of growth by which a living body acquires its due quantity.

3. The *generative* or reproductive power, by which a bodily living being produces a numerically distinct being of the same specific nature.

N.B. The sensitive and intellectual operative potencies will be studied in subsequent chapters, in which we shall make a careful analysis of their operations.

CHAPTER IV

KNOWLEDGE IN GENERAL

General Description of Knowledge: What is knowledge? What is this mysterious process through which we sense and understand the real? Perhaps, to a philosopher the most general notion of knowledge is that it is a kind of becoming, an acquiring of the form of other things, an extension of being. One individual being, the knower, somehow *becomes* and *is* another, the object known. Although the knower becomes, that is, receives the form of another, he nevertheless retains his identity. Hence, this "becoming" of knowledge cannot be precisely a corporeal or material becoming; rather, consequent upon an *immaterial* receiving of form, the knower by his own operation becomes and is the known in an intentional ("representative") union. This union of knower with known constitutes actual knowledge.

In a celebrated analogy,[1] Aristotle compares the "becoming" which occurs in knowledge to the impress which wax used for sealing letters receives from a signet ring. The wax receives the form, the impress of the signet ring without the gold or bronze. In a sense, the wax becomes and *is* the signet ring. Obviously, such a comparison can only give us a very limited understanding of the process which we call knowledge.

Division: In this brief and general description of knowledge, we

[1] Aristotle, *De Anima,* II, 12, No. 424[a].

may discern various implied elements which we shall examine in the following order: (1) The becoming that occurs in knowledge demands that the knower be in some way independent of matter; in fact, immateriality is the root of knowledge. (2) While becoming intentionally another, the knower remains the same physical individual. (3) In order to become — and hence to be — another, man's faculty of knowledge must first of all be actuated by an immaterial likeness (form) of the object. (4) Once the faculty is informed, that is, actuated by this representative image, the knower places the immanent action of knowledge. (5) This operation unites the knowing subject and the known object in an intentional union which is actual knowledge. (6) This intentional union is so perfect that the actual knower *is,* in a way, the thing actually known. (7) The degree of perfection of this union will vary according to the degree of immateriality of both subject and object. (8) Finally, a "definition" of human knowledge.

1. Immateriality Is the Root, the Ultimate Reason for Knowledge: There is a vast difference between knowing and non-knowing beings. Non-knowers possess only their own form, while knowers acquire the forms of other beings while retaining their own form. A plant, as long as it retains its own identity, cannot become another. It is true that the plant, for example a tree, may become something else — dead wood, smoke, ashes; such a becoming, however, implies the destruction of the plant. As the form of another thing is acquired, the plant itself ceases to exist. Since the plant, however, is a living, vegetative being, it can assimilate other beings, such as the various chemicals in the soil, through its own nutritive processes. In this act of assimilation, we note that the plant does not in any manner become the chemicals which it assimilates; it does not take on the form of minerals. On the contrary, the minerals, being assimilated by the plant according to their physical reality (form and matter), undergo a substantial change and become something of the plant. In knowledge, on the other hand, the knowing subject does not receive the object according to its physical reality (matter and form). Rather, the knower somehow receives (is actuated by) a form which is a representation, an "intention," a formal likeness of the object. Because of this actuation, the subject—while remaining itself—through its own operation somehow becomes the object in the union which is knowledge, without destruction of the object. We may say, then, that the knowing subject "acquires" or "receives" the form of the object *without the matter.*[2]

There is, then, this vast difference between knowing and non-knowing beings:

> . . . The latter [non-knowers] possess only their own form; whereas the knowing being is naturally suited to have also the form of some other thing, for the species [the likeness] of the thing known is in the knower. Hence, it is manifest that the nature of a non-knowing being is more contracted and limited; whereas the nature of knowing beings has a greater amplitude and extension. That is why the philosopher says that the soul is in a sense all things.[3]

But what is there in the nature of the knower that makes it capable of this dilation and extension which we call *knowing?* The ultimate explanation, according to St. Thomas, is the freedom of the knower from the limitation of matter; immateriality is the reason why a thing is capable of knowing. For it is matter which restricts a being by limiting its form and preventing it from being anything beyond what it is. From this we conclude that the more perfectly the knowing subject is independent from matter, the more perfect will be its act of knowledge.

---

[2] ". . . the sensible form is in one way in the thing which is external to the soul, and in another way in the senses, which receive the forms of sensible things without receiving matter, such as the color of gold without receiving gold." (*S. Th.*, I, 84, 1, *c.*)

[3] *Ibid.*, 14, 1, *c.*

> . . . The contraction of a form comes through the matter. Hence . . . according as they are the more immaterial, forms approach more nearly to a kind of infinity. Therefore, it is clear that the immateriality of a thing is the reason why it is cognitive, and that . . . according as they are the more immaterial, forms approach Hence, it is said . . . that plants do not know, because of their materiality. But sense is cognitive because it can receive species without matter; and the intellect is still further cognitive, because it is more separated from matter and unmixed. . . . Since, therefore, God is in the highest degree of immateriality . . . it follows that He occupies the highest place in knowledge.[4]

"There is, then, a considerable gap between that which is never anything but itself, and that whose being is, on the contrary, capable of dilating and taking up within itself the being of other things; this is precisely the gap which separates the 'material' from the 'spiritual.' "[5] And, in the last analysis, this gap is founded on the difference between the material and the immaterial "to be." If the "to be" is material in a complete sense, that is, if it depends absolutely and entirely upon matter, the being can be only what it is; it can never become another; it can never know. If, on the contrary, the "to be" is at least somewhat immaterial, and therefore not "buried" in matter, the existing subject, besides being what it is, can somehow be other things as well.[6]

---

[4] *Loc. cit.* The same principle is expressed in another excellent text from the *Summa Theologica:* ". . . the material things known [by the human intellect] must exist in the knower, not materially, but rather immaterially. The reason for this is that the act of knowledge extends to things outside the knower; for we know even the things that are outside us. Now by matter the form of a thing is determined to some one thing. Therefore, it is clear that knowledge is in inverse ratio to materiality. Consequently, things that are not receptive of forms, save materially, have no power of knowledge whatever — such as the plants. . . . But the more immaterially a being receives the form of the thing known, the more perfect is its knowledge. Therefore, the intellect, which abstracts the species not only from matter but also from the individuating conditions of matter, knows more perfectly than the senses, which receive the form of the thing known without matter, indeed, but subject to material conditions." (I, 84, 2, *c.*)

[5] Etienne Gilson, *The Philosophy of Saint Thomas,* trans. by Edward Bullough (St. Louis: Herder, 1937), p. 283.

[6] "The two modes of existing (*esse*) differ as follows: according to the material 'to be,' which is restricted by matter, an individual thing is only itself, for example,

2. The Knowing Subject Remains Itself While Becoming Another: It might appear that we are professing some sort of Idealism when we say that to know is to "become" and hence to know is "to be" the object known. It must be understood, however, that knowledge does not imply that the knower ceases being himself while becoming another. When anyone perceives a mountain, he certainly does not turn into that mountain. If he did, a substantial change would take place; the knower would cease being himself; and, having become a mountain, he would no longer be capable of knowing anything; in fact, *he* would no longer be. John of St. Thomas expresses this fundamental truth in these words:

> Beings that are capable of knowing are superior to the non-knowing beings because they can receive in themselves that which is other in its otherness, that is, what remains distinct as another, so that while they remain what they are, they can become other beings.[7]

This "becoming another" without losing one's own individuality may seem an implicit denial of the principle of contradiction. In point of fact, however, there is no such denial here, for the simple reason that the knower becomes the object *in the order of intention* (the order of immaterial, formal likeness) while remaining what he is *in the order of nature.* The object is received in the knower not *physically* (that is, by a material reception of form), but *intentionally,* that is, by means of an immaterial likeness of the object in the knowing subject.[8]

3. Necessity of a "Representative" Species: The faculty of knowl-

---

this rock is none other than this rock; but according to immaterial 'to be,' which is more extensive and after a fashion infinite, inasmuch as it is not restricted by matter, a thing is not only itself, but is also, after a fashion, other things." (*In II De Anima,* lect. 5.)

[7] *In Tres Libros De Anima,* Q. IV, a. 1. This important article should be read in full.

[8] "We see that the same thing can be found at one and the same time in the world of nature where it exists, and, when it is known, in the world of the soul or of thought; and it is necessary for us to distinguish the thing as thing, existing or able to exist by itself, and the thing as object, set before the faculty of knowing and made present to it." (Jacques Maritain, *The Degrees of Knowledge,* trans. by B. Wall and M. Adamson [New York: Scribner's, 1938], p. 110.)

edge in man, whether intellect or sense, is primarily a passive and indeterminate potency. It must somehow be actuated, moved from potency to act, by the object, since the object is a real cause of knowledge. This actuation implies the reception in the faculty of an immaterial form which renders the object present. We call this form the "representative" species or image. We should note, however, that the being of the object "received" in the knower is not the physical object which exists distinct from the knower, but a form or species[9] — a more or less perfect likeness — which "represents" not merely the *form* of the object, but the whole object, the composite of matter and form. This likeness, this species, is called the object in the intentional order. This same species, when viewed not as a "representation" but according to its own reality in the order of *nature,* is an accidental form, and as such it is united physically with the operative potency, the cognoscitive faculty of which it is the actuation.

Now, if we consider the union which takes place in the order of nature between the species (as an accidental form) and the operative potency (which is an accidental form of the knowing subject), we must say that this union is a *physical* union of act and potency. This is so because the species is the actuation of the operative potency, and the resulting composite is neither of its parts; it is something else, a third "something," namely, the actuated faculty. If, however, we consider that the form received is the *likeness* of the object, and that by means of this likeness the subject knows the object; and if, moreover, we consider that both

---

[9] Exceptions to this distinction are noted in the case of pure spirits (angels) and more so in the case of God, regarding the knowledge of their own essence. The object here is intelligible in itself, immediately present to the subject, and proportioned to its mode of knowledge. At this peak of reality, the order of nature is identical with the order of intention, and, therefore, no representative species is required. If, however, it were objected that the soul of man, which is an immaterial form and therefore intelligible in itself and immediately present to the knower, is not known except by means of a very imperfect representative species, the answer, as we shall explain later, is that this object is not proportioned to the human intellect, which has for its proper object material essences.

forms — the operative potency and the species — are acts (perfections) and are immaterial,[10] we must infer that this union is a peculiar union of act (perfection) with act, through which the subject becomes the object in the operation we call knowledge.

That the species must be *immaterial* is easily shown. The reason is that the subject must be somehow immaterial in order to know. The object, being received in the knower, must also be free from matter according to the degree of immateriality of the subject, since whatever is received must be received according to the nature of the receiver. It follows, then, that a corporeal object will have to be received in the knower as a "representative," *immaterial form, a species,* by means of which the operative potency will unite itself to the object.[11] It is unthinkable that a corporeal, individual substance, existing by its natural "to be," could be received in an immaterial subject, and be united to the knower in an intentional

[10] The subject must somehow be immaterial in order to know. The species, being received in the knower, must also be free from matter according to the degree of immateriality of the subject, since whatever is received must be received according to the nature of the receiver. " . . . the sensible form is in one way in the thing which is external to the soul, and in another way in the senses, which receive the forms of sensible things without receiving matter, such as the color of gold without receiving gold. So, too, the intellect, according to its own mode, receives under conditions of immateriality and immobility the species of material and movable bodies; for the received is in the receiver according to the mode of the receiver." (*S. Th.,* I, 84, 1, *c.*)

[11] ". . . the known material things must exist in the knower not materially, but rather immaterially. The reason for this is that the act of knowledge extends to things outside the knower." (*S. Th.,* I, 84, 2, *c.*) When a material object is known, it is "received" in the knower. This reception is not a material reception. Rather, this "reception" of the object means that a representative species is educed from the operative potency (in the case of human knowledge) by the action of the object. Now, to exercise this action, the object must somehow be in act. This, however, would not be possible if the corporeal object did not possess a faint vestige of the immaterial, of actuality.

All limited beings, even those that are lowermost in the scale of reality, participate in immateriality. The reason is that all limited beings, precisely because they are beings, must participate in the Being that is the pure act of existence and which therefore is pure Immateriality. Consequently, no matter how weak this participation is, no matter how deeply immersed in matter the form may be, there remains a trace of that which it shares, of that which makes it real, which makes it be. It is by reason of this actual element that a material object is able to actuate, to move the human cognitive potency.

union.[12] We conclude: the species, which is the actuation of the cognoscitive faculty, is an immaterial form.

4. The Immanent Action of Knowing: The eduction of the species is not the act of knowledge; rather, it is a preparation for knowledge, which is a vital operation. Now a being acts (operates) in so far as it is in act, that is, in so far as it possesses a perfection. It follows that once the faculty of knowledge has been actuated by the immaterial likeness of the object, it must elicit an operation by which the knowing subject attains the object, i.e., by which the knower becomes "intentionally" united with the thing known. This operation is the act of knowledge. It is an immanent action of the highest type, the act of a perfect being (*actus perfecti*). This operation, although terminating in the knowing subject, somehow unites the subject with the object in the intentional union we call knowledge.

5. Intentional Union of Actual Knowledge: The intentional union, which constitutes actual knowledge, is a union so perfect, so intimate, that *the actually knowing subject IS the actually known object.* In other words, the act of knowledge renders a thing actually known; knower and known are united in one act, which is the act of knowledge. This explanation of the intentional union is expressed by St. Thomas in several key passages:

> . . . The sensible in act is the sense in act, and the intelligible in act is the intellect in act. For the reason why we actually sense or understand something is that our intellect or sense is actually informed by the species of the sensible or intelligible object.[13]

> The forms that are actually understood become one with the intellect actually understanding.[14]

[12] We should not imagine that the intentional "to be" of the species is a reality distinct from the "to be" of nature of the same species. In reality, they are one and the same act of existing. There is, we may say, one immaterial "to be" in which we distinguish two functions: the natural physical union between two immaterial accidental forms and the intentional union or immaterial reception of the formal likeness of an object in an operative potency which is made to know. From this unique mode of union, the fact of knowledge necessarily results.

[13] *S. Th.*, I, 14, 2, *c.* [14] *C. G.*, I, 44, 4^{m} arg.

> The thing understood is in the knower by its own likeness. It is in this sense that we say that the thing actually understood is the intellect in act, because the likeness of the thing understood is the form of the intellect, just as the likeness of a sensible thing is the form of the sense in act. It does not follow that the abstracted intelligible species is what is actually understood; but rather it [the species] is the likeness thereof [of the thing understood].[15]

These texts indicate the manner in which the knower becomes the object known, and in what sense the classical phrase, "the intelligible in act is the intellect in act," must be taken.[16] The intelligible in act, that is, the thing actually understood, does not signify the species, but rather the object as denuded of the matter which prevented it from being actually understood. It is *because of* and *by means of* the species that the thing itself becomes actually understood. This fact must be carefully noted, for it is of extreme importance. What is actually understood is not the species, but the object itself.

a) The Intellect in Act: The phrase, "intellect in act," signifies the intellect which has been actuated by the eduction of a species.[17]

---

[15] *S. Th.,* I, 85, 2, ad 1^m^.

[16] For the sake of brevity we are limiting our discussion to human *intellectual* knowledge.

[17] Relative to the text from the *Contra Gentes* quoted above, Sylvester of Ferrara has a lengthy and important commentary. According to the *Commentary on the Sentences* (*In I Sent.,* dist. 35, a. 1, ad 3^m^), Ferrara thinks that we should not understand the phrase, "the form actually understood becomes one in act with the intellect," to mean that the form becomes the very essence or part of the essence of the possible intellect; rather, the form is to be considered as inhering in the intellect. From the conjunction of the two forms — species and intellect — a unit results which we call the intellect in act, just as from the conjunction of the soul and the body a unit (man) results which is capable of human operations. We do not say, however, that the body becomes the soul or the soul becomes the body. Hence, this comparison is not exact in all particulars, but only in so far as in each case a union which is a unit for operation results. From the union of species and intellect results a unit which is in act to know. The intellect in act is not the species, nor is the species the thing actually understood. Rather, the intellect is one with the species, in as much as from the union of these two factors the intellect in act results. Consequently, the "thing actually understood" really signifies the mental "word." For, as we shall explain, in the forming of the "word," the intellect finds the object and becomes the object in the intentional union which is knowledge. Hence, in intellectual knowledge, "the intellect in act is the thing understood in act."

The intellect in act is not the species, nor is the species the thing actually understood. Rather, the intellect is one with the species, in as much as from the union of these two the intellect in act results. And thus species and intellect are one by composition.

b) The Thing Actually Understood: By the "thing actually understood" is meant the known object, not the species. The reason for this is that the intellect acts according to the form which it has received. Now this form (the intelligible species) is the same form *according to its intelligible content*[18] as that of the object outside the intellect. They differ, however, in the mode of existence. In the order of individual realities, the form has a "to be" of nature, whereas the form received in the intellect has an intelligible "to be."[19] The very nature, the very perfection of the thing which exists outside the mind is received in the intellect.[20]

Now, since everything is what it is by its form, it follows that the intellect in act—because it has the form of the object—becomes by its action the thing understood.[21] This the intellect does through the act of understanding, by forming the mental "word" (*verbum*). In this intellectual expression of the object, the intellect finds the object as in a mirror and becomes one with it in a union of knowledge. Thus, one who understands a stone *is* a stone in a true sense, just as a being having the form of a stone is a stone; in both instances the formal element is the same. And yet, since the form of the stone as existing in the intellect has no natural "to be" as a stone, but only an intelligible "to be," it follows that the intellect cannot be called a stone absolutely, but only intelligibly.

[18] We do not mean, to be sure, the same identical form, but one that represents not merely the form but the essence of the object.

[19] "The intelligible species is the likeness of the essence of the object, and in a certain sense it is the quiddity and nature of the thing, not with the 'to be' of nature, as in things outside the mind, but with an intelligible existence." (*Quodlibet*, VIII, 2, 4.)

[20] Cf. *De Ver.*, II, 2. That is why St. Thomas declares that even a stone, when known, perfects the intellect.

[21] *"Sic enim actu intelligit res, cum species rei facta fuerit forma intellectus possibilis. Propter quod dicitur quod intellectus in actu est intellectum in actu."* (*Compendium Theol.*, c. 83.)

In brief, the intellect in act by its operation becomes the object in the *intentional* order.[22]

c) The Subject Is the Object: The intellect informed by the species of the thing understood is said *to be* the thing understood because the intellect has the form of the object by means of which the intellect is in act. For the same reason, the thing understood is the intellect in act, because it is actually understood by means of the same form which actuates the intellect. This form is the intelligible species existing in the intellect.

As to the nature of the union between the understood object and intellect, we may truly say that a more intimate unit is effected here than that of matter and form. The reason is that a new being — a third something — does not result from this union, as it does in the composite which is effected in the union of matter with form. For, as we have explained, when the thing is understood, the intellect becomes one with it, so that the intellect *is* in a true sense that which is understood. Matter, on the contrary, does not become form, but from the union of matter and form a third something results. Consequently, the unity between the intellect in act and the thing understood in act — that is, between the actually understanding intellect and the actually understood object — is more perfect than the unity of a matter and form composite.[23]

6. Degrees of Intentional Union: Knowledge, we have seen, is a *union,* an immaterial or *intentional* union, between the knowing

[22] "It is manifest that the intelligible species, by which the possible intellect is in act, are not the object of the intellect. For they are not related to the intellect as that which is understood, but as that by which the intellect understands. For, just as the species which is in the sight is not that which is seen but is that by which the sight sees — what is seen is the color which is in the body — likewise, what the intellect understands is the quiddity, which is in things — not the intelligible species, except through the intellect's reflection on itself." (*In III De Anima,* lect. 8, No. 718.)

[23] Cajetan proposes the same conclusion regarding the perfection of the union between knower and known. "The knower is the thing known, either actually or potentially. But matter is never form. And from this difference as to being follows a difference as to unity: namely, that knower and known are more one than matter and form." (*In S. Th.,* I, 14, 1.)

subject and the known object.[24] Now this mode of union with the object will vary according to the degree of immateriality of both subject and object; for matter is the obstacle both to knowing and to being known. Moreover, since in the actual union the object must share in the mode of existence of the subject, we may say that the perfection of the act of knowledge is proportioned to that of the "to be" of the knower. This will become clear if we compare four types of knowledge: the knowledge of God, of the angels,[25] the intellectual knowledge of man, and the sense knowledge of both man and the brute animal.

a) *God's knowledge* is perfect because He is His own "To Be," and, consequently, the act of knowledge in God is identical with existence, which is His very essence. "God alone, therefore, understands all things through His essence; but neither the human soul nor the angels can do so."[26] Both the knowing subject and the object known are Pure Act, and hence Pure Immateriality; the act of knowing is absolutely perfect, for the subject is perfectly one with the object. Consequently, knowledge in God is most perfect.[27]

b) *Angelic knowledge* is necessarily less perfect than God's knowledge. The reason is that an angel's essence is distinct from and limits its "to be." Consequently, no act of knowledge in an angel, not even the knowing of its own essence, can be so perfectly united with that essence as to be identical with it. Thus, even

---

24 "The noblest way of possessing a thing is to possess it in an immaterial manner, that is, by possessing its form without its matter, and this is the definition of knowledge." (*In Librum de Causis,* lect. 8.)

25 Although we do not know of the actual existence of angels from the natural light of unaided reason, still we must consider the possibility of beings whose essences are pure forms. In a treatise on knowledge, it will be an aid to our understanding to contrast the knowledge of these "possible" beings with the knowledge of man.

26 *S. Th.,* I, 84, 2, *c.*

27 ". . . it is clear that the more a thing is understood, the more closely is the intellectual conception joined and united to the one understanding, since the intellect by the very act of understanding is *made one with* the object understood. Hence, as the divine understanding is the very supreme perfection of God, the Divine Word is of necessity *perfectly one* with the source whence He proceeds, without any diversity [italics added]." (*Ibid.,* 27, 1, ad 2^m^.)

angelic knowledge, although far superior to human knowledge, is limited and imperfect precisely because of the distinction between essence and "to be." But, since the essence of an angel is a pure form, the problem of matter — the primary hindrance to knowledge — does not enter into the question of angelic knowledge. Accordingly, an intelligible species distinct from the essence is not required for the angel to know its own essence.[28]

c) *Intellectual knowledge in man:* With regard to man's knowledge, the influence of matter is all-important. Man is a rational animal, composed of a body and a spiritual soul which is the form of the body. Accordingly, his mode of being is partly material, and hence his knowledge is far less perfect than that of an angel. It is true that he possesses an intellectual soul made to know the intimate reality of substances. Nevertheless, because this intellectual soul is the substantial form of the body, man must derive his intellectual knowledge from the sensory data provided by cognitive contact with corporeal objects through the senses. For this reason, the proper and proportionate object of man's intellect is the essences of material things. Now this object is intelligible only in potency, because it is immersed in matter. It cannot be received in a purely immaterial potency of knowledge unless it is in some way immaterialized. Consequently, the potential intelligibility of this object must be rendered actual by an abstraction from matter. It will be manifest that in the act of knowledge, which follows the abstractive process, only an imperfect union between subject and object can be had.

d) *Sense knowledge:* Finally, since a sense faculty is partly material, and since the objects of sense cognition are the sensible manifestations of material reality, namely, the appearances of things, the union between subject and object in cognition of this kind is necessarily weak and ephemeral.[29]

---

[28] Its essence — being pure form — is intelligible in act and is immediately united to the angelic intellect.

[29] "The more immaterially a being receives the form of the thing known, the

We conclude from this brief survey of the various types of knowledge that the degree of perfection of knowledge varies according to the mode of existence of the knower. The notion of knowledge, therefore, which we attribute to diverse beings must be attributed *analogously,* and this analogy, since it depends on the nature of the act of existing, may be termed an "analogy of proportionality."

7. Definition of Human Knowledge: We are now able to give a descriptive "definition" of man's knowledge. *Human knowledge is an immanent operation enacted through an operative potency which has been actuated by a representative species of the object, thus enabling the knowing subject by its operation to become intentionally united with the object.*

In conclusion, let us state that the explanation of knowledge which we have just proposed is an *existential* metaphysics of cognition. It is because of the perfection of the act of existing that a limited being, even a corporeal supposit such as man, is able to become and to be other things in the act of knowledge. For to know is *to be* in a fuller manner. Not only does a knowing subject *become* the object known; in a true sense, in the act of knowing it *is* the object known.

SUMMARY

1. The *root of knowledge* is the *immateriality* of the knowing subject. For non-knowers possess only their own form; whereas knowers receive also the forms of other things, for the species (likeness) of the thing known is in the knower. Hence, the nature of knowing beings is less limited, less restricted. Now it is matter that limits and restricts form. Therefore, the immateriality (freedom from matter) of a being is the reason why it is cognitive.

2. The knowing subject *remains itself* while becoming another. The

---

more perfect is its knowledge. Therefore, the intellect, which abstracts the species not only from matter, but also from the individuating conditions of matter, knows more perfectly than the senses, which receive the form known without matter indeed, but subject to material conditions." (*S. Th.,* I, 84, 2, *c.*)

knower "becomes" the object known in the order of *intention* (of immaterial representation) while remaining what it is in the order of *nature*. In sense knowledge, the knower "receives" the form of the object *without matter* but *with* the individuating conditions of matter. In his intellectual knowledge, man "receives" the form of the object without matter and even *without* the individuating conditions of matter.

3. *Necessity* of representative *species*. Man's faculties of knowledge are primarily passive (operative) potencies. They must, therefore, be *actuated,* that is, determined and specified somehow by the object, since the object is a real cause of knowledge. The form educed from the potentiality of the cognitive potency is the form of the thing *without matter*—an immaterial representation or likeness which we call the *species*. By it the cognitive faculty, which of itself is indeterminate, is in act to operate immanently.

4. The *immanent action* of knowing. The reception or eduction of the representative species is not actual knowledge but a preparation for the act of knowing, which is the act of a being (faculty) *in act,* that is, an immanent operation.

5. *Intentional union* of actual knowledge. The immanent action of knowing unites the knower with the known in an intentional union. This union is so perfect that the actually knowing subject *is* the actually known object. *"The intellect in act IS the thing understood in act."* "For the reason why we actually understand something is that our intellect or sense is actually informed by the species of the intelligible or sensible object."

6. *Degrees of intentional union.* Knowledge is an immaterial (intentional) union between knowing subject and the object known. The mode of union will vary in perfection according to the degree of immateriality of both subject and object, since matter is the obstacle to knowledge. Thus the perfection of the union differs in: (*a*) God's knowledge, (*b*) angelic knowledge, (*c*) human intellectual knowledge, (*d*) sense knowledge.

7. *Definition of human knowledge.* Human knowledge is an immanent operation enacted through an operative potency which has been actuated by a representative species of the object, thus enabling the knowing subject in its operation to become intentionally united with the object known.

CHAPTER V

THE SENSES

PROLOGUE

Man has a very complex nature. In his highest operation, that of intellection, he attains to a knowledge of being as being. In the lower functions of human life, however, he has operations in common with the plants. Between these two extremes — intellection and vegetation — his sense knowledge holds a unique position, sharing somewhat in the nature of both. Like vegetation, it is an operation depending essentially on matter; it is material. Like intellection, for which it provides the data, sensation shares somehow in the immaterial; it is an action with some freedom from matter. This immateriality cannot be termed immateriality in the strict sense, that is, the immateriality which we attribute to the soul (spirituality), for the operation of sensation can never occur except with and in matter. Yet, there is a real immateriality in sensation in that the subject of sense knowledge becomes intentionally another being by means of a representative species. But the action of sensing, which results from such an actuation, remains so restricted by matter that it cannot attain the essential perfection of the object, but only its individual and material manifestations. In brief, sensation implies a change in the operative potency of sense that is material as well as immaterial.

Division: At the outset, we should distinguish carefully between external sensation and the operation of the internal senses. These two distinct types of sensory operations will be discussed in the two questions which comprise this chapter.

Question I

THE EXTERNAL SENSES

This question is divided into three articles in which we shall endeavor (1) to analyze the reality which we call external sensation, and (2) to study the nature and distinction of the external senses. To this we shall add (3) an article on the validity of sense knowledge.

ARTICLE I: Analysis of Sensation[1]

Problem: Sensation, though obviously an operation material in nature, is also somewhat immaterial. For it is a process of knowledge, an operation in which a corporeal knowing subject becomes ("receives the form" of) another corporeal thing without losing its own identity. The philosopher must account for this immaterial element in his explanation of sensation; he cannot rest with an explanation that does not rise above the realm of mere material and transient action. It is his role to give an explanation that takes into account the immateriality found in all knowledge, even in knowledge of the lowest sort — sensation.

Procedure: In the discussion of sensation, we shall show that (1) the sense faculty is primarily a *passive* and indeterminate operative potency, and, consequently, that it must be actuated by the object which is the initial cause in sense knowledge. (2) This actuation is had by the action of the object on a material sense organ of which an immaterial sense faculty is the quasi-form.

[1] *S. Th.*, I, 78, 3.

(3) The sensory species is educed from the potency of the immaterial faculty, and (4) is, therefore, a form without matter. But since the faculty is united to the sense organ as its form, this species exists with the conditions of matter; hence, the species is a particular, not a universal likeness of the object. (5) Once the sense faculty has been actuated, it must act. Consequently, the immanent action of sensation follows, in which the knowing subject is united to the object, which is intentionally present in the species by its action.

1. The Sense Faculty Is Primarily Passive and Must be Actuated: "Sense is a passive (operative) potency, and is naturally changed (*immutatur*) by the exterior sensible."[2] It is clear that man's sense faculties are primarily passive, for man is not always sensing; rather, he senses successively. Since sensation is the action of an operative potency in act, a sense faculty must first be actuated so that it can perform the immanent action of sensing. This prompts us to ask: How is the sense faculty actuated in order that it may operate immanently? To this we answer that the sensed object brings about this actuation of the sense; it is the initial cause in sensation. With regard to sight, for example, the object acts by reflecting light; in an auditory sensation, a vibrating body affects the sensing subject through the medium of sound waves. As a matter of fact, all external sensation implies a transient action of the object upon the sensing subject; hence, all sensation has a passive element.[3] Moreover, of itself, the sense is indeterminate and must be acted upon by the external object in order to be in act to the production of a *specific* sensation.

2. Conjunct of Material Organ and Immaterial Operative Po-

---

[2] *S. Th.*, I, 78, 3, *c*.

[3] "*Sentire consistit in quodam pati et alterari.*" (*In II De Anima*, lect. 13, No. 393.)

"*Sensus postquam factus est in actu a sensibili, est similis ei; sed ante non erat similis.*" (*Ibid.*, lect. 10, No. 357.)

"*Et quia quod est receptivum alterius, comparatur ad ipsum sicut potentia ad actum . . . ideo hoc modo dicitur passio.*" (*Ibid.*, lect. 11, No. 366.)

tency: The sensible object by its action, either immediate or mediate, causes a material change in the sense organ, a change which can be accurately determined and measured by experimental methods. This transient material action in the sense organ, however, cannot constitute sensation. *Otherwise, all bodies which are the subjects of transient action would have sensation.*[4] There must, therefore, be another change, a reception of form in the immaterial order, simultaneous with and in some way dependent on the passion in the sensory organ. This reception of form is the eduction of the sensible species[5] from the sensory operative potency and is pre-required for the immanent action of sensation. This form, a representation of the sensible object, is an immaterial form and is the term of an *immaterial* mutation. In fact, St. Thomas himself applies the term "spiritual" to this type of change.

> . . . Change (*immutatio*) is of two kinds, one natural and the other spiritual. Natural change takes place when the form of that which causes the mutation is received according to its natural being (*esse*) into the thing changed, as heat is received into the thing heated. But spiritual change takes place when the form of what causes the change is received according to a spiritual mode of being into the thing changed, as the form of color is received into the pupil, which does not thereby become colored. Now, for the operation of the senses, a spiritual change is required, whereby an intention of the sensible form is effected in the sensory organ. Otherwise, if a natural mutation alone sufficed for the action of the sense, all natural bodies would have sensation when they undergo alteration.[6]

---

[4] For example, water while being heated would sense the heat.

[5] The cognitive power, indetermined of itself, is determined or specified by this form. Hence, this representation is aptly called a *species*.

[6] *S. Th.,* I, 78, 3, *c.* A parallel text of the *De Anima* may help to clarify this difficult point. "I call that change natural in which a quality is received in the patient according to its natural mode of being, as when something is cooled or heated or moved locally. But a spiritual change is one in which a species is received in a sense organ or in a medium as an intention and not as a natural form. For the sensible species is not received in the sense according to that mode of being which it has in the sensible thing." (*In II De Anima,* lect. 14, No. 418.)

As we have explained, it is the object which actuates the sense, and it does this by its transient action through some sort of contact[7] upon the organ of the sense faculty.[8] If, as is necessary to explain the immaterial element in sensation, this same passion is accompanied by an immaterial change in the faculty (an eduction of a representative species from the operative potency of sense), there must be an intimate union between sense organ and sense faculty. We can explain this close unity as being analogous to that of matter and form, the organ being the quasi-matter and the operative potency being the quasi-form.[9] We may express this same notion by saying that the sense faculty is the "act of the sense organ." By this we mean that the human eye, for example, is *human* precisely because matter is informed by the rational form in such a way that in the resulting composite, a certain quantitative part of the body, possessing a specific structure, is the subject of a specific operation, the operation of seeing. This means that the soul exercises its operation through its distinct operative potency of sight in a definite quantitative part of the body of which the soul is the substantial form. The union, therefore, between operative potency and the sense organ is most intimate and can be designated as that of quasi-matter and quasi-form; or we may say that the faculty is the act of the organ. This unit, which is the subject of a twofold passion or change and the immediate principle of the operation of sensing, we shall call the sensory *conjunct.*

3. Eduction of the Sensible Species: This, then, is the genesis of sensation: The corporeal object, being sensible in act,[10] acts

[7] "*. . . organum tactus sine quo nullus sensus esse potest.*" (*In II De Anima,* lect. 24, No. 557.)

[8] Obviously, a corporeal object cannot act directly on the immaterial operative potency.

[9] "*Potentia enim est quasi forma organi.*" (*In II De Anima,* lect. 24, No. 555.) "*Organum sensus cum potentia ipsa est idem subiecto. . . .*" (*Loc. cit.*)

[10] "Sensible in act" signifies that a corporeal object is capable of actuating a sense faculty. All corporeal things are sensible in act, whether they are actually sensed or not by a sentient subject, which must first be actuated by the object before it can sense.

upon the sense organ by some sort of contact, either immediate or mediate. Because the sense organ is material, the change which takes place in it is primarily material. But since the faculty, which is the quasi-form of the organ, is somewhat immaterial, its mutation (which must accompany the change in the organ) will be more or less immaterial according to the perfection of the faculty. Accordingly, this mutation or change, which terminates in the sensible species, must be both material and immaterial. The dual nature of the subject of reception (the sensory conjunct) necessitates two distinct types of becoming for any alteration of the senses. Consequently, the sensible species, in so far as it is received in an immaterial potency, will be a representative form (a form *without* matter); but, since the faculty depends on a material organ, it will be a form representative of the individual.

4. Nature of the Sensible Species: The form, or sensible species, which results from this twofold mutation, has a manner of existence which is peculiar to sense knowledge. To express this mode of existence, St. Thomas has a terse formula. The sensible species, he says, is a form which exists in the faculty *without matter, but with the conditions of matter.* Or, to express the same in his own existential terminology: "in the sense the thing has a 'to be' without matter, but not without the conditions of matter."[11] This formula must be explained.

a) *Without matter:* The difference in the mode of being of the "received" form from that of the form that is being communicated by an extrinsic agent will be due principally to the mode of reception. For, whatever is received in another is necessarily received according to the mode of being of the receiver. Now, sometimes we find that a form has the same mode of existence in both agent and subject, as occurs in the heating of water. This identity of mode of existence is due to the fact that the subject has the same

---

[11] *In II De Anima,* lect. 5, No. 284.

kind of disposition to the form as has the agent. In this instance, the form which is received in the patient exists in the same manner as it exists in the agent, namely, *with matter.*

In sense knowledge, however, the form is received in the subject according to a different mode of existence from that which it enjoys in the agent. The reason must be that the disposition of the subject toward the reception of the form is not the same as that of the agent. In the case of sensation, the form is received in the subject *without matter,* in as much as the subject is assimilated to the agent *according to form, but not according to matter.* Thus the form has a different "to be" in the sense than it has in the sensible object. In the object, the form has a natural "to be"; in the sense faculty, it has a "to be" that is intentional and immaterial.[12]

b) *With the conditions of matter:* To explain this phrase, we can do no better than to quote a passage of the Commentary on the *De Anima,* in which St. Thomas compares the natural material act of existing with the immaterial "to be" (*esse*). The principal inference from this passage is that knowledge is possible only when a form exists by an immaterial "to be," since a thing can be only what it is if its natural existence depends absolutely upon matter. Now there are two kinds of immaterial "to be," namely, the "to be" of intellection and of sensation. The "to be" of the intellectual species is absolutely immaterial, having no dependence upon matter; consequently, since the individuating principle is matter, intellectual knowledge can be only of universal essences. On the other hand, an individual likeness of a corporeal object (the sense species) must necessarily be educed from some partly *material* subject, such as the unit composed of organ and sense faculty. Since the senses know individuals, they must be partly material, though

---

[12] Cf. *In II De Anima,* lect. 25, Nos. 552 and 553.

as subjects of knowledge they must also be partly immaterial.[13] Because the senses are immaterial, the sensible species, being proportioned to its subject, will be *without matter;* because the senses are also material, the same sensible species will represent an individual object.[14] This latter fact is implied by saying that in sense the object has a "to be" *with the conditions of matter.*

The following is the passage taken from the Commentary on the Second Book of the *De Anima* of Aristotle:

> Since, therefore, each thing has a proper operation in accordance with its "to be," in virtue of the fact that everything operates in so far as it is being, it is necessary to consider the operations of the soul as it is found in living things.
>
> Now lower living things, whose act is the soul, with which we are at present dealing, have a twofold "to be." One indeed material, in which they have a common lot with the other material things; the other immaterial, in which they share in some degree with higher substances.
>
> There is, however, a difference between these "to be's" because, according to the material "to be," which is contracted by matter, each thing is that alone which it is, as this stone is not other than this stone. But according to the immaterial "to be," which is fuller and after a fashion infinite, inasmuch as it is not limited by matter, a thing is not only that which it is, but also in a manner other things. . . .
>
> In these lower things, however, the immaterial "to be" has two grades. One is entirely immaterial — namely, the intelligible "to be"; for in the intellect things have "to be" both without matter and without the material individuating conditions, and over and above that, without a bodily organ. But the sensible "to be" is a mean between these two, since in the sense a thing has "to be"

[13] This is more precisely expressed by the words of St. Thomas. Those living beings which have sensible cognition, he says, have a twofold "to be," (*habent duplex esse*). He does not say, of course, "two distinct 'to be's,' " since he is speaking of the substantial act of existence by which a being is one. We might say that such a "to be" fulfills two functions.

[14] Since individuating matter is made known to us by the conditions of matter, for example color, weight, size, etc., it follows that a species whose "to be" is *with* the conditions of matter will cause knowledge of an individual, not universal knowledge.

without matter, yet not without material individuating conditions nor without a bodily organ. For the sense deals with singulars, but the intellect with universals. And it is with regard to this twofold "to be" that the Philosopher says in the third book of this work that the soul is somehow all things.

Hence, operations which belong to living things according to a material "to be" are operations which are attributed to the vegetable soul — operations which, although ordered to that to which the actions in inanimate things are also ordered, namely, to seek and conserve "to be," are nevertheless in living things so ordered in a higher and nobler way. . . . But operations which are attributed to living things according to an entirely immaterial "to be" pertain to the intellective part of the soul; whereas those which are attributed to them according to a "to be" which is a mean between the strictly material and the strictly immaterial pertain to the sensitive part of the soul.[15]

c) *A formal representation of the object:* The sensible species is a formal and not merely a virtual representation of the sensible object. By a *formal* representation, or similitude, we mean that the species is a real likeness of the object according to the object's own form (*secundum propriam formam*). It is, we maintain, formal and not — as some have claimed — merely a virtual principle which together with the faculty is capable of causing a true image of the object. Of course, we must admit that the accidental form which is the species has an altogether different mode of existence (intentional) from that of the corporeal object; otherwise, it could never be the medium by which the object is known. But the likeness of the species to the object is real and actual, not merely potential. This important truth of realistic philosophy is well expressed in the following passage from the *De Veritate:*

. . . The mutual likeness of two things can be regarded in a twofold way. In one way according to their agreement in very nature. Such a likeness is not required between the knower and the known. Indeed, we sometimes see that precisely in so far as a likeness of

[15] *In II De Anima,* lect. 5, Nos. 281–286.

> this is less, the more penetrating is the cognition: as the similarity of the likeness in the intellect of a stone is less than that which is in the sense, since it is farther removed from matter. And yet the intellect knows more penetratingly than the sense does. In the second way, this mutual likeness can be regarded according to *representation* [italics added]; and this likeness of knower to known is required.[16]

5. The Act (Action) of Sensation: The sense faculty, as we have pointed out, is primarily a passive faculty. Knowledge, however, is an operation, an immanent action. That is true of all knowledge, and, therefore, it is true also of sensation. Since the sense faculty of itself is only in potency to know, it cannot act unless it be put in act, for a being acts only in as much as it is in act, and certainly not because it is in potency. We have already explained the process by which the sense faculty is actuated, that is, how the sense species, an accidental form, is educed from the potentiality of the sense faculty by the transient action of the object on the sense organ, of which the faculty is the quasi-form. The sense operative potency, having been put in act by the eduction of the species, must act.[17] The act, or operation, is the act of a perfect being (*actus perfecti*). Our present problem is concerned with the nature of this operation. To solve it we must ask and answer the following questions: (*a*) What is the complete, immediate principle of the act of sensation? (*b*) What is the term of this operation? (*c*) Since knowledge is fundamentally a union, how can the knowing subject be united to the known object by means of such an operation?

a) We may infer at once that the *immediate principle*[18] of the act of sensation is not the sense faculty alone, nor the organ alone, nor the species alone; all these three must be considered as factors of the same operational unit. The reason is that the actuated sense

---

[16] *De Ver.*, II, 3, ad 9^{m}.

[17] "Regarding the act which follows the perfecting of the sense faculty by the species, sensation is an operation." (*In I Sent.*, dist. 40, q. 1, a. 1, ad 2^{m}.)

[18] We should never forget that the subject of knowledge — the knower — in an absolute sense is the supposit, not the faculty, nor even the soul.

faculty is the quasi-form of the sense organ. We may also infer that since the immediate principle of operation, the conjunct, has a material element — the sense organ — the action of sensation, although it does possess a qualified immateriality, must unqualifiedly be termed a material operation. Consequently, this operation will attain its object according to its individual manifestations, not as a universal essence.

b) In order to understand the union of the knower with the term of the operation of sensing, we should recall that the operation in question is an immanent action, and that such an action does not cause an effect produced in a distinct object. For an immanent action is the perfection of the agent and must terminate *in the subject itself*. We should also recall that immanent action does not fall under the predicament, transient action; rather, the act of sensation, like all truly immanent actions of a limited being, belongs to the predicament, quality. This operation does not, therefore, necessitate a becoming (*motus*) in a distinct being (the patient) as does transient action. On the contrary, the action of sensation is produced in the very being which causes it, and which is already in act to act, since this being is the agent. This indicates what is implied by this very mysterious entity: the act of a perfect being (*actus perfecti*).

c) This immanent action of sensing, this quality, is the *immediate means of the cognitive union* which we call sense knowledge — a union which takes place between the knower and the known. Such an action must begin in the knower who is the agent. But since it is a means of union, the action must terminate somehow in the known object. Our question, therefore, is: How is this union effected?

Several opinions[19] have been advanced in response to this ques-

[19] One opinion, proposed by Suarez, affirms that another species — an expressed species it is called — which is truly representative of the object must be produced as the term of the act of sensation. In this new species the knower knows the known as in a mirror. The reason for postulating such a species is that the ad-

tion. We think it best, however, to explain this union according to the principles of St. Thomas, allowing ourselves to be guided by clear and definite texts. Our task, then, is to indicate how an immanent action, the action of sensing, can attain an extrinsic term — the object.

Let us recall that the sensible species is educed from the potency of the sense faculty through the action of the external object upon the sense organ, of which the faculty is the quasi-form. This action is transient and is, therefore, in the patient (*actio est in passo*).[20] Hence, we must say that *the object is present immediately by its own action* and that the object by its operation immediately *actuates the faculty* so that the faculty must act immanently. Let us recall the metaphysical principle that an effect is produced only as long as its cause continues causing it.[21] The effect being pro-

---

vocates of this opinion think that the first species — they call it the impressed species — is not a formal but a *virtual* representation of the object, and, therefore, in order really to know the object, the sense must produce a new species which is truly representative of the object. We have already explained why the sensible species is a *formal* representation. Indeed, there is no valid reason why it should not be such a representation. Hence, we cannot see any need for postulating an expressed sense species.

A second opinion, defended by many Thomistic philosophers, declares that the object itself is immediately present to the external sense, and, consequently, the intentional union is had without need of any other species. The union between subject and object is immediate. This is an attractive theory because it is extremely realistic — perhaps too much so. Unfortunately, it seems erroneous. In the first place, the union we speak of, as St. Thomas explains, is an intentional union. It is clear, therefore, that the members of this union must be in the intentional order, that is to say, they must be immaterial. According to the opinion we are now considering, the object and term of this union is a *corporeal* entity. It exists by a natural "to be," and its union with the subject is immediate. If that is so, certainly no intentional union is possible. Moreover, in this theory it would seem that the operation or act of knowledge necessary to effect such a union would have to be a transient, not an immanent action, since it would terminate not *in* the subject but in the object.

[20] Cf. *The Philosophy of Being,* pp. 137–150.

[21] It is true that the operation of an internal sense faculty does not require that the object be present here and now by its action upon the subject. The reason is that we are able to recall the species which has been retained in the memory or imagination. Here we are considering the act of an external sense, not the memory, which is an internal sense; hence, there can be no question of recalling a species. On the contrary, the species of the external sense must be caused here and now by the external object of sensation. But why is the external species not retained? Why

duced in this instance is the eduction of the sensible species; this species must be caused here and now by the object. This amounts to saying that, in order to have sensation, or an act of knowledge by the external sense, the *object must be actually present* by its action in causing the eduction of the sensible species without which the faculty cannot be in act to operate immanently. Accordingly, when this actuation of the faculty is not had, no act of sensation follows. Consequently, the immanent act of the faculty of sensation, which follows immediately upon this actuation, must terminate not in the object existing corporeally — this would make sensation a transient action — nor in another distinct species, but in the *object actually present intentionally* by its action in causing the eduction of the sensible species. Through the sensible species, which terminates the action of the object, the knowing subject becomes united with the object present by its action.

> . . . The species which is in the sense is abstracted from things themselves, and *through this species* [italics added] sense cognition is continued to the sensible things themselves. . . .[22]

> . . . The likeness which is in the sense is abstracted from the thing as from a knowable object, and therefore the thing itself is known directly through that likeness. . . .[23]

> External sense cognition is brought about solely by the mutation of the sense by the sensible. Hence, by the form which is impressed by the sensible, it senses [i.e., by eliciting the operation of sensing]. The sense itself, however, does not produce any sensible form.[24]

We shall close this important article with a remark concerning the position of sense knowledge in the life of man. While we frankly admit that sensation is found in all animals, man and

---

must it be caused here and now? The reason is that the external sensible species is not a complete form. Rather, it is like a motion, and a motion as such cannot be retained.

[22] *De Ver.*, II, 6.

[23] *Loc. cit.*

[24] *Quodlibet,* V, 9, ad 2^m^.

beast, there is a great difference in the finality of this operation. Sense cognition is the most perfect operation in the life of brute beasts. It is a sort of reciprocal end in itself; the brute animal lives to sense and senses to live. In man, however, sense knowledge is only a beginning, a means ordered to his highest and most perfect operation, the act of understanding. In man, sense cognition — in fact, all the operations of sense life — is a means and not the end.

ARTICLE II: Nature and Distinction of External Senses[25]

Why Many Senses? Our experiences of reality in the world of sensation are many and varied. The reason is that corporeal reality presents itself under different aspects. But why is there such diversity of aspects? Why must bodies constantly manifest themselves to the apprehension of sense from various points of view? It must be that the sensible cognition of material reality under one aspect — for example, under the formality of color or of sound — does not give us sufficient data for the intellectual knowledge compatible with our nature. To attain an adequate knowledge of the real, man must possess a wealth of varied sense experience. These experiences, these sensory operations, since they differ specifically, suppose distinct sense faculties proportioned to various aspects of the world of bodies. Man's nature demands many senses.[26]

Norm for Distinction Between Faculties: What we wish to discover at present is the norm, the criterion, for determining the distinct senses in man. To this end, let us recall the general principle which enables us to distinguish between operative potencies.

---

[25] *S. Th.,* I, 78, 3.

[26] "As nature does not fail in necessary things, there must be as many actions of the sensitive soul as may suffice for the life of a perfect animal. If any of these actions cannot be reduced to one and the same principle, they must be assigned to diverse [operative] potencies, since a potency of the soul is nothing else than the proximate principle of the soul's operation." (*Ibid.,* 4, *c.*)

Since the *object specifies the operation,* and since the *operation*—in this case, the sensation as referred to a sentient subject—*specifies the faculty,* it will be sufficient to examine the various formal aspects of sensed reality to discover what these distinct faculties are.[27]

From the general observation of men, we find that there are at least five distinct formalities under which we commonly experience the world of bodies: *color, sound, taste, odor,* and the manifold *tactile aspects.*[28] These are the formal objects of the external senses; they are specifically diverse modes in which bodily things can actuate a sentient subject. These formal objects of the external senses we designate as *proper sensibles.* From the diversity of formal objects (proper sensibles) we infer that there are (at least) five distinct external senses: sight, hearing, smell, taste, and touch, which enable us to attain an experiential knowledge of the world of bodies.

> . . . The reason for the number and distinction of the exterior senses must . . . be ascribed to that which belongs to the senses properly and *per se.* Sense is a passive (operative) potency, and is naturally changed by the exterior sensible. Hence, the exterior cause of such mutation is what is *per se* perceived by the sense, and according to the diversity of that exterior cause are the sensitive potencies diversified.[29]

We do not deny that there may be other aspects under which

[27] The sensible qualities are distinct aspects of corporeal beings when they are referred to a sentient subject viewed as sentient. The reason is that the sentient nature can know material reality only as limited by a material organ, and therefore under a limited aspect. When corporeal being and its sensible qualities are referred to an intellectual nature, which understands independently of matter and bodily organs, they are all viewed as *being,* and, therefore, there can be only one intellectual faculty.

[28] Bodies can be perceived under various tactile aspects: as hot or cold, smooth or rough, wet or dry. To these we may add, as regards our own body, the formal aspects of pain and kinesis. Whether these are all distinct formal objects which diversify distinct operative potencies of touch is not a matter of great philosophical moment. There does not seem to be any difficulty in admitting the existence of several senses of "touch." ". . . the sense of touch is generically one, but is divided into several specific senses, and for this reason extends to various contrarieties." (*S. Th.,* I, 78, 3, ad 3^{m}.)

[29] *Ibid.,* 3, *c.*

we could, and perhaps do, attain the world of corporeal things in sense knowledge; but we leave it to the experimentalist to discover the data necessary for the discussion of such a question. From the point of view of the philosopher, the solution of this problem—if it exists—is not of great importance. It matters little to the philosopher whether we have five or fifty distinct sense faculties. What really matters is whether our sensory experience provides us with the data necessary for the intellectual knowledge of essences which our rational nature demands. We are, let it be remembered, studying sensation primarily as a means ordered to a more perfect cognitive act, the act of intellection.

Various Kinds of Sensibles: The sense faculty, we have seen, is specified by its operation, and the operation is specified in some way by the object, the *sensible.* Now there are two general types of sensibles: (*a*) the *per se* sensible, namely, that which is sensible of itself, like color or size; (*b*) the *per accidens* sensible—that which is sensible by reason of something else. Man, for example, is a sensible *per accidens,* that is, by reason of his color and size.

A. "Per Se" Sensibles: Of the *per se* sensibles, there are two types: the *proper* and the *common,* which now come up for detailed consideration.

1. *Proper Sensibles:* The distinct, formal aspects of sensible reality (color, sound, etc.), which are the fundamental reasons for the specification and distinction of the sense operative potencies, are called by St. Thomas the *proper sensibles,* or proper sensible qualities. Primarily and essentially (*primo et per se*) they produce a change in the sense faculty terminating in a representative species, which is more or less immaterial according to the degree of perfection of the faculty. Consequently, when a corporeal object actuates a sense faculty according to a definite proper sensible quality, the likeness of the sensible exists in the sense primarily[30]

---

[30] The object is not perceived to be colored (proper sensible) because it is already known to be of a certain shape, but rather vice versa. It is by virtue of a color

and essentially,[31] as in the sight there is a likeness of the object according to its color aspect. The various likenesses which the various proper sensibles cause to be educed from the sense faculties are specifically distinct; for example, a sound species is specifically distinct from the color species caused by the same material object. Moreover, the immanent operation of a faculty which has been informed by one species, for example that of color, will be specifically different from that of a faculty informed by a specifically distinct likeness. For this reason, the senses are ultimately diversified according as the proper sensible qualities differ. These qualities, which cause the alteration in the sense, primarily affect but one sense, and for that reason are called *proper* sensibles; they are: color, sound, taste, smell, "touch."

2. *Common Sensibles:* The common sensibles, on the other hand, are perceivable by more than one sense, for they can affect more than one sense. They are five in number: *size, shape, number, motion, rest.* They do not cause a specifically distinct representation to be educed from the sense as do each of the proper sensibles. For example, whether the colored object be large or small, the color species is specifically the same. As regards the actuation of the sense, the common sensibles differ among themselves, not because of the difference in the species which they cause, but because of the *mode* of action. This mode of action varies according as the object, for example, something colored, is in motion or at rest, is large or small, is spherical or cubic, etc. In the case of common sensibles, the likeness of a thing exists in the sense of itself, that is, essentially (*per se*), but not primarily (*primo*). The reason is that the common sensibles do not actuate the sense except by reason of a proper sensible quality, as, for

---

sensation that we apprehend the shape (common sensible) of the object. Hence, we say that the proper sensible quality is known primarily.

[31] Whether the colored thing is a man or a dog is accidental to the sense of sight, which apprehends the object merely under the limited aspect of color.

example, a surface moves the sense of sight, not directly, but by reason of its color.[32]

The five common sensible qualities are all reducible to quantity, which is the proximate subject of the qualities (proper sensibles) that cause alteration[33] in the sense. Obviously, then, the common sensibles do not move the senses primarily, that is to say, directly, but by reason of a proper sensible quality.

B. "Per Accidens" Sensibles: The accidental sensibles do not cause knowledge or mutation (the preparation for knowledge) in the sense essentially (*per se*) as do the proper and common sensibles, but only accidentally. It is accidental to the sense whether a white thing is man or beast. Thus, the likeness of man is in the sight only in as much as the colored object happens to be a man rather than some other colored object.[34] The reason is that the change in the sense is produced not by man as man, but by

---

[32] We can perceive a surface as large or small only if we apprehend it as colored, or under some other primary formal aspect. "The knowledge of things by the senses is in proportion to the existence of their likeness in the senses. Now the likeness of a thing can exist in the senses in three ways. In the first way, primarily and essentially (*per se*), as in sight there is the likeness of colors and of other sensibles proper to it. Secondly, essentially, though not primarily; as in sight there is the likeness of figure or bodily shape, and of other sensible objects common to more than one sense. Thirdly, neither primarily nor essentially, but accidentally; as in sight, there is the likeness of a man, not as man, but in so far as the colored object happens to be man." (*S. Th.*, I, 17, 2, *c.*)

[33] ". . . The common sensibles are all reducible to quantity. As to size and number, it is clear that they are species of quantity. Shape is a quality about quantity, since the nature of shape consists in fixing the bounds of magnitude. Movement and rest are sensed according as the subject is affected in one or more ways in the magnitude of the subject or of its local distance, as in the movement of growth or of locomotion, or again, according as it is affected in some sensible qualities, as in the movement of alteration; and thus to sense movement and rest is, in a way, to sense one thing and many. Now quantity is the proximate subject of the qualities that cause alteration [proper sensibles] as surface is of color. Therefore, the common sensibles do not move the senses first and of their own nature, but by reason of sensible quality; as the surface by reason of color. Yet, they are not accidental sensibles, for they produce a certain diversity in the mutation of the sense. For sense is changed differently by a large and by a small surface. . . ." (*Ibid.*, 78, 3, ad 2^m.)

[34] Obviously, anything that is perceived as colored must be something with a definite essence or nature. Essence, or nature as such, however, is not perceivable by the senses.

man *as colored*. The accidental sensibles, therefore, do not produce a mutation in the external sense of themselves, that is, essentially (*per se*), but by reason of the proper and common sensibles. Consequently, another cognoscitive faculty — the intellect — is required in order that the accidental sensible may be known essentially.

Hierarchy of Sense Faculties: Now there is obviously an order of perfection among the various sense faculties. We may speak of a hierarchy of faculties analogous to the hierarchy of beings. The reason for this order is that the different formal aspects of the proper sensibles manifest corporeal reality to us in a more or less perfect manner. The sensible objects, as initial causes in sensation, by their action on the conjunct of sense organ and faculty, move the sense faculties under diverse formal aspects, thereby causing the eduction of sensible species which vary specifically in perfection. The less immaterial and hence the more perfect the change which terminates in the species, the more perfect must be the sense faculty and its consequent operation of sensing.[35]

ARTICLE III: Validity of Sensation

Problem: Since the data for man's intellectual knowledge are gathered through the senses, it is of the greatest importance to discern not whether, but *how* — that is to say, under what conditions — a true knowledge of the object is obtained by the sense

---

[35] St. Thomas was of the opinion that the sight was the most immaterial — he uses the term *spiritual* — and hence the most perfect of the senses. Following the faulty physiology of his time, he considered that there was no material change involved in sensory vision. ". . . in some senses we find spiritual mutation only, as in sight, while in others we find not only a spiritual but also a natural mutation. . . . Now, the sight, which is without natural mutation either in its organ or in its object, is the most spiritual, the most perfect, and the most universal of all the senses. After this comes the hearing, and then the smell. . . . Touch and taste are the most material of all. . . ." (*S. Th.*, I, 78, 3, *c.*)

faculties. We say advisedly "not whether, but how" such knowledge is attained for this simple reason: To ask *whether* true knowledge is attainable by the sense faculties implies a real doubt regarding the capacity of these operative potencies to know reality; it is to pave the way to skepticism. For, once we cast an irrational doubt upon the validity of our faculties of sense knowledge, we are faced with this insoluble difficulty: How can we ever arrive at a satisfactory solution of this very problem if the sensory data for intellectual judgments depend upon the use of faculties whose validity is doubtful?

Intellectual Knowledge Is Derived From Sense Knowledge: We may recall that we began our study of philosophy by stating the principle of intelligibility: *being is intelligible.* Now, in order to understand being, man needs the data of sense knowledge. The reason is that the soul of man is not created with the likenesses of things already impressed in the intellect. Rather, man comes into existence devoid of all actual knowledge; he must acquire knowledge by operations. Now, because man is a corporeal being, because his soul is the substantial form of the body, his knowledge is obtained primarily by a sense operation, which results from some bodily contact with other corporeal beings. Even the initial data for intellectual knowledge of the true and for intellectual love of the good is presented by sense cognition. It is evident, then, that unless the knowledge provided by sense is true, that is to say, in accord with reality, there can be no hope that man may ever understand the true and love the good. To ask *whether* the real can be known by the sense operative potency is to doubt and, in the last analysis, to deny all true knowledge; it is an affirmation of absolute skepticism and puts an abrupt end to all sane efforts to philosophize. Our problem, therefore, is limited to the *how* of valid sense knowledge, that is to say, under what conditions the object is known in accord with truth.

General Principle: To the question, "Under what conditions is a true knowledge of reality obtained by the senses?" St. Thomas gives this general answer:[36]

a) The senses *have no false knowledge* concerning the *proper* sensible objects, *except accidentally* (*per accidens*) *and rarely,* for these are the specifying objects proportioned to the sense faculties. Error in regard to knowledge of proper sensible qualities will be due to some defect either in the sense organ or in the medium through which the sense organ is stimulated.

b) As regards the *common* sensibles and the *accidentally* sensible objects, the "judgment" of sense can of itself be erroneous, even when the sense organ is properly disposed and when there is no defect in the medium. The reason is that these objects are not directly related to the sense faculty and are not absolutely proportioned to its nature.

> . . . The sense is not deceived concerning its proper object (as sight in regard to color) except accidentally, through some chance impediment to the sensory organ. For example, the taste of a person stricken with fever judges (*iudicat*) a sweet thing to be bitter, because his tongue is filled with evil humors. As regards the common sensibles, the sense is [sometimes] deceived, as when judging the size or the shape [of an object]; as when, for example, it judges the sun to be only a foot in diameter, whereas in reality it exceeds the earth in size. Much more is the sense deceived concerning accidentally sensible

---

[36] ". . . the knowledge of things by the senses is in proportion to the existence of their likeness in the sense. Now the likeness of a thing exists in the sense in three ways. In the first way, primarily and essentially, as in sight there is the likeness of colors and of other sensible objects proper to it. Secondly, essentially, though not primarily; as in sight there is the likeness of figure, or size, and all the other common sensibles. Thirdly, neither primarily nor essentially, but accidentally; as in sight, there is the likeness of a man not as man, but in so far as it happens that this colored object is a man. Now sense has no false knowledge concerning the proper sensibles, except accidentally (*per accidens*) and rarely, on account of this, that owing to an indisposition in the organ, it does not receive the sensible form rightly; just as other passive subjects because of their indisposition receive defectively the impressions of the agent. Hence, for example, it happens that because of an unhealthy tongue sweet seems bitter to a sick person. But as to common and accidental sensibles, even a rightly disposed sense may have a false judgment (*iudicium*), because the sense is related to them not directly, but accidentally, or as a consequence of being related to other objects." (*S. Th.,* I, 17, 2, *c.*)

> objects; as when it judges that vinegar is honey because the color is similar. The reason for this is obvious. Every [operative] potency is of itself (*per se*) ordered to its proper object, according to the potency which it is (*secundum quod ipsa*); and things of this kind are always uniform [i.e., are always naturally inclined according to the same finality, and consequently are always naturally ordered to the same perfection or act]. Hence, as long as the [operative] potency remains, its judgment concerning its proper object cannot fail.[37]

The key to the solution of our problem is a principle stated in the last few lines of the passage just quoted: potency is necessarily ordered to its act; potency and act are necessarily correlated. Given the potency, the proper act to which it is ordered will always be proportioned to the capacity of the potency; the potency is made for the act which is its perfection. As long, therefore, as the potency is what it is, the act which actuates the potency will be this act and none other. Now the potency which we call the sense faculty is ordered to a certain object, i.e., the proper sensible. The faculty is just for that object; it is made to attain its proper object by knowledge. Once the potency is actuated by the likeness of its proper object, it cannot but place the necessary action by which it truly knows the object. Under normal conditions, when its organ is properly disposed, the sense faculty cannot fail to judge its proper object truly. To deny this is to deny the metaphysical law of act and potency; it is to deny that being is intelligible.

On the other hand, the non-proper objects, whether common or accidental sensibles, are either not primarily (in the case of common sensibles) or essentially (in the case of accidental sensibles) related to the sense faculty as act is related to potency. The common sensibles are known secondarily, and the accidental sensibles do not impress their likeness in the sense according to their mode of existing, but according to the mode of being of the proper and of the common sensibles. Consequently, there is no necessary relation, no necessary order to the true knowledge of

[37] *Ibid.*, 85, 6, *c.*

either the common sensibles, and much less so of the accidental sensibles. Accordingly, as regards the common and accidental sensibles, there can be a false judgment, even in a sense conjunct which is properly disposed. The reason is that ". . . the sense is related to these [objects] not directly, but accidentally, or as a consequence of being related to other objects."[38]

Question II

THE INTERNAL SENSES

This question is divided into three articles: (1) the need for four internal sense faculties; (2) the functioning of the internal senses in man; (3) the connection between all the senses.

ARTICLE I: Need for Four Internal Senses[39]

Human knowledge begins with the operation of the external sense—sensation. It is caused initially by the action of a sensible object on the sense. This knowledge, however, is imperfect and incomplete. Even in animals it has no meaning except as a preparation for the act of knowledge of the internal senses which the animal's nature requires. This is true *a fortiori* of man's knowledge, since his rational nature requires a far more perfect type of cognition. At this juncture, however, our prime concern is to show the connection between the external and internal senses and the necessity for internal senses in the life of an animal and especially in that of the rational animal, man. St. Thomas offers four arguments establishing the need for four internal senses. These arguments are based on the general principle that operations which cannot be reduced to one and the same principle—because they

[38] *S. Th.*, I, 17, 2, *c.*
[39] *Ibid.*, 78, 4.

have distinct formal objects — must be assigned to diverse operative potencies. The four internal senses are: the unitive or "common" sense, the imaginative, the estimative, and the memorative senses.

Need for the Unitive ("Common") Sense: Concrete, external sensations do not remain disconnected activities; rather, they are integrated in a unified cognitive operation. Now this *integration* of external sensations is not an operation that can be carried out by the external senses themselves, since their specifying objects are color, sound, taste, etc. Accordingly, there must be another faculty on the sensory level which performs this necessary operation of integration. ". . . To it, as to a common term, all apprehensions of the [external] senses must be referred. . . ."[40]

Because this sense functions as an integrating factor in sensory experience, it is able to *discern between the proper sensible qualities* of things. The white cube of sugar, for example, is known on the sensory level not only as "the *white* thing," but also as "the *sweet* thing"; indeed we habitually identify the sweet cube by its white color, and we would be amazed if perchance we find that the white cube is not sweet, but salty. Now "that which discerns between two things must know both."[41] Neither sight nor taste nor any of the other external senses is capable of this discernment, because each of them is limited to one formal object. Hence, this discerning judgment between proper sensibles must be assigned to a sense by which all the formal objects, "all the intentions of the senses are perceived."[42]

Moreover, a sentient agent, besides having unified experiences, in which it discriminates between the various sensibles, also perceives itself to be the source of these various operations; it is *aware that it senses,* ". . . as when someone sees that he sees."[43] This operation, too, cannot be attributed to the external senses,

---

[40] *Ibid.,* ad 2m.
[41] *Loc. cit.*
[42] *Loc. cit.*
[43] *Loc. cit.*

but must be a function of the unitive sense, which has for its object sensation itself.

Need for the Imaginative Sense: To retain and preserve the species received from the external senses in the unitive (common) sense, a distinct faculty, *a sensory memory,* is required. The reason for this is that the species caused by the object in the external sense (and in the unitive sense) is present only as long as the object is acting upon the external sense. Yet an animal must be able to apprehend things when they are no longer actuating the sense, for otherwise an animal would not be able to seek something which is absent. Accordingly, the species of sensible things must be retained by some power. "Since to receive [as do the external and unitive senses] and to retain are in corporeal things reduced to distinct principles,"[44] the operative potency which *preserves* these species must be really distinct from both the external senses and the unitive sense.

> Now we must observe that for the life of a perfect animal, the animal should apprehend a thing not only when it is present but also when it is absent. Otherwise, since animal motion and action follow apprehension, an animal would not be moved to seek something absent; the contrary of which we may observe especially in perfect animals, which are moved by progression, for they are moved toward something apprehended and absent. Therefore, through the sensitive soul an animal must not only receive the species of sensible things, when it is actually affected by them, but it must also retain and preserve them. Now to receive and retain are, in corporeal things, reduced to diverse principles. . . . Therefore, since the sensitive potency is the act of a corporeal organ, it follows that the [operative] potency which receives the species of sensible things must be distinct from the potency which preserves them.[45]

We see, therefore, that the reception of sensible forms is the function of the various proper senses and the unitive sense. "But

---

[44] *S. Th.,* I, 78, 4, *c.* A being "receives" a perfection in so far as it is in potency and "retains" it in so far as it is in act.

[45] *Loc. cit.*

for the retention and preservation of these forms, the . . . imaginative is appointed, being as it were a storehouse of forms received through the senses."[46] This role of the imaginative sense is commonly termed "memory."

Besides this memory function, the imaginative has a secondary role, that of *combining and dividing imagined forms,* ". . . as when from the imagined form of gold and the imagined form of a mountain, we compose the one form of golden mountain, which we have never seen. But this operation is not to be found in animals other than man . . . "[47] in whom it can be directed by the intellectual powers and used creatively in the production of artistic works. A commonly used term for this function of the imaginative sense is the *phantasy.*

Need for the Estimative Sense: Animals have certain activities which are performed regardless of whether the objects of these actions are pleasant or disagreeable. Thus a bird will gather straws, which are not particularly pleasant to the taste, because it perceives that the straw is useful for building its nest. A sheep will flee from the oncoming wolf (even when seen for the first time), not because its color or shape is unpleasant, but because of a sensory "estimation" that this object is harmful or inimical. These estimations move the sense appetites and give rise to external activity which is more or less uniform within the species (all orioles build their nests the same way) and proper to the species (orioles construct nests in a manner different from swallows). Moreover, the knowledge which gives rise to this appetitive and external activity is not learned nor is it necessarily dependent on previous experience; rather, it is a ready-made sensory "judgment" that comes into act because of certain external and internal sensations.

This function of sensory discernment of what is useful or harmful, friendly or inimical to the individual and to the species,

---

[46] *Loc. cit.*
[47] *Loc. cit.*

cannot be an operation of any of the sensory potencies already studied. For, their knowledge ("sensate intentions") moves the appetite only in so far as the object is "judged" pleasant or disagreeable. Moreover, "friendly-unfriendly," "useful-harmful" are not the formal object of the external senses, nor of the unitive sense, nor of the imaginative sense; rather, they are what St. Thomas calls "insensate" intentions. Accordingly, in animals there must be a distinct internal sense for forming these intentions, which we shall call the estimative sense or estimative power (*vis aestimativa*).

> Again, we must observe that if an animal were moved only by things pleasing and disagreeable to the sense, there would be no need to suppose that an animal has an apprehension beside that of the sensibly perceived forms in which it takes delight or from which it shrinks with horror. But the animal needs to seek or to avoid certain things, not only because they are pleasing or not pleasing to the senses, but also because of other advantages and uses, or disadvantages; just as the sheep runs away when it sees a wolf, not because of its color or shape, but as from a natural enemy. So, too, a bird gathers together straws, not because they are pleasant to the sense, but because they are useful for building its nest. Animals, therefore, need to perceive such intentions, which the exterior sense does not perceive. Now some distinct principle is necessary for this, since the perception of sensible forms comes by a mutation caused by the sensible, which is not the case with the perception of the above intentions.[48]

In man, corresponding to the estimative sense of lower animals, is a similar power which is under the control of the universal reason. It is called the *cogitative power* or particular reason, ". . . for it compares individual intentions, just as the intellectual reason compares universal intentions."[49]

Need for Memorative Sense: It will be seen at once that since the estimative power is concerned with the apprehension of intentions which are not the result of external sense experiences (estima-

---

[48] *S. Th.*, I, 78, 4, *c.*
[49] *Loc. cit.*

tions of harmfulness, suitableness, etc.) a faculty of retention distinct from the imaginative will be required to conserve these "insensate" intentions and to recall them when needed.

> . . . For the apprehension of intentions which are not received through the senses, the estimative power is appointed; and for their preservation, the memorative power, which is a storehouse of such intentions. A sign of which we have in the fact that the principle of memory in animals is found in some such intention, for example, that something is harmful or suitable.[50]

ARTICLE II: Functioning of the Internal Senses in Man

Functioning of the Unitive ("Common") Sense: It would be a serious mistake to imagine that the proper objects of the unitive or "common" sense are the common sensibles to the exclusion of all other sensible objects. Rather, the "common" sense is that operative potency in which the operations of all the external senses terminate; its object, therefore, includes *proper* as well as common sensibles. The immanent operation of external sensation, which occurs in the various external senses, causes the eduction in the common sense of a complex sense species which has the intentional elements found in all the external senses. The common sense, being now in act, performs the vital operation of sensory perception. In this operation, the knowing subject attains the object (as actually sensed) under all the aspects presented here and now through the various external senses which make their proper contribution to the act of the common sense. Since the external senses primarily and directly attain the proper sensible qualities and attain the common sensibles *in* and *through* the proper sensibles, it is manifest that the "common" sense is in no way limited to the common sensibles as its proper object. Accordingly, the common sense receives its name, not because it has for its object the common

---

[50] *Loc. cit.*

sensibles, but because it ". . . is the common root and principle of the external senses."[51]

It should be noted that the common sense species elaborated from the intentional elements received from the external senses may also be completed and perfected by intentional elements recalled by the sense memory (imaginative sense), which is, as it were, a continuation of the common sense. When one has a sensory perception of an object which has been experienced before, elements of the previous experiences, which have been retained in the sense memory, may be recalled and combined in the total sensory perception. Accordingly, the species of the imaginative sense can become more complex with added experiences, as the knowing subject "learns" more and more about the object of external sensation.

Functioning of the Imaginative Sense: The imaginative sense is an operative potency that is really distinct from the common sense. We have seen that the common sense can know what the external senses know, but only *when* they know. The reason is that the common sense is not in act to operation unless it receives the term of the mutation which is caused here and now by the sensible object in each of the external senses. The imaginative, on the other hand, retains and recalls the species communicated to it by the common sense, even when the external object is no longer actuating the senses. Sometimes, too, from the sensory data received, the imagination forms new phantasms, new sensory "percepts."[52]

Although these two senses—the imaginative and the common sense—are distinct, nevertheless, they are so closely connected in function that the imagination can be spoken of as a continuation of the common sense. Just as the common sense perfects and completes the sensation of the external senses, so the imagination

---

[51] *S. Th.*, I, 78, 4, ad 1m.
[52] Cf. *De Memoria et Reminiscentia,* II.

perfects and completes the operation of the common sense. Indeed, without this function of the common sense, the external sensations would be incomplete and devoid of perceptual integration; thus, man would experience only a disconnected series of sensations. In like manner, through the imagination, the knowledge obtained by the common sense is completed by a stable and permanent impression of the apprehended object. This impression[53] can be brought into consciousness even when the object is absent. As a matter of fact, the only way in which an absent object can be made present is by a RE-presentation, by an immanent operation in which the imaginative sense produces a distinct intentional term, which is called the *phantasm*.

The imagination, however, does not only reproduce the data of the common sense; it can even "create" new impressions by combining and rearranging the different elements of these sensory data. This last function, the creative use of the imagination, is had only in conjunction with the intellect; obviously, this operation does not require a distinct internal sense. It is by reason of the use of imagination conjoined to intellect that man is able to invent and to make constant progress in the arts of civilization.

Functioning of the Estimative Sense: The impressions received in the estimative sense are sometimes designated as "insensate intentions" (*intentiones insensatae*). By this expression we understand those sensory apprehensions which are not the operations of the common sense, nor of the imaginative sense. These "insensate" apprehensions are really sensory "judgments" of value which are not the result of previous sense experience of an object; rather,

---

[53] This impression is a sensible species distinct from that in the common sense. It actuates the imaginative and remains in it as a habit, as an imperfect act. Now when this habitual species is brought into consciousness, it fully actuates the imaginative, which thereupon breaks forth into operation. This action of the imaginative unites the faculty with the object. Now the object is never present to the imaginative sense. Consequently, the imaginative by its operation must form a phantasm, an intentional term, which represents the object and in which the faculty finds its object and unites with it intentionally. The phantasm, therefore, is distinct from the sensible species. Cf. *S. Th.*, I, 85, 2, ad 3^{m}.

these "judgments" of suitability or unsuitability are formed instinctively as soon as a certain object is sensed. Hence, no proper images corresponding to these "insensate intentions" are produced either in the external senses or in the common sense and the imagination. Examples of "insensate intentions" are utility, harmfulness, friendship, enmity.

The estimative sense is distinct from the imaginative because the formal objects of these senses are distinct. The object of the imagination is received from the common sense; it is an elaboration of external sensation, of *sensed* intentions. On the other hand, the object of the estimative power comprises the *"insensate* intentions," which are neither proper nor common sensibles and hence cannot be sensed by either the external or common sense. Consequently, the estimative power is distinct from the imaginative sense.

Nevertheless, these "insensate intentions" are dependent in some way on the external and common senses. This is evident from the fact that without some sort of sensation and perception in these other faculties, the estimative power, which is in some way a continuation of them, could never form the "insensate intentions." The sheep, for example, estimates as harmful the oncoming wolf which it knows here and now through the operation of both the external and common senses.[54] In a way, the estimative forms the "insensate intention" of something inimical from the data provided by the external and common senses. For this reason, St. Thomas remarks that the functioning of the estimative power is similar to that of the intellect.[55] Like the intellect, which also

[54] These senses only give knowledge of the presence of the wolf. They cannot give a foundation for a judgment of value the first time the wolf is apprehended. The judgment of the estimative is instinctive and originating from nature itself.

[55] "Brutes possess something similar to reason in that they participate in a sort of natural prudence in as much as the lower nature in some manner attains to the perfection of the higher nature. This similarity consists in their possession of an ordered judgment concerning certain things. But this judgment results from a natural estimation, and not from a comparison, since they do not know the reason for their judgment. Consequently, a judgment of this kind does not extend to all things, as does the judgment of reason, but only to certain definite objects. Brutes likewise possess something similar to freedom of judgment and choice (*liberi arbitrii*). . . ." (*De Ver.*, XXIV, 3.)

depends on the senses, the estimative power is able to obtain a knowledge which the external senses and the common sense are not able to reach.

> Although the operation of the intellect has its origin in the senses, yet, in the things apprehended through the senses, the intellect knows many things which the senses cannot perceive. In like manner does the estimative [operative] potency, though in a less perfect way.[56]

The estimative power, then, is the most perfect of the senses. It is analogous to reason, being farther removed from matter than the other senses. It may even be called a sort of participation of intellect in brute animals, for it perceives the end of action in a vague way and orders an operation to that end.

In brute animals, therefore, the estimative power—or "instinct,"[57] as it is often called—is a sort of natural prudence. We observe that some of the higher animals are able to learn, that is, to acquire new modes of behavior, for example, to avoid danger and to obtain food in a prudential manner, so that they seem to be capable of choosing the proper means to an end. Because of these striking facts, some experimentalists have maintained that the brute animals, like human beings, possess an intellect, or "mind," with the same power of abstraction and reasoning, though admitting that these powers are quite undeveloped in the present stage. Such assertions show a lack of philosophical reflection. While an animal can learn particular facts, it can never abstract a universal principle and apply it to particular cases. This is evident from the fact that through the ages each species (not necessarily the individuals) of animals has operated in the same unchanged manner and has learned no new mode of action. Moreover, these same animals manifest at times far more sagacity than man, and this clearly indicates that their nature is determined to operation by an extrinsic intellect greater than that of mere man.

---

[56] *S. Th.,* I, 78, 4, ad 4^{m}.

[57] This term has a vague meaning in popular discourse and is apt to be misleading if used as a synonym for estimative sense.

> . . . The power of the mover appears in the movement of that which it moves. Accordingly, in all things moved by reason, the order of reason which moves them is evident, although the things themselves are without reason; for through the motion of the archer the arrow goes straight toward the target, as though it were endowed with reason to direct its course. The same may be seen in the movements of clocks and all devices put together by the art of man. Now as artificial things are in comparison to human art, so are all natural things when compared to the divine art. Accordingly, order is to be seen in things moved by nature, just as in things moved by reason. . . . And thus it is that in the works of irrational animals we notice certain marks of sagacity, in as much as they have a natural inclination to certain highly ordered processes through being ordained by the supreme art. For this reason, too, certain animals are called prudent or sagacious; and not because they reason or exercise any choice about things. This is clear from the fact that all that share in one nature invariably act in the same way.[58]

The Cogitative Power: In man the estimative sense is called the cogitative power. It apprehends the individual objects as the real and concrete subjects of the universal essences conceived by the intellect. For that reason, and because it can compare these individual intentions, it is called the *particular reason.*[59]

"The cogitative power owes its excellence . . . to a certain affinity and proximity to the universal reason, which, so to speak, overflows into it."[60] Because of this conjunction with the intellect, the cogitative participates somewhat in the action of the intellect which is to compare and infer; and in this manner it finds "insensate intentions" by a sort of comparison and inference. In this it is unlike the estimative sense in the brute, which immediately apprehends these intentions. The cogitative does not, of course, infer

[58] *S. Th.,* I–II, 13, 2, ad 3m.

[59] ". . . contingent things can be considered as individual existents and thus they are variable and do not fall under the apprehension of the intellect except through the medium of the sensitive potencies. Hence, among the parts of the sensitive soul there is one [operative] potency which is called the particular reason, or cogitative power, which compares particular intentions." (*In X Libros Ethicorum ad Nicomachum,* Liber VI, lect. 1.)

[60] *S. Th.,* I, 78, 4, ad 5m.

what is suitable or unsuitable from a consideration of the natures and properties of things; only the universal reason does that. Rather, it discovers these intentions (suitable, unsuitable) by proceeding from one individual intention to another.

> Now, we must observe that as to sensible forms there is no difference between man and other animals, for they are similarly moved by external sensibles. But there is a difference as to the above intentions: for other animals perceive these intentions only by some sort of *natural instinct,* whereas man perceives them also by means of a *certain comparison* [italics added]. Therefore, the power which in other animals is called the natural estimative, in man is called the cogitative, which by means of some sort of comparison discovers these intentions. Therefore, it is also called the particular reason . . . for it compares individual intentions, just as the intellectual reason compares universal intentions.[61]

The Memorative in Man Has Reminiscence as Well as Memory: It is necessary to distinguish between the act of a simple memory and the act of reminiscence. The act of simple memory, of simple recall, is a sudden recollection of the past. This act occurs when, without any intermediate knowledge, without passing from one intention to another, we recall the object which had been known in the past. The act of *reminiscence,* on the other hand, is had when we seek "syllogistically, as it were, for a recollection of the past by the application of individual intentions."[62] In this operation we come to a remembrance of the object known in the past, by means of mediating knowledge or intentions. We pass from one thing to another, seeking by means of what is well remembered to recall that which is but poorly remembered, as occurs in our attempts to find a lost object. We may, then, compare the act of reminiscence to the process of intellectual reasoning.

It should be noted that sensory memory, in man as well as in brute animals, requires two distinct faculties: the imaginative

[61] *Ibid.,* 4, *c.*
[62] *Loc. cit.*

sense, which retains the "sensate" intentions, and the memorative, which preserves the "insensate." Fundamentally, however, we must say that the memorative is the principle of all sense memory. For the primary "insensate" intentions of usefulness and harmfulness are really the reason why the species of sensible objects are retained and recalled. Moreover, the memorative is the sense which apprehends the past as past.[63]

ARTICLE III: The Connection Between All the Senses

Interdependence of the Faculties: The unity of man postulates an interdependence of the operative potencies[64] so that while we must insist upon the distinction of these faculties, we must not forget that they are separate powers of *one existential unit,* the supposit man. Perhaps, then, the best way to summarize this treatise will be to indicate the necessary connection between the sense faculties, which makes it possible for them to attain their end. This end, we have noted, is to perfect man by preparing the way for intellection.

Beginning with the five distinct aspects of sensible reality, we posited five external senses. These, we discovered, vary in the perfection of knowledge which they attain, precisely because of the degree of immateriality of the species educed from the potentiality of the sense faculty. But because these distinct external senses are not able to unify their various experiences, it is necessary for the good of man that there exist an internal sense to which is communicated an impression of the discrete knowledge of the external senses. This is the "common" sense, whose function it is to integrate the diverse sensations of the external faculties.

---

[63] Cf. C. Boyer, *Cursus Philosophicus* (Paris: Desclée, 1937), Vol. II, p. 45.

[64] "Just as one power arises from the soul by means of another . . . so likewise the soul is the subject of one power through another." (*S. Th.,* I, 78, 4, ad 3^{m}.)

Moreover, since the act of the external and common sense can endure only as long as the external object is present to the sense,[65] there is need of another faculty whose function will be to retain these experiences and to recall them when needed. These impressions are communicated by common sense to this internal sense faculty which we call the imaginative sense.

From the immediate experiences which have been unified and organized by the common sense, and from the sensory data retained in the imaginative sense, man is able by a sort of particularized reasoning to conclude to what is useful or harmful to his nature. This faculty (the cogitative power in man, the estimative in brutes) is not immediately actuated by the external senses, but by the common sense and the imaginative, and it depends upon these two for new knowledge. Yet, once it has "intuited" (as in brutes) or has "reasoned" (as in man) to new "insensate" knowledge, it is able to communicate this knowledge to a distinct faculty called the memorative sense, in which this knowledge is retained.

Order of Dependence: This, then, is the order of dependence of the sense faculties: the external sense depends upon the external object for its actuation; common sense upon the external senses; imaginative sense upon the common sense, by which it is put in act to produce an intentional term, or phantasm, in which it knows the object. The cogitative sense is moved by the external senses, the common sense, and the imaginative sense to formulate its "judgment" as to the usefulness or harmfulness of the object. Finally, the memorative sense depends upon the cogitative, from which it receives the species which it retains and recalls.

---

[65] The reason is that the object is united with the external sense through the sensible species. Now, the sensible species of the external sense never reaches the state of a complete form. It may be viewed as analogous to a motion. Hence, it cannot be supported by the subject of knowledge, but must depend here and now upon the extrinsic agent or object. Such is not the case as regards the sensible species of the internal senses.

SUMMARY

QUESTION I

THE EXTERNAL SENSES

Article I: *Analysis of Sensation*

1. The *sense faculty* is primarily a *passive* and indeterminate operative potency. It is actuated by the object, which is the initial cause in sensation.

2. *Conjunct:* This actuation is had by the (transient) action of the object on a material sense organ, of which an *immaterial* operative potency (the sense) is the quasi-form.

3. *Sense species:* The sensory species is educed from the potentiality of the immaterial sense faculty.

4. *Nature of the species:* Hence, the sense species is a form *without* matter. But, since the faculty is united to the sense organ as its quasi-form, the species exists *with* the conditions of matter; hence, the sense species is a particular, not a universal representation of the object.

5. *Act of sensation:* Once the sense faculty has been actuated, it produces the *immanent* action of sensation, in which the knowing subject is united to the object which is intentionally present in the species by its *action.*

Article II: *Nature and Distinction of External Senses*

1. From the diversity of *formal objects,* we infer that there are (at least) five distinct external senses: sight, hearing, smell, taste, touch.

2.

- *Per se* sensible: That which is sensible of itself (*per se*).
  - *a*) *Proper* sensibles: are qualities perceived primarily and essentially, and by *one* sense; they cause specifically distinct representative species in the sense: color, sound, taste, smell, texture.
  - *b*) *Common* sensibles: are perceived essentially but not primarily and by more than one sense: size, shape, number, motion, rest.
- *Per accidens* sensible: that which is sensible by reason of something else, e.g., man by reason of his color and size.

Article III: *Validity of Sensation*

1. *Problem:* To ask *whether* reality can be known by the senses is to doubt all true knowledge, for even the data for intellectual knowledge is presented by the senses. Rather, the problem is: *under what conditions* is a true knowledge of the object obtained by the senses?

2. *Principle:*

a) The senses have *no false knowledge* concerning the *proper sensibles* (their proper object) except accidentally (*per accidens*) and rarely owing either to defect in the sense organ or in the medium through which the sense organ is stimulated. The reason is that the sense is ordered to the proper sensible as potency to its proper act.

b) As regards the *common* and *accidental* sensibles, the "judgment" of sense can of itself (*per se*) be erroneous even when there is no defect in the organ or in the medium, for these sensibles are not related to the sense as act to potency.

Question II

THE INTERNAL SENSES

Article I: *Need for Four Internal Senses*

Operations which cannot be reduced to one and the same principle (because they have distinct formal objects) must be assigned to distinct operative potencies.

1. *Unitive ("Common") Sense:*
   - *a*) to integrate external sensations
   - *b*) to discriminate between proper sensibles
   - *c*) sensory awareness
2. *Imaginative:*
   - *a*) sense memory — to retain and recall species of common sense
   - *b*) phantasy — to construct new species by combining elements of old; dreams
3. *"Instinctive":*
   - *a*) *estimative:* to form instinctive, insensate intentions, i.e., sensory "judgments" of what is useful or harmful, friendly or unfriendly
   - *b*) *cogitative* in man
4. *Memorative:*
   - *a*) to retain insensate intentions of the estimative sense
   - *b*) also "reminiscence" in man

Article II: *Functioning of the Internal Senses in Man*

1. The operations of all the external senses terminate in the *common sense.* Its object, therefore, includes proper as well as common sensibles.

2. The *imaginative* sense often is used creatively in conjunction with intellect.

3. The *cogitative* power compares experiences and infers a particular judgment. Hence, it is called the *particular reason.*

4. The *memorative* in man, besides simple memory and simple recall, has "reminiscence," a sort of syllogistic memory.

Article III: *The Connection Between All the Senses*

External senses depend upon the external object for their actuation; common sense upon the external senses; imaginative sense upon the common sense. The cogitative sense is moved by the external senses, the common sense, and the imaginative to formulate its "judgment" as to the usefulness or harmfulness of the object. The memorative retains the species of the cogitative sense.

CHAPTER VI

THE INTELLECT

The greatest among the perfections of things is that a thing be intellectual, because thereby it is, after a fashion, all things, having in itself the perfection of all.[1]

PROLOGUE

In an earlier chapter, we established the fact that the human soul performs its highest operation, the act of understanding, without dependence on a corporeal organ, and, therefore, that it is immaterial in the strict sense. Consequently, it will not be necessary, at this point, to demonstrate the spirituality of the human *intellect.* Such a demonstration would be superfluous. In view of the fact that we have proved the spirituality of the *intellectual* soul, it is obvious that if a distinct faculty be shown necessary to explain the soul's spiritual operation, such a faculty must itself be spiritual.

It is essential, of course, for those writers who reserve the treatise on the nature of the soul to the very last to propose at this point a formal proof of the spirituality of the intellect.[2] For without this basic truth, the problem of the origin of intellectual knowledge

[1] *C. G.,* I, 44.

[2] The problem of human intellectual knowledge — how can a material object actuate a strictly immaterial intellect — presupposes that the spirituality of the human intellect has been firmly established.

in man cannot be properly presented and solved. In this matter we are following the Angelic Doctor, to whom the strict immateriality of the intellect seems to have been so evident that he seldom bothered to discuss it, having once established that the intellectual soul is a subsisting form.

Division: In this treatise we shall consider: first, the nature of the human intellect; second, the act (operation) of the intellect; third, how the intellect knows its various objects; fourth, special functions of the human intellect.

Question I

NATURE OF THE HUMAN INTELLECT

This question is divided into three articles: (1) the human intellect is a passive operative potency; (2) an agent intellect is needed to actuate the possible intellect; (3) the process of abstraction.

ARTICLE I: The Human Intellect Is Primarily a Passive Potency

The Human Intellect Is an Operative Potency of the Soul:[3] It is impossible for the human soul to operate immediately by its essence. "For then alone is the essence of that which operates the immediate principle of operation when operation itself is its 'to be.'"[4] Now in God alone is operation identified with "to be." We conclude that in God alone is the essence the immediate principle of operation and the intellect identified with essence. Accordingly, in all limited intellectual beings, the intellect is an operative potency really distinct from the essence. The human intellectual soul, therefore, being a limited reality, operates through a distinct operative potency, the intellect.[5]

[3] *S. Th.,* I, 79, 1, *c.*
[4] *Loc. cit.*
[5] The general principles presupposed here were studied in the chapter on the operative potencies.

The Human Intellect Is a Passive Potency:[6] Furthermore, we must also admit that the human intellect is a passive potency,[7] that it can pass from potency to act, that it is actuable. Indeed, it is a common fact of experience that we constantly acquire intellectual knowledge not previously possessed; consequently, our intellect must pass from potency to act; for, in order to produce the immanent operation of understanding, it must be in act. Only an intellect that is Pure Act — an intellect which is identical with its "to be," and which is, therefore, virtually all being — cannot be actuated further, and consequently cannot be in potency to knowledge. On the other hand, every created intellect, no matter how perfect, precisely because it is not Pure Act, remains in potency to knowledge.

Now there are two ways in which an operative potency may be related to act: (1) there is a type of potency which is always in act, always actuated;[8] (2) another type of potency is not always in act and proceeds from potency to act. The human intellect is a potency of this second type.[9] It is not in act of itself with regard to knowledge, but must acquire its species by a laborious process originating in sensory experience. In the beginning of its existence, it is, as Aristotle states, like a clean tablet on which nothing has

---

[6] *S. Th.*, I, 79, 2, *c.*

[7] "*. . . intelligere est pati. . . .*" (*Ibid.*, *sed contra.*)

[8] Such is the angelic intellect. Because of its perfection and proximity to God, it is in act regarding its intelligible objects. The reason is that the intelligible species necessary for the knowledge required by the nature of angels were infused at the time of their creation. This is the theory which St. Thomas proposes regarding the actuation of the angelic intellect: ". . . the species whereby the angels understand are not drawn from things, but are connatural to them. . . . Consequently, they attain their intelligible perfection through an intelligible outpouring, whereby they received from God the species of things known, together with their intellectual nature." (*Ibid.*, 55, 2, *c.*)

[9] The human intellect is proportioned to a nature that is not a pure form, but a composite of spiritual soul and matter. ". . . the lower spiritual substances (souls) have a 'to be' related to a body, in so far as they are the forms of bodies; and, consequently, from their very mode of existing it is necessary for them to seek their intelligible perfection from bodies and through bodies. Otherwise, they would be united to bodies in vain." (*Loc. cit.*)

been written.[10] The nature of the intellect of man, then, is primarily that of a passive (operative) potency. Following the terminology of Aristotle and St. Thomas, we shall call the intellectual faculty of man the *possible intellect.*

We may say, then, that the possible intellect primarily is a passive operative potency, really distinct from the essence of the soul. It is an accidental form which performs the operation of understanding once it is put into act. The problem now is to discover *how this passive operative potency is actuated.*

ARTICLE II: Need of the Agent Intellect to Actuate the Possible Intellect[11]

Problem: The intellectual faculty in man is a spiritual *passive* potency. It must, therefore, somehow be actuated by an object, which is the initial cause in human knowledge. But how can the material objects that surround us actuate a faculty that is strictly immaterial?

Object of the Human Intellect: The fundamental difficulty in solving this problem is that the *proper* object of the intellect of man in this life is the essences of material things. By the proper object we mean that which our intellect knows primarily (*primo*) and *per se,* that is, according to the mode of existing of the object, and not through another being.

In technical philosophical language: the proper object of the human intellect is *material quiddity,*[12] the essence or nature of corporeal things. Our first, our proper conceptions are of material beings: man, horse, house.[13] True, the human intellect goes be-

[10] ". . . mind is in a sense potentially whatever is thinkable though actually it is nothing until it has thought. What it thinks must be in it just as characters may be said to be on a writing tablet on which as yet nothing actually stands. . . ." (*De Anima,* III, 4, 430a, 1.)

[11] *S. Th.,* I, 79, 3.

[12] ". . . the proper object of the human intellect, which is united to a body, is the quiddity or nature existing in corporeal matter. . . ." (*Ibid.,* 84, 7, *c.*)

[13] Why must the proper object of the human intellect, which is a strictly immaterial faculty, be a material and not a spiritual essence? The reason is that the soul, although it is spiritual, is the substantial form of the human body, and is not united to the body in vain.

yond the data of sense; man understands the essences of things. Still, these essences exist with the conditions of matter; they are material. Hence, our knowledge of immaterial things is non-proper and, therefore, imperfect; it can be attained only by reflection upon the essences of material things—by using the data received from corporeal things. From this proper knowledge of material things, we construct our knowledge of immaterial realities.[14] Accordingly, in our conceptions of immaterial things, we retain, we might say, the material viewpoint of our understanding of material beings. This fact cannot be too strongly emphasized: the material essence is the proper object of the human intellect. ". . . It is proper to the [human intellect] to know a form existing individually in corporeal matter. . . . Our intellect understands material things. . . ."[15]

Now, if matter is not intelligible, and is, as we have observed, the one obstacle to intelligibility, how can a material object actuate an immaterial potency[16] so that it becomes in act to understand? *How can the object, which is material, or its phantasm, which is partly material, move a spiritual operative potency, the possible intellect, from potency to act?*

This difficulty is so enormous and so fundamental that many of the philosophical errors which have arisen throughout the ages are based on a faulty solution of it. The most important of these errors, because of its pervading influence even to this day, is that of Plato.

Solution of Plato: Plato seems to have held a previous existence of the soul in a "world of Ideas" before its union with the

---

[14] ". . . it is through these natures of visible things that the [human] intellect rises to a certain knowledge of things invisible." (*S. Th.*, I, 84, 7, *c.*)

[15] *Ibid.*, 85, 1, *c.* We grant, of course, that any created intellect is capable of knowing every being, its adequate object. What philosophers term the adequate object of any intellect is ". . . something universal, namely *being* and the *true* [italics added]. . . . The first [proper] object of our intellect according to its present state is not every being and every true, but being and the true as found in material things. . . ." (*Ibid.*, 87, 3, ad 1^{m}.)

[16] "Nothing corporeal can make an impression on the incorporeal." (*Ibid.*, 84, 6, *c.*)

body. It was there that the soul somehow acquired intelligible species which are presumably participations in the separate intelligible "Ideas." This doctrine is a fundamental form of *Innatism*. According to this explanation, the intellectual soul does not acquire ideas in this life, since it already possesses them; it is already somehow in act. The soul merely recalls its "ideas" on the occasion of coming in contact, through sensation, with the individual material participations of these same "Ideas." For Plato, accordingly, intellectual knowledge is had by recollection. St. Thomas states Plato's view in these words:

> . . . Plato supposed that the forms of natural things subsisted apart from matter, and, consequently, that they are intelligible; for a thing is actually intelligible from the fact that it is immaterial. And he called such forms *species* or *Ideas* [italics added]. From a participation in these, he said that even corporeal matter was formed, in order that individuals might be naturally established in their proper genera and species, and also that our intellect was formed by such participation in order to have knowledge of the genera and species of things.[17]

Thus, "Plato held that there are separate Ideas (*species*) of all things, and that individuals are named from them (*denominantur ab eis*) as participating in the separate Ideas; for instance that Socrates is called man according to the separate form of man."[18] The source of this strange metaphysical error is a fundamental fault in Plato's theory of knowledge.

> . . . He thought that the form of the thing known must of necessity be in the knower in the same manner as in the thing known. Then he observed that the form of the thing understood is in the intellect under the conditions of universality, immateriality, and immobility. . . . Therefore, he concluded that the things which we understand must subsist in themselves under the same conditions of immateriality and immobility.[19]

Although Plato is often called an exaggerated *realist* because of

[17] *S. Th.*, I, 79, 3, *c.* [18] *Ibid.*, 6, 4, *c.* [19] *Ibid.*, 84, 1, *c.*

his assertion that knowledge corresponds exactly to reality (the separated species or "Ideas"), nevertheless, he was forced by this position to posit innate species (ideas) in the intellect of man in order to solve the problem of the origin of intellectual knowledge; consequently, he deserves rather to be called the father of all *idealists*. For the various theories which under one form or another deny the objectivity of knowledge and affirm the supremacy of thought over being are but natural outgrowths of the pure position of Plato, whether it be the agnosticism of the Neo-Platonists, the skepticism of Ockham, the distinct idea of Descartes, the *esse est percipi*[20] of Berkeley, the Kantian *a priori* forms, or even the absolute identification of thought and reality by the modern neo-Hegelians.

Materialist Position: For the materialist, the problem of intellectual knowledge in man simply does not exist. Having reduced all reality to matter, he can see no difficulty in having a material object act upon a material intellect. For him, intellectual knowledge is but a more complex type of sense knowledge, which is undoubtedly material in nature. As we have noted before, Materialism is really an evasion of a philosophical problem rather than an attempt at a solution.

The True Solution: Need of the Agent Intellect: Since we have no innate ideas, no infused species, and since, moreover, the proper objects of our intellect — sensible beings — are not intelligible to us in act (that is, are not capable of actuating the spiritual human intellect), in order to explain the fact of intellectual knowledge, there must be in the soul a special spiritual power, always in act, which we shall call the *agent intellect*. Like a beacon of light, it renders sensible objects actually intelligible, somewhat as the light of the sun renders colors actually visible.[21] Illuminating the

---

20 "To be is to be perceived."

21 ". . . Aristotle's comparison of the agent intellect to light is verified in this, that as light is required for seeing, so is the agent intellect required for understanding, but not for the same reason." (*S. Th.*, I, 79, 3, ad 2^{m}.)

phantasm, which is the sensible representation of the corporeal object, this spiritual light transforms it and by its instrumentality produces in the possible intellect the intelligible species, by which the possible intellect is in act to operate immanently.[22]

> . . . Since forms existing in matter are not actually intelligible, it follows that the natures or forms of the sensible things which we understand are not actually intelligible. Now nothing is reduced from potency to act except by something in act; as the senses are made actual by what is actually sensible. We must, therefore, assign on the part of the intellect some power (*virtus*) to make things actually intelligible, by the abstraction of the species from material conditions. And such is the necessity of an agent intellect.[23]

For an accurate understanding of the passage quoted above, several technical expressions must be clarified:

Actually intelligible (intelligible in act): ". . . A thing is actually intelligible from the very fact that it is immaterial."[24] Such a form, if it is united to the intellect, will put the intellect in act to knowing (*intelligere*). "Now the intelligible in act is not something existing in nature, provided, of course, that we are thinking of the nature of sensible things, which do not subsist without matter."[25] Neither sensible objects nor their representative forms in the sense—the phantasms which exist with the conditions of matter—are intelligible to us in act; they cannot of themselves actuate a spiritual passive intellect, that is, move it from potency to a specific act.

Potentially intelligible (intelligible in potency): Any corporeal reality is a potentially intelligible being. Such a being—whether

---

[22] Why could not the possible intellect, which is an immaterial faculty, act directly upon the phantasm? The reason is that the possible intellect is in potency. It would have to be actuated in order to place an action. Hence, the agent intellect is absolutely necessary to explain human intellectual knowledge.

[23] *S. Th.*, I, 79, 3, *c*.

[24] *Loc. cit.* It is not the universality which makes something intelligible, but the immateriality. *"Ex hoc enim aliquid est intellectum in actu quod est immateriale, non autem ex hoc quod est universale."* (*Quaestio Unica de Anima,* art. II, ad 5^{m}.)

[25] *S. Th.*, I, 79, 3, ad 3^{m}.

existing intentionally (phantasm) or in nature—is not of itself capable of actuating the human intellect, although it does contain some intelligibility (by reason of form and the act of existing). This intelligibility can be rendered actual if abstracted from matter. The phantasms, therefore, are potentially intelligible; they become actually intelligible by a process of abstraction from the conditions of matter.[26]

ARTICLE III: The Process of Abstraction

Formation of the Intelligible Species: The agent intellect, being a spiritual power always in act,[27] illumines and transforms the phantasm.[28] Using the transformed phantasm as its instrument,[29] the agent intellect educes from the potency of the possible intellect an accidental form (the intelligible species), which—since it is without the individuating conditions of matter—is strictly immaterial, and, consequently, can represent the object according to its universal nature.

Nature of the Intelligible Species: With regard to the intelligible species we should carefully note: (1) It is strictly immaterial, because it is received in (educed from) a strictly spiritual faculty and caused principally by a *spiritual* operative power, the agent intellect, through the instrumentality of a phantasm "separated" from the conditions of matter. (2) Because the intelligible species is strictly immaterial, it is intelligible in act; and, being received in and united to the possible intellect, it actuates the intellectual faculty so that the intellect in act must produce the operation of knowledge. (3) Because this form is strictly immaterial, it is not

[26] "The agent intellect causes the phantasms received from the senses to be actually intelligible by a process of abstraction." (*Ibid.*, 84, 6, *c.*)

[27] The agent intellect ". . . is in act according to its substance." (*In III De Anima,* lect. 10, Nos. 732 and 733.)

[28] We could compare the agent intellect to the X-rays, which allow the observer to visualize the bone structure as if the flesh had been removed. Like all examples, however, this is not an exact comparison.

[29] Cf. *The Philosophy of Being,* p. 141.

only stripped of all matter, but even of the individuating conditions of matter. Therefore, it does not and cannot represent an individual essence, for matter is the principle of individuation.[30] (4) Consequently, intellectual knowledge resulting from this actuation must be of universal, indeterminate essences.

Role of Possible Intellect, Phantasm, and Agent Intellect in the Process of Abstraction: In order to delineate the precise role of possible intellect, phantasm, and agent intellect in the abstractive process, that is, in the formation of the intelligible species, we present the following classic text from the *Contra Gentiles:*

> Nothing hinders one thing from being in one respect in potentiality with regard to some other thing, and in act in another respect. . . . Now we find this same comparison between the intellective soul and the phantasms; for the soul has something in act to which the phantasm is in potency, and is in potency to something which is found in act in the phantasms. Because the substance of the human soul has immateriality, it consequently possesses an intellectual nature, since such is every immaterial substance. Yet it does not follow that it is likened to this or that determinate thing, which is required in order that our soul may know this or that thing determinately; for all knowledge results from the likeness of the known in the knower. Hence, the intellective soul remains itself in potency to the determinate likenesses of things that can be known by us, and these are the natures of sensible things. It is the *phantasms* that *offer us these determinate natures of sensible things;* these phantasms, however, have not yet attained an intelligible "to be," since they are images of sensible things even as to material conditions, which are the individual properties, and, moreover, they are in material organs. Wherefore, they are not actually intelligible. And yet, since in the individual man whose image the phantasms reflect, it is possible to conceive the universal nature apart from (*denudatam*) all individualizing conditions, they are intelligible potentially. Accordingly, they have intelligibility potentially, though they are actually (*in actu*) determinate as images of things: whereas it was the other way about in the intellective soul. Consequently,

[30] Cf. *The Philosophy of Being,* p. 216.

there is in the intellective soul an active power (*virtus*) in respect of the phantasms, *rendering them actually intelligible,* and this power of the soul is called the *agent intellect.* There is also in the soul a power (*virtus*) which is in potency to the determinate images of sensible things, and this is the *possible intellect. . . .*

The intellective soul is in potency to the likenesses of things which are the phantasms, not according to the mode in which they are there, but according as these images are raised to something higher, *by being abstracted from* the individualizing conditions of matter, so that they become actually intelligible. Consequently, the action of the agent intellect on the phantasm precedes the reception by the possible intellect. . . .

Consequently, Aristotle was moved to assert that those things which are intelligible to us are not certain existing things that are intelligible in themselves, but that they *are made intelligible from sensibles.* Hence, he had to posit a power (*virtus*) which would do this; and this is the agent intellect. Wherefore, the reason for positing the agent intellect is that it makes intelligibles proportionate to us [all italics added].[31]

Joint Causality of Agent Intellect and Phantasm: In the abstractive process, the agent intellect is a principal cause using the phantasm as an instrument. The patient is the possible intellect. The effect is the eduction of the intelligible species from the potency of the passive intellect. Both agent intellect and phantasm are true causes in the production of this effect, but in a different manner. The agent intellect is in act with respect to spirituality—it is aptly compared to a beacon of light—but is *indeterminate* with regard to any determinate likeness of things. The phantasm, on the other hand, is a *determinate* likeness of a sensible object, but is partly material. Consequently, neither agent intellect nor the phantasm can of itself produce the effect that actually occurs, that is, the actuation of the possible intellect by the eduction of a *strictly immaterial likeness* of the object. But through the exercise

---

[31] *C. G.,* II, 77.

of a joint causality, the agent intellect (as principal cause) and the phantasm (as instrumental cause) bring about the eduction of this strictly immaterial likeness of the object, the intelligible species. The agent intellect, as principal cause, contributes strict *immateriality* to the effect; the phantasm, as the instrumental cause, contributes *representativeness* to the same effect. The intelligible species, accordingly, is a strictly immaterial representation of the object, for it is produced according to the condition of both agent intellect and phantasm exercising a joint causality.[32]

The phantasm is not an exemplar, nor a material cause, but an *efficient* instrumental cause. Hence, we must not conceive the process of abstraction as the taking out of a form from the phantasm and the placing of it in the possible intellect. That would be rank materialism. Rather, the intelligible species is a spiritual accidental form educed from the potency of the possible intellect by the joint efficiency of agent intellect and phantasm. Consequently, when we speak of the "illumination and elevation" of the phantasm, our meaning is simply this: from the agent intellect, the phantasm receives a "virtue" (*virtus*), not with its complete "to be," but with a flowing, spiritual "to be" (*esse fluens*), like

---

[32] "In the reception by which the possible intellect receives the species of things from phantasms, the phantasms function as an instrumental and secondary agent, the agent intellect indeed as a primary and principal agent; and, therefore, the effect of the action remains in the possible intellect according to the condition of both, and not according to the condition of the agent intellect only. Wherefore, by virtue of the agent intellect, the possible intellect receives the forms as actually intelligible, but from the cognition of the phantasms it receives them as likenesses of determined things; and thus the actually intelligible forms do not exist *per se* either in the imagination or in the agent intellect, but solely in the possible intellect." (*De Ver.*, X, 6, ad 7^{m}.)

"With reference to the possible intellect, things are insufficient agents; for the action of sensible things themselves does not stop even in the imagination, but, in addition, the phantasms move the possible intellect. Of themselves, to be sure, they are not capable of doing so, since they are potential intelligibles and the intellect is not moved except by the actually intelligible. On this account, the action of the agent intellect, by whose illumination the phantasms become actually intelligible, must supervene. And thus it is clear that the agent intellect is the principal agent which produces the likenesses of things in the possible intellect, whereas the phantasms which are received from external things are as it were instrumental agents." (*Quodl.*, VIII, 3.)

that of a becoming, which terminates in the intelligible species in the possible intellect.[33]

Agent Intellect and Possible Intellect Are Really Distinct: The distinction between the agent and possible intellects is evident from a consideration of their functions. The agent intellect *produces* the intelligible species; the possible intellect *receives* the species. The agent intellect, therefore, is in act;[34] the possible intellect is in potency regarding the same object. The agent intellect is an operative power, like a beacon of spiritual light, which makes intellectual knowledge possible in man; it is not, however, a cognoscitive power. The possible intellect, on the other hand, is a faculty of knowledge; although it is primarily passive, nevertheless, when actuated by the agent intellect acting in conjunction with the phantasm,[35] it elicits the act of knowledge. There are, then, two distinct operations of two distinct powers; yet there is only one action of knowing (*intelligere*), namely, the operation of the possible intellect consequent upon its actuation.[36]

---

[33] "In a corporeal thing there cannot be a spiritual power with a complete 'to be'; however, it can be present by way of intention." (*In IV Sent.*, d. I, q. I, a. 4, sol. 2, ad 4^{m}.)

[34] The agent intellect is not a pure act; it is an accidental power which is constantly actuated by the prime mover, God. We could express this truth by saying that the agent intellect in us postulates a higher intellect in which it participates: "There must be some higher intellect, by which the soul is helped to understand. . . . This separate intellect . . . is God Himself, who is the soul's Creator, and only beatitude. Therefore, the human soul derives its intellectual light from Him." (*S. Th.*, I, 79, 4, *c.*)

[35] The internal senses which furnish the phantasm for the actuation of the possible intellect are the imaginative and the cogitative. For, on the one hand, the intellect understands the nature of objects that have been *sensed,* for example, the nature of a tree, rose, cat. In such cases the sensory data for the intelligible species is from a phantasm in the imaginative sense. On the other hand, the intellect also understands such notions as usefulness, friendship, and the like, which can in no way be sensed. The data for such notions must be derived from the cogitative sense, which forms *insensate* intentions.

[36] ". . . we must maintain that the two intellects, namely the possible and agent intellects, have two distinct actions. For the act of the possible intellect is to receive intelligibles; but the action of the agent intellect is to abstract intelligibles. Nevertheless, it does not follow that man has two actions of understanding; for both actions concur in the one action of understanding (*intelligere*)." (*Quaestio Unica de Anima,* art. 4, ad 8^{m}.)

Conclusion: The doctrine of the agent intellect is of extreme importance. We might say that it is a strategic point in the philosophy of man. As a matter of fact, it is the only intelligible position that can be taken with respect to intellectual knowledge in man.[37] If one rejects it, there remain only two untenable and erroneous positions. The first is *materialism,* which postulates that intellectual knowledge is only a highly developed form of sense cognition. Against such an unphilosophical assertion, we need only recall our chapter on the spirituality of the intellectual soul. The other position, some sort of *innatism,* we have already explained, and have shown not only that it is against all experience, but that it must lead to idealism and skepticism.

Question II

THE ACT (OPERATION) OF THE INTELLECT

This question is divided into four articles: (1) the need of the mental "word"; (2) the two types of mental "word"; (3) in the forming of the mental "word," the object is known first; (4) the truth of the mental "word."

ARTICLE I: Need of the Mental "Word" (Verbum)

We have noted that the intellectual cognoscitive faculty, the possible intellect, because it is primarily a passive potency, requires to be informed and actuated by the intelligible species. This species is obtained through the process of abstraction by the joint

---

[37] A curious theory regarding the agent intellect was proposed by Averroes, the great Arab commentator on the works of Aristotle. Because this doctrine was adopted in the early Middle Ages by many philosophers, St. Thomas often refutes it. Briefly, the doctrine is this: The agent intellect is not to be found multiplied in individual men; rather, it is one, unique; it exists separated from all human nature as a distinct entity. Cf. *S. Th.,* I, 79, 4 and 5.

causality of the agent intellect and the phantasm. Once the possible intellect has been thus informed and actuated, it is in act as regards operation. The immanent action which follows is the act of understanding. It is to this operation that we must now direct our attention. We shall examine the nature of this action and the product, the mental "word" (*verbum*), in which the act of understanding terminates.

Presence of the Object of Knowledge: Knowledge is an intentional union of subject with object. With regard to the cognition of the external sense, we saw that for such a union there was no need of an intentional term because the sensible object is actually present in the intentional species by its action here and now in causing the eduction of the species.[38] Since the action of an agent is *in* the patient, it follows that the agent — in this case the sensed object — is somehow present in the sensible species.

In the operation of the imaginative sense, we discovered that an intentional term is needed, since the external object is not present to this sense by its action. This term, this form, which terminates the operation of the imaginative sense we have called the *phantasm*. Now in studying the act of intellection, we shall see that the need for a term is much more clearly realized, since the object (a material individual) *as such* is never present in the intellect.[39] Hence, it must be "*re*-presented" in order that the intentional union which is knowledge may take place.

Intentional Union of Intellect With Object in the "Word": To understand the need of a term distinct from the operation of understanding, we must consider that intellection is an *immanent* action. Accordingly, it is not sufficient that the external object be present to the intellect in as much as its intelligible species is received in the possible intellect. The actuation of the possible intel-

[38] The species in the external sense is more like a passing change than like a complete form and does not endure and remain in the faculty.

[39] The object as existing is a corporeal individual; it is in the intellect, however, according to its universal nature.

lect by the eduction of this species is not the intellectual operation of knowing (*intelligere*); rather, it is merely the preparation for that act; it is but the actuation of the intellectual faculty in order that this faculty may produce its proper operation, the act of understanding—"to understand" (*intelligere*).

Now the act of understanding, which the actuated intellect produces, is a quality uniting the faculty with the object, for *knowledge is a union.* But, since the object (a material individual) is not present *as such* in the faculty, it cannot be united with the faculty unless in the intellectual operation the intellect form for itself an intentional term. This becomes all the more evident when we consider that the intellect understands a thing whether it is present or absent. Moreover, the intellect understands the object as separated from the material conditions without which it does not exist in reality.

The intellect must, therefore, produce an *intention,* a form of the object known; it must "conceive" the object. The product of this intentional conception—the *concept* or "word"—is the thing as understood. It is an intellectual expression of the thing known, and is therefore aptly called the mental "word" (*verbum*) by analogy with the words of human speech, which in turn are the external expression of this internal "word."[40] In the internal "word," the intellect becomes united intentionally with the object and understands that object as in a mirror; this mental "word" is a medium in which (*medium in quo*) the existing object is known. All this is set forth by the Angelic Doctor in the following text:

---

[40] ". . . the spoken word is something uttered by the mouth of man, and expresses that which is signified by the human word. The same applies to the human mental word, which is nothing else than something conceived by the mind, by which man expresses mentally the things of which he is thinking." (*S. Th.,* I–II, 93, 1, ad 2m.) ". . . what the intellect forms in its conception is the word." (*Ibid.,* I, 34, 1, ad 2m.) "The concept (*conceptus*) of the mind is called the interior word." (*Ibid.,* 107, 1, *c.*) ". . . the interior concept (*conceptus*) of the mind is called the word." (*Ibid.,* 34, 1, *c.*)

. . . It must be observed that the external objects which we understand do not exist in our intellect according to their own nature, but it is necessary that our intellect contain their species whereby it becomes intellect in act. And being in act by this species, as by its proper form, it understands the object itself. And yet the act of understanding is not an action passing into the object understood, as heating passes into the object heated, but it remains in the one who understands; although it bears a relation to the object understood, for the very reason that the aforesaid species, which is the formal principle of intellectual operation, is the image of that object.

It must furthermore be observed that the intellect, informed by the species of the object, in the act of understanding *produces in itself a kind of intention of the object understood,* which intention reflects the nature of that object and is expressed in the definition thereof. This indeed is necessary, since the intellect *understands indifferently a thing absent or present,* and in this point agrees with the imagination. Yet the intellect has this besides, that it understands a thing as *separate from material conditions,* without which it does not exist in reality; and this is impossible unless the intellect forms for itself the aforesaid intention.

Now this understood intention, since it is the term, so to speak, of the intellectual operation, is distinct from the intelligible species which makes the intellect in act and which we must look upon as the principle of the intellectual operation, although each is an image of the object understood; since it is because the intelligible species, which is the form of the intellect and the principle of understanding, is the image of the external object, that the intellect in consequence forms an intention like that object; for such as a thing is, such is the effect of its operation. And since the understood intention is like a particular thing, it follows that the intellect by forming this intention understands that thing [all italics added].[41]

---

[41] *C. G.,* I, 53. A parallel passage in the *Summa Theologica* compares the operation of the intellect to that of the imagination and shows that besides the impression of a species, there is need of a mental term (the "word") in the intellectual faculty corresponding to the image (the phantasm) produced by the imagination. This operation St. Thomas calls a ". . . formation inasmuch as the imaginative power forms for itself an image of an absent thing, or even of something never seen. Both of these operations [the impression of a species and the act of the faculty which forms an intention] are found in the intellect. For in the first place, there is a passion in the possible intellect inasmuch as it is informed by the intelligible species; and the possible intellect, thus informed, then forms a definition, or a division, or

Four Distinct Factors in Man's Intellectual Knowledge: From this exposition of the act of human intellection, we can conclude that:

a) The mental "word" is really distinct from the act of understanding, as a term of operation is distinct from operation itself;

b) The intelligible species is really distinct from the operation of the intellect, as the principle of action is distinct from action in all limited beings;

c) The intelligible species is distinct from the intellect, since act is distinct from potency;

d) The intelligible species is also distinct from the mental "word," as a principle is distinct from that which proceeds from the principle.

Hence, we must distinguish four diverse elements in the act of intellectual knowledge in man: (1) the possible intellect, which is the operative potency; (2) the intelligible species, which is the actuation of that potency; (3) the act of understanding, the act of a perfect being (*actus perfecti*) by which man knows; (4) the mental "word" (*verbum*), in which man knows the object. That these factors are really distinct in human knowledge is an indication of the imperfection of man's knowledge, since knowledge is intentional *union*. Accordingly, that knowledge is most perfect in which all these factors are identified.[42]

---

a composition, which is expressed through words. And so, the notion (*ratio*) signified by a noun is a definition; while an enunciation signifies the intellect's composition and division." (*S. Th.*, I, 85, 2, ad 3^{m}.) Cf. *In S. Ioannis Proemium*.

[42] "The life of the angels does not reach the highest degree of perfection, because, though the understood intention is altogether within them, it is not their very substance, because in them 'to understand' and 'to be' are not the same thing. Therefore, the highest perfection of life belongs to God in Whom 'to understand' is not distinct from 'to be.' Wherefore, the *understood intention* [the Word] must be the divine essence itself.

"By *understood intention,* I mean that which the intellect itself conceives of the thing understood (*de re intellecta*). Now, in us, this [understood intention] is neither the thing itself that is understood, nor the substance of the intellect, but it is a likeness conceived in the intellect of the thing understood, and is expressed by external speech. Wherefore, this intention is called the *internal word* and is expressed by an external word.

ARTICLE II: Two Types of Mental "Word"

Logical Order: The traditional division of the operations of the intellect as given in a course of Logic is into three general types: (*a*) simple apprehension, (*b*) judgment, and (*c*) reasoning. This division of intellectual operations is based on mental relations, for the "simple apprehension," the "judgment," and the "reasoning" of the logician are *second intentions;* that is to say, they are relations of reason established by a reflection of the intellect upon terms (mental products) already existing in the mind; in other words, these relations are formed by a reflection on things *as known.* The only reality which these logical "acts" of the intellect possess consists in this, that the mind places such relations while considering terms already in the mind, as it does when it forms subject-predicate relations, genus-species, and antecedent-consequent relations.

Real Order: In reality, in as much as the intellect is informed by an intelligible species, there is only one specific act of the intellect — "to understand" (*intelligere*). In this operation, the human intellect forms a mental "word" (object as known, an understood intention) and becomes united with the object. This mental "word," which is formed through the operation of understanding (*intel-*

"That this same *intention* is not the thing which we understand is evident from the fact that to understand a thing is quite different from understanding its understood intention; and the intellect does this when it reflects on its own production (*opus*). For this reason, sciences that treat of things are distinct from those that treat of *understood intentions.*

"Again, it is clear that in us the understood intention is not the intellect itself, because the 'to be' of the understood intention consists in a 'to be understood' (*in ipso intelligi*); not so with our intellect whose 'to be' is not its 'to understand' (*intelligere*). . . .

"The *Word* of God is the divine 'to be,' and the essence of God, and God in very truth (*ipse verus Deus*). It is not so with the *word* of the human intellect. For when our intellect understands itself, the 'to be' of the intellect is not identified with the act of understanding, because the substance of the intellect was understanding in potency before it would actually understand. Consequently, the 'to be' of the understood intention is distinct from the 'to be' of the intellect; since the 'to be' of the understood intention consists in being understood [all italics added]." (*C. G.,* IV, 11.)

ligere), is either: (*a*) a *definition* (concept), in which the object is grasped according to its quiddity (essence), or (*b*) a *composition* or *division*[43] (attributive judgment), in which the intellect understands also the properties and accidents of the essence. These mental "words" are not relations established by the mind. Rather, they are the thing *as understood*. First, we understand the quiddity, the essence of an object (definition); we then proceed to composition or division. This second type of mental "word" (composition or division) is, in a way, the term of a deeper probing into reality, of a more profound understanding of the thing understood (*res intellecta*). Finally, we should note that in reasoning the intellect proceeds from one composition (or division) to another; such an act terminates in a more complex composition (or division).

> . . . The human intellect does not acquire perfect knowledge of a thing by the first apprehension; but it first apprehends something of the thing, such as its quiddity, which is the first and proper object of the intellect; and then it understands the properties, accidents, and relations that modify the essence of the thing. Thus it necessarily composes one apprehension with another or divides it therefrom; and from one composition or division it necessarily proceeds to another, and this is to reason.[44]

We see, therefore, that the logical "acts" of the intellect — "simple apprehension, judgment, and reasoning" — do not signify the act of knowing the real (*intelligere*). Rather, they signify mental constructs resulting from a reflection upon several mental conceptions. On the other hand, the definition and the composition (or division) are mental "words" formed as terms of the operation of understanding. Both, definition and composition (or division), are understood realities (*res intellectae*), not relations of reason.[45]

[43] ". . . the possible intellect thus informed [by the intelligible species] . . . forms a definition, or a division, or a composition, which is expressed by words. And so the knowledge (*ratio*) signified by a noun is a definition; and an enunciation [proposition] signifies the intellect's division or composition. Words . . . signify . . . that which the intellect forms for itself for the purpose of judging of external things." (*S. Th.*, I, 85, 2, ad 3^{m}.)

[44] *Ibid.*, 5, *c.*

[45] ". . . sciences that treat of things are distinct from those that treat of understood intentions [e.g., Logic]." (*C. G.*, IV, 11.)

ARTICLE III: In the Forming of the Mental "Word" the Object Is Known First

Objectivity of Intellectual Knowledge: ". . . That which is understood primarily (*primo*) is the thing (*res*) of which the intelligible species is the likeness."[46] ". . . The intelligible species is not what is actually understood, but that *by* which the intellect understands."[47] We find these statements recurring in the writings of St. Thomas whenever he discusses the question of intellectual knowledge in man. They express a fundamental position in his epistemology as well as in his psychology.

Many philosophers, however, have held a different doctrine about human knowledge. They have thought that the impression made upon the mind by the thing is what is first understood, and not the thing itself. That we do know these impressions—whether intellectual or sensible—is, of course, true. But such knowledge is had solely by reflecting upon them. They are neither the only things we know, nor the first things. In point of fact, the reflective act by which we know them presupposes and demands what we may call a first knowledge, a knowledge of the thing, of objects.

Error of the Subjectivists: St. Thomas, in examining and solving this problem,[48] begins by giving us two extrinsic reasons why the doctrine which would limit our knowledge to our impressions, that is, to the knowledge of representative forms, is false. He then presents an analysis of knowledge which establishes the truth of his own realist position.[49] It will be sufficient merely to quote and paraphrase his explanation.

To say that we know only our impressions of the real is false for two reasons. First, there would be no science of objects outside

---

[46] *S. Th.*, I, 85, 2, *c.*
[47] *Loc. cit.*
[48] *Loc. cit.*
[49] In the strict sense, realism is not a "position" (a mere viewpoint) regarding reality.

of us, but only a science of ideas.[50] This is the doctrine of the Platonists, a doctrine which leads directly to skepticism. Second, we would have to conclude that truth is not objective, but purely subjective, and that "whatever seems is true," since we would be able to judge only of our impressions and not of reality.[51] Thus, we would be committed to an irrevocable relativism as regards truth.

The Mental "Word" Is the Intelligible Prolongation of the Object: The complete solution to our problem lies in an analysis of the act of understanding. In the first place, the intelligible species is a prolongation of the object; it is an intelligible likeness of the object. Accordingly, it can only be a medium *by which* the intellect knows; it is not the object known.

> . . . Action is twofold . . . one which remains in the agent (for example, to see and to understand), and another which passes into an external object (for instance, to heat and to cut). Each of these actions proceeds by virtue of some form. And just as the form from which proceeds an action tending to something external is the likeness of the object of the action, as heat in the heater is a likeness of the thing heated, so the form from which proceeds an action remaining in the agent is a likeness of the object. Hence, that *by which* the sight sees is the likeness of the visible thing; and the likeness of the thing understood, that is, the intelligible species, is the form *by which* the intellect understands [italics added].[52]

Second, the intelligible species is not the act of knowledge; rather, this species is the form (a likeness of the thing understood) which is the actuation of the possible intellect.[53]

---

[50] This is equivalent to maintaining that Logic is the one and only true science.

[51] This basically is the position of all Subjectivists, as exemplified in the theories of cognition of Kant, Berkeley, and Hegel.

[52] *S. Th.*, I, 85, 2, *c*.

[53] "It is the species of the thing which becomes the form of the possible intellect." (*Compendium Theologiae*, c. 83.)

Finally, the immanent action of intellection, which is consequent upon this actuation, will terminate in a mental "word" of the same intentional form as that of the intelligible species and of the object. The reason is that every agent — in this case the actuated intellect — acts in so far as it is in act, or according to its form. In brief, the actuated intellect by its operation generates a form (the mental "word") similar to that of the generator, *in which* the intellect understands the *thing*.[54]

If the mental "word" were obtained by a sort of reflection upon the intelligible species, not the object, but the species would be the first thing known by the intellect. But that is not what occurs in knowledge. "Our intellect does not form the word by looking at the intelligible species. . . . The reason is that the intellect cannot understand unless it be one with the species. . . . It is the species which first directs the intellect to the object."[55] The species as such is not known, since it is but a principle of knowledge in as much as it is a (formal and efficient) cause not only of the act of understanding, but also of the intelligibility of the "word" in which the object is known. The species, therefore, must be considered as a sort of "prolongation" of the thing, *by which* the subject knows the object. For the intellect forms the "word" in as much as it is in act through its information by this same intelligible species, which is the likeness of the object. The mental "word" is *intelligible only because of the intelligibility* of the object, which by its prolongation — the species — causes this "word." Hence, that which is first known is neither the intelligible species nor the "word," but the object understood in the "word."

---

54 ". . . that this same intention [the "word"] is not the thing which we understand is evident from the fact that to understand a thing is quite different from understanding its understood intention; and this the intellect does when it reflects on its own production." (*C. G.*, IV, 11.)

55 *"Non enim intellectus noster inspiciens hanc speciem [intelligibilem] . . . aliquid facit quasi verbum eius . . . cum intellectus non intelligat nisi factus unum cum specie . . . Species enim semper ducit in objectum primum."* (*De Natura Verbi Intellectus.*)

ARTICLE IV: The Truth of the Mental "Word"[56]

Pseudo-Problem of Idealism: The problem of formal truth is an epistemological one which cannot be treated here. One fundamental point, however, must be established in order to understand the Thomistic position toward Idealism, and, in particular, the Thomistic solution — or lack of solution — to what is called the critical problem.

The problem is often formulated in this wise: How can the intellect know *that* it knows the real? How can the intellect *prove* to itself that the knowledge of the object which it attains in the mental "word" is truly knowledge of *that which is?*

To such a question there can be no answer. To ask it is implicitly to affirm some form of skepticism, from which there can be no reasoned escape. For one cannot hope to lay a foundation for true and certain knowledge by using as "proof" other knowledge whose validity has already been questioned. One cannot "prove" that one's knowledge corresponds to the real through the mediation of a knowledge whose reliability is doubted. Accordingly, to a follower of St. Thomas, the critical question as stated above has no meaning. For to state the fact of knowledge is to affirm the union of intellect with the object understood; *"intellectus in actu EST intellectum in actu."* Error in the very act of understanding is inconceivable, since it is the external reality which begins, specifies, and in a way terminates the process of knowledge, thereby "prolonging" its own intelligibility in the mental "word."

> . . . A power of knowing (*virtus cognoscitiva*) cannot fail in the knowledge of that thing by the likeness of which it is informed; it can fail, however, as regards something consequent upon that form or accidental to it. . . . Now as the sense is directly informed by the likeness of its proper object, so is the intellect informed by a likeness of the quiddity of a thing. Hence, as regards the essence (*quod quid est*) of a thing the intellect is not deceived, just as the

[56] *S. Th.*, I, 85, 6, *c;* cf. *ibid.*, 17, 3, *c.*

senses are not deceived regarding the proper sensibles. In composing, however, or in dividing, the intellect may be deceived. . . .[57]

A complete explanation of knowledge does away with the initial critical problem. A theory of knowledge in which the mental "word" is one with the thing understood, and is fundamentally caused by it, allows no possibility of error in the knowledge of *what* a thing is (*quod quid est*). Hence, for one who accepts the philosophy of knowledge of St. Thomas the so-called problem of idealism is a pseudo-problem. The Thomistic metaphysics of cognition establishes the fact that ***the intellect in act is the thing understood in act.*** Such a metaphysics renders the very existence of the problem of idealism impossible.

Problem of Error: The problem of error, however, still remains and may be stated thus: Under what conditions can the intellect, which obviously can and does attain the real, be false?

The general answer which St. Thomas gives on this point is that:

a) The human intellect cannot be in error *per se* as regards its proper object, the quiddity (essence) of corporeal things. As regards its knowledge of "simple" things (knowledge of substance, of accidents), in whose definition there is no composition, the intellect can *in no way* be deceived. The same also is true for self-evident principles, since they are known as soon as the quiddity of their terms is known. Moreover, those conclusions that are seen to follow necessarily from these principles cannot be perceived falsely.

b) In forming a composition or division and *a fortiori* in the process of reasoning, the intellect *can be in error.*

c) The intellect may be in error *per accidens* regarding the quiddity of a thing whose "definition" involves a composition of incompatible elements, or when the definition is erroneously affirmed of another thing.

Every power, as such, is directed of itself (*per se*) to its proper object; and things of this kind are always uniform. Hence, so long

[57] *S. Th.,* I, 17, 3, *c.*

> as the power exists, its judgment concerning its own proper object does not fail. Now the proper object of the intellect is the quiddity in a thing. Hence, properly speaking, the intellect is not in error concerning this quiddity; whereas it may go astray as regards the accompaniments of the essence or quiddity in the thing, when it orders one thing to another by composing or dividing, or even by reasoning. That is why it is also true that the intellect cannot err in regard to those propositions which are understood as soon as the quiddity of their terms is understood. Such is the case with first principles, from which there also arises infallible truth with the certitude of science with respect to its conclusions.
>
> The intellect, however, may be accidentally deceived in the quiddity of composite things, not by the defect of its organ, for the intellect is a power that is independent of an organ, but on the part of the composition which may take place as regards the definition in this way, that the definition of one thing is erroneous when said of another, as the definition of circle when said of a triangle. . . . Hence, as regards simple things [knowledge of substances, of accidents], in whose definition there is no composition, we cannot be deceived; but if we fail, we fail completely to attain them. . . .[58]

"Since everything is true according as it has the form proper to its nature, the intellect, in so far as it is knowing, must be true according as it has the likeness of the thing known, which is its form as a knowing power."[59] It cannot err, therefore, in the knowledge of a corporeal essence, which is attained in its mental "word." "The quiddity [of corporeal beings] is the proper object of the intellect, so that just as the senses are true in knowing the proper sensibles, so is the intellect true in knowing what a thing is."[60] The reason for this is that ". . . the operation by which the intellect engenders the concept is a *natural* operation; in performing it, therefore, it performs simply what is natural to it, and — the

[58] *S. Th.*, I, 85, 6, *c.*

[59] *Ibid.*, 16, 2, *c.*

[60] *"Quidditas autem rei est proprie objectum intellectus; unde sicut sensus sensibilium propriorum semper est verus, ita et intellectus in cognoscendo quod quid est. . . ."* (*De Ver.*, I, 12.)

process being as described — we may conclude that its result is necessarily infallible. . . . The intellect conceives the essences as infallibly as hearing perceives sound or sight perceives color."[61] ". . . In the absolute consideration of the quiddity of a thing and of those things that are known thereby, the intellect is never deceived."[62]

Question III

OBJECTS OF THE HUMAN INTELLECT

This question is divided into four articles: (1) the proper object of the human intellect; (2) its knowledge of corporeal beings; (3) its knowledge of itself; (4) its knowledge of immaterial beings.

ARTICLE I: Proper Object of the Human Intellect

The nature of an operative potency such as the human intellect is understood through its operations. Actions, however, manifest their nature through their objects. It is, therefore, of importance to ascertain the various types of objects of the intellect in order to rise to a better understanding of its nature.

Material, Formal, and Proper Objects: In general, we may distinguish between the *formal* and the *material* objects of an operative potency.[63] Now the latter as regards the intellect of man is twofold. We speak of: (1) an *adequate* or "extensive" material object, that is, an object which comprises every being which can be known by the human intellect, and beyond which it can attain nothing; and (2) the *proper* or "intensive" material object, which

---

[61] Gilson, *The Philosophy of St. Thomas,* pp. 271–272; cf. *S. Th.,* I, 12.

[62] *S. Th.,* I, 85, 6, *c.*

[63] We should recall that the material object of a faculty of knowledge comprises those beings which can be known through the operation of that faculty. The formal object is the aspect under which the material object is attained by the faculty.

is limited to those beings to which the human intellect is *connaturally proportioned*. By this phrase we mean that the object is similar, not superior, to the knower according to its mode of existing. Such an object can be "received" in the faculty of human knowledge and determine its operation. Consequently, an object of this nature can be known primarily and as it is in itself.

Formal Object of the Human Intellect: The formal object of an operative potency is that by reason of which the material object is related to the potency.[64] St. Thomas demonstrates that on the level of a purely immaterial faculty of knowledge, there can be no other operative potency besides the intellect. While proposing this demonstration, he explains the nature of the formal object of the human intellect.[65] He states that whenever an operative potency according to its specific or proper make-up (*secundum propriam rationem*) is related to a certain object according to a common aspect (*secundum communem rationem*), there can be no other distinct faculty (on the same level) as regards this object. For example, there can be but one sight which is related to its object under the common aspect of color. Now the intellect apprehends every object, every being, in so far as it is being (formal object). This viewpoint (*ratio*) clearly has the widest extension; it is the most common or "extensive" aspect, that is to say, it underlies and comprises every reality. It follows, then, that there can be no other purely immaterial faculty of knowledge besides the intellect. The point of this argument is that the material object of the one human intellect is every being precisely because its formal object is being *as being;* not being under a restricted aspect, as color, which would limit the material object to *the colored*.

It is clear that whatever the intellect apprehends, it views pri-

---

64 ". . . the [formal] object of an [operative] potency . . . is that under the formality of which (*ratio*) all things are related to that power . . . as man and stone are related to sight in that they are colored. Hence, the colored is the proper object of sight." (*S. Th.*, I, 1, 7, *c.*)

65 *Ibid.*, 79, 7, *c.*

marily *as being,* and any other knowledge it may possess is some determination of being. It is by virtue of this all-embracing formal object that the intellect has a limitless material object—all being.[66]

Adequate ("Extensive") Material Object of Human Intellect: By the material object of a faculty of knowledge, we mean those objects which can be attained by that faculty in its act of knowing. Now it is obvious that an operative potency whose formal object is being *as being* can attain any being. There is nothing, therefore, which the intellect cannot attain in some way, either mediately or immediately, directly or indirectly, properly or analogously. At least the intellect can know these objects in so far as they are or can be. The intellect can reach them either in themselves or in their effects, or in their causes, or in their manifestations, or through anything connected with them. For the intellect, therefore, the *adequate* object comprises the whole field of reality, whether possible or actual, abstract or concrete, intentional or real, material or immaterial, finite or infinite, substantial or accidental. In a word, the *adequate material object* of the intellect is every being.

Proper ("Intensive") Material Object of the Human Intellect: The first or proper object of our intellect, that to which the human intellect is primarily directed in this state of life, is not any and every being, but *being as found in material things.* It is from these proper objects that the human intellect arrives at a knowledge of all other things.[67]

What do we mean by the proper object, and why is the proper object of the human intellect limited to bodies? The *proper object* is one that is connaturally proportioned to the knower. By this statement we wish to signify that the mode of existing of the proper object must not exceed in perfection the mode of existing

---

[66] Sometimes the true (*verum*) is called the formal object of the intellect. (Cf. *S. Th.,* I, 87, 3, ad 1m.) This, however, does not mean that the true, and not being as being, is the formal aspect (*ratio*) of the object of the intellect, but rather that the true necessarily implies being as related to intellect.

[67] *S. Th.,* I, 87, 3, ad 1m.

of the knower, for the known object is "received" in the knower according to the conditions of the knower. Man, for example, is not a connatural object of a brute's knowledge. By the proper object, therefore, we mean that object which can be known as it is in itself, directly, and not merely through the knowledge of another, that is, by a knowledge which is partly negative (non-proper).

> . . . Knowledge takes place according as the thing known is in the knower. But the thing known is in the knower according to the mode of the knower. Hence, the knowledge of every knower is according to the mode [of being] of its own nature. If, therefore, the mode of existing of the thing known surpasses the mode of the nature of the knower, it follows that the knowledge of that thing is above the nature of the knower.[68]

Although man's soul is spiritual, it is the substantial form of the body, and it derives its intellectual knowledge from the data obtained through the senses; without this sensory data it can in no wise know. Owing to this peculiar origin of man's intellectual knowledge from sensation, the proper object of the human intellect can be only sensible realities, the world of bodily things.[69] The human intellect is able to cognize only corporeal objects according to their mode of existence, that is to say, as they are in themselves. In brief, bodily beings are the proper material object of the human intellect.[70]

On the other hand, immaterial beings are attained in human knowledge not directly, but indirectly; not according to *their* mode of existing, but through our knowledge of beings which exist in

---

68 *S. Th.*, I, 12, 4, *c.*

69 ". . . the proper object of the human intellect is the quiddity of a material thing which [material thing] is apprehended by the senses. . . ." (*Ibid.*, 85, 5, ad 3^m.)

70 "It is, therefore, connatural for us to know those things which have 'to be' in individual matter, because our soul by which we know is the form of some definite (*alicuius*) matter. . . . To know natures, [however] which do not exist in matter . . . is above the natural capacity of the intellect of the human soul in the state of its present life, in which it [the soul] is united to the body." (*Ibid.*, 12, 4, *c.*)

matter. Our knowledge of immaterial beings is non-proper; it is not connatural knowledge.[71]

Object of Metaphysics: The object of the intellect is closely related to the "object" of metaphysics. The reason is that this science is *"maxime intellectualis,"*[72] the intellectual science par excellence. What, then, is the "object" — St. Thomas calls it the *subject* — of metaphysics?[73]

Metaphysics is a speculative science, an intellectual habit of demonstration. Now a speculative science is concerned with a study of the real viewed according to a definite intelligible aspect, that is, according to a definite mode of consideration. The science of metaphysics is concerned with all beings regarded from the point of view that they are *being*.

1. Problem: The problem now at hand is this: How can the metaphysician rise to a knowledge of all reality under this aspect? To do so, he must discover a unifying principle, a subject which is like a genus (*genus-subjectum*) regarding all beings in so far as they are being. To this subject all the predicates in the conclusions reached will be attributed. This subject St. Thomas calls "common being" (*ens commune*).

Now a speculative science is concerned *directly* with abstracted natures (*rationes universales*) and not with this or that individual

[71] In the remaining articles of this question, we shall discuss the various material objects of the human intellect.

[72] *In Met. Prooemium.*

[73] The position presented here is treated at length in the author's article, "What Is St. Thomas' Approach to Metaphysics?" in *The New Scholasticism* (Jan., 1956), XXX, 1, pp. 64–83. St. Thomas discusses the subject of metaphysics, "common being," in his commentary *In Librum Boethii De Trinitate,* qq. V and VI. This knowledge is a metaphysical notion (*ratio*) and is quite different from the first intellectual knowledge of being (meaning "thing") in a child. According to St. Thomas, the knowledge of *common being* (*ens commune*) is the last conception in the process of resolution which is the way of analysis and reasoning. ". . . according to the way of resolution, the process of reasoning (*rationalis consideratio*) terminates in an intellectual [conception] in as much as the reasoning power from the consideration of many culls one simple truth. . . . Now those things are most universal which are common to all beings. Hence, the last term in the way of resolution is the consideration of being and of those things which belong to being as being." (*In Boeth. De Trin.,* VI, 1, 3, *c.*)

existent. For, although human knowledge must, in the last analysis, depend on a sense experience of the individual material existent, a speculative science — since it seeks necessary, not contingent, truths — must consider natures (*rationes*) in their absolute intelligibility, that is, as abstracted from matter and from motion.

2. Knowledge of "Common Being" (Ens Commune): How does the human intellect rise from sense experience of material existents to an understanding of "common being," the unifying *ratio* of the metaphysician? First of all, by means of a total abstraction, we proceed to a conceptual knowledge of the various material natures (*rationes*) such as man, dog, white object, and the like. By considering (analyzing) the intelligible contents of these natures, we infer that *to exist in matter* belongs to the very intelligibility of these natures. Consequently, these abstract natures (*rationes*) cannot as such fall under the direct study of the metaphysician. For being limited to the world of matter, they cannot embrace immaterial reality. Hence, they cannot help us in obtaining the *ratio* which will unify our knowledge.

We must make a further examination of these natures (*rationes*), no longer viewing them in their essential (specific) determinations, but only as regards their relation (*habitudo*) to existence, that is to say, in so far as these abstracted natures (*rationes*) express various modes of existing. Thus we arrive at a knowledge of the various genera of beings, such as substance, quality, etc. By considering (analyzing) the intelligible content of these natures, of these various modes of existing, we infer that *to exist in matter does not belong* to the very intelligibility of some of these natures (*non est de ratione eorum*), even though these *rationes* were abstracted from material existents. Hence, they can exist without matter.[74]

---

[74] Let us note in passing that the knowledge thus obtained through consideration (analysis) and reasoning is expressed in a negative judgment in which the possibility of existing without matter is expressed. This judgment is called by St.

Now we come to the final step in our search for the subject (*genus-subjectum*) of metaphysics, a subject which will unify our philosophical knowledge of reality whether material or immaterial. We now examine the various modes of existence, the various genera of being (substance, quality, etc.), to discover in them some common principles under which they could be unified. (For there are in every genus certain common principles which extend to all the principles of that genus.) We find that the supreme modes of existing—and consequently, together with them, all (limited) beings—communicate in being precisely because of the relation (*habitudo*) of their essence to a distinct "to be" (*esse*). Each and every existent (known ultimately from experience) has two principles in common: "to be" and essence, that is, act and potency in the existential order.

By a consideration (analysis) of the *rationes* of the various modes of existing, the metaphysician understands that the relation (*habitudo*) of these essences to their respective *esse*—since this *esse* is many and therefore limited—is to an existential act which is not identical with, but distinct from, its potency. From this consideration of "quiddity related to a distinct *esse*" the metaphysician forms a *ratio* (a concept) which is common to the various genera, that is, to the various modes of existing, and consequently common to all limited beings. The content of this notion is "essence related to a distinct 'to be.'" St. Thomas calls this *ratio* "common being" (*ens commune*), for it expresses what is common to any limited being. It is the subject (*genus-subjectum*) of Thomistic metaphysics.

3. Knowledge of God: The realization that "to be" is distinct from the essence (of limited existents) which it actuates enables us

---

Thomas a "separation." It expresses the knowledge that a substance, for example, need not be in matter to exist.

N.B. The judgment of separation, according to St. Thomas, does not state that in limited beings essence is not *esse*—that is taken for granted—for separation is a judgment which looks to existence, which states that one can exist without the other. Certainly, limited essence or existence cannot exist separately. The judgment of separation does not affirm the real distinction. In this instance, it affirms that certain modes of existence do not require matter.

to rise through causality to the first principle of existence who IS Existence (*Ipsum Esse*). Thus we know God, the cause of all limited existents. Since the subject of metaphysics is "common being," which expresses an *esse* distinct from essence, God is not part of the subject of metaphysics. Rather, He is attained and known only as the *principle* of the subject, that is, as first cause of all creatures. We know in this science *that* He is, not *what* He is.[75] In a science whose subject is *ens commune,* we can never study God's whatness; we cannot have a natural theology as part of such a science.

4. "Transcendental Being" (Ens Transcendentale) and Natural Theology: No doubt, a natural theology is not only possible but is also today an extremely necessary science. To establish such a science, however, we shall have to form another subject—"transcendental being" (*ens transcendentale*). This *ratio* will abstract from the determination of the relation (*habitudo*) of essence to "to be." This *ratio,* which embraces God as well as creatures, will be needed as the first of all predicables and as the foundation for all predication in a science in which God is part of the subject. This notion, however, will be attributed to God and creatures *analogously* (by the analogy of proportionality), since the relation to *esse* in God and in creatures is found to be diverse: God is His own "To Be," whereas the creature's essence is distinct from its "to be." By abstracting from the determination of the relation to *esse,* the intellect is able to form the notion (a concept), *transcendental being,* which in no way implies whether essence is distinct or identical with "to be." Accordingly, the content of this *ratio* is: essence with non-determined relation to "to be." "Transcendental being" (*ens transcendentale*) is the subject of a "meta-

[75] For St. Thomas, the science whose subject is God is not a philosophical theology; it is sacred theology, a science founded upon the revealed word. *"Theologia ergo philosophica determinat de separatis secundo modo, sicut scilicet, de principiis subiecti; theologia vero Sacrae Scripturae tractat de separatis primo modo, sicut de subiectis."* (*In Boeth. De Trin.*, V, 4, c.)

physics" which is concerned with Divine Being and creatures. Consequently, the Divine Being is part of the subject of this metaphysics, by means of which we are able to know God, not only through causality but also by analogous predication.

ARTICLE II: Knowledge of Corporeal Beings[76]

1. Knowledge of the Essences of Corporeal Beings: It will not be necessary to give a detailed explanation of how man understands the essences of corporeal objects. That has already been done in a previous question of this same chapter. It should be noted, however, that, in this knowledge, man's intellect attains the corporeal object according to its *absolute* nature, without the individuating conditions of matter. Yet, the real existents which are the objects of our knowledge are not absolute essences; rather, they are individual natures with their own material conditions.

2. Knowledge of Singular Corporeal Beings: Obviously, we *do* know singular material beings by our intellect as well as by sense. Certainly, the intellect forms and uses many judgments which we express in propositions whose subjects represent singular corporeal realities, as, for example, "*Socrates* is a man." Moreover, the practical intellect directs us to actions which are concerned with singular things, and, therefore, it must know singular things; our acts of choice are concerned with particular means which must be intellectually known. What is more, the intellect understands itself. But the intellect is an individual faculty. Hence, it does understand singulars.

On the other hand, against these reasons there remains the fact that both the intelligible species and the mental "word," which are media of intellectual knowledge, represent only absolute (or universal) natures, since they abstract from the conditions of matter and are received in a strictly spiritual operative potency.

---

[76] *S. Th.*, I, questions 84–86.

Consequently, it would seem that the intellect cannot understand the singular.

To solve this problem, we must distinguish between direct and indirect knowledge of singulars. The intellect cognizes its object by means of an intelligible species and in a mental "word" which communicates a nature not as individualized but absolutely. Consequently, the intellect *cannot directly* know the singular. Rather, the intellect

> . . . indirectly, however, and as it were *by a kind of reflection* . . . can know the singular, because . . . even after abstracting the intelligible species, the intellect cannot by means of these (*secundum eas*) understand actually unless it *turn to the phantasms* in which it understands the intelligible species. . . . Therefore, it understands the universal directly through the intelligible species, and indirectly the singular represented by the phantasm. And thus it forms the proposition, "Socrates is a man" [italics added].[77]

Difficulty: Even with this explanation, however, a seemingly formidable difficulty remains. As we pointed out when discussing the process of abstraction, the phantasm of itself cannot act upon the possible intellect, precisely because no proportion can be found between what is strictly immaterial (spiritual) and what still retains the conditions of matter. To answer this difficulty, we must observe that while it is unquestionably true that the corporeal can have no contact with, and make no impression upon, the spiritual, the reverse is not true; the intellect can *contact* the phantasm. That the spirit can move the body, as is manifest in the union of body and soul, is quite understandable.

"Turning" to the Phantasm: How, then, is this *contact* made when the intellect knows the material singular? What precisely is the process by which the intellect gets at the singular? What, in other words, is the true meaning of St. Thomas' expressions, "as it were by a kind of reflection" and "the intellect needs to turn

---

[77] *S. Th.,* I, 86, 1, *c.*

to the phantasm"? Evidently, there is question here of a *prolongation* or *continuation* of the intellectual act, in which the intellect intuitively pushes on, so to speak, to know the intelligible species, which is the principle of the direct cognition it has obtained of the essence of the object.

Now, while it is true that the intelligible species is representative of the object and not of the phantasm, it is also true that this species is the term of an intelligible mutation *caused* by the phantasm. Consequently, in its "reflection" upon the intelligible species, the intellect not only knows it as representing a universal nature, but also understands it to be the term of an intelligible mutation caused by the phantasm, which in turn represents the object according to its *individuating* conditions. It is impossible, therefore, for the intellect to know the intelligible species without knowing its immediate cause—the phantasm.

Now, if a singular and material phantasm can by the action of the agent intellect be elevated so that it can determine the possible intellect to a spiritual operation, most assuredly the intellectual faculty in act can know the phantasm reflexly by cognizing the principle of that operation.

"Prolongation" of the Intellect's Reflective Act: We have seen that an individual corporeal object can prolong and project itself through the external sensation and the imaginative sense and, being elevated by the power of the agent intellect, can continue even into the intellect through the eduction of an immaterial representative species. In similar fashion, the intellect, which is able to know its own act, can by the cognition of this act—which is determined by and proportioned to the material phantasm—reach a certain knowledge of that phantasm. This knowledge, of course, is not had by a likeness or similitude of the phantasm in the intellect, nor by an inference, but solely through a prolongation of the intellect's reflective act, by which it cognizes the phantasm as the origin and medium of direct intellectual knowledge.

We arrive, therefore, at the following important conclusion: In this life, in order to understand reality — which is the existing singular — we must *turn* to the phantasm.[78] By this "turn," or reversion, we do not mean that the intellect tends toward the phantasm by a direct cognition — since the phantasm is not its object of knowledge — but that it does so by a reflection, that is to say, by a prolongation of the act of understanding. Knowing its own act, the intellect comes to the knowledge of the intelligible species which is the principle of the act, and, at the same time, it knows the phantasm from which the agent intellect abstracted the species. *Through this operative contact with the phantasm the intellect perceives the singular.*

3. Knowledge of the Existing Singular Corporeal Being: But even in its reflective act, the intellect has not yet attained a knowledge of the existing individual, the supposit, *as existing;* it has only a faint realization of the individual essence as manifested by the phantasm, but not of the "to be" (*esse*), not of the fact that the individual exists. For that reason, the intellect continues its seeking after the reality which is the existing singular — the existent. It does so by a prolongation (*continuatio*) of its reflective act, reaching beyond the phantasm even to the species of the external sense. Because the species of the external sense is being caused *here and now* by the object, we may say that the object is present in the species by its operation. Hence, through the prolongation of the intellectual reflection, there is effected some sort of operative contact between the intellect and the existing individual. On the basis of this contact, the intellect judges that the individual *is*. Only in this operation, in which the intellect affirms the existential *actuation* of what it knows through the reflective act, does the intellect attain the singular *as existing*.

Conclusion: It will appear that the immediate existential judgment implies several stages in the knowledge process. To begin

---

[78] *S. Th.*, I, 84, 7, *c*.

with, the intellect by its first act of understanding, which results from an intelligible species, knows in the first understood intention only an indeterminate, absolute essence. Then, by a sort of reflection, in which it comes in contact with the individual, the intellect is, as it were, actuated anew — not by a new intelligible species, but by a knowledge of the individual essence seen somehow in the action of the object as it causes the sensible species in the external sense. This contactual knowledge, though very imperfect, is sufficient to direct the intellect to produce a judgment.[79] It is in this judgment that the intellect affirms the existence (*esse*) of the subject which is the individual known in the reflective act; in this judgment, the intellect knows *that* the subject *is*.

ARTICLE III: The Intellect's Knowledge of Itself[80]

The Intellect Does Not Know Itself by Its Essence: The question here is not whether the intellect is distinct from the soul, for that has already been established. The problem is simply this: Does the human intellect understand itself by its own essence,[81] without the medium of a representative species? Does the human intellect have immediate cognition of itself?

To answer this question we must consider that a thing is knowable in so far as it is in act, not in so far as it is in potency. Now the human (possible) intellect is only potentially understanding, and, consequently, it can understand (and be understood) only when it is actuated. But the intellect is naturally put in act by an intelligible species abstracted from the phantasms of sensible material things, which in this life are its proper object. Con-

[79] "*Iudicium . . . humanae mentis fit secundum vim intellectualis luminis.*" (*Ibid.*, II–II, 173, 2, *c.*)

[80] *Ibid.*, I, 87.

[81] The essences of angels are intelligible in act because they are pure forms. The angelic intellect, therefore, although distinct from the angelic essence, is immediately united to, and actuated by, that essence. Hence, an angel does not need a distinct species representing his essence. He understands himself by his own essence without the medium of a representative species.

sequently, it is not connatural to the human intellect to understand itself immediately; rather, an intelligible species is required which causes the intellect to perform the act of understanding. Accordingly, the intellect knows itself, not by its essence (immediately), but in its very act of understanding.

This can occur in two ways: (1) *individually,* when in the very action of understanding something else, a man is aware that he himself understands, and hence, that he must have an intellect as the principle of this operation;[82] (2) *universally,* by a reflection upon the nature of human intellection, by which we come to a knowledge of the nature of the intellect as such. In either case, an intelligible species derived from a sensory phantasm is required in order that the intellect can know itself. Hence, it cannot know itself directly by its very essence.[83]

Habits Known Through Operations: Habits are principles of action, intermediate between operative potency and operation. They are, therefore, only partially in act. Now nothing is known except that which is in act. Therefore, in so far as a habit falls short of being in act, it falls short of being knowable. It is only by inquiring into the intensity, facility, and pleasureableness of the operation which is the act of the habit that we are enabled to know the nature and character of the habit.[84]

The Intellect Knows Its Own Action: "The first thing of (*de*) the intellect that is understood is its own act of understanding."[85] This truth rests on the principle that a thing is actually known according as it is immaterial and in act. Now the perfection or act of the intellect (an immaterial potency) consists in its own operation. For this operation does not tend to a distinct patient which is perfected by the action of the agent, as building is the

---

[82] Man knows that he has an intellectual *soul* through a knowledge of his intellectual operations.

[83] *S. Th.,* I, 87, 1, *c.*

[84] *Ibid.,* 2, *c.*

[85] *Ibid.,* 3, *c.*

perfection of the thing built; rather, this action, being immanent, remains in the agent as its perfection and act.[86] Accordingly, the first thing *of the intellect* that is understood is its own act of understanding. We know that we know.

> . . . The human intellect . . . is not its own act of understanding, nor is its own essence the first object of its act of understanding, for this object is the nature of a material thing. And therefore that which is first known by the human intellect is an object of this kind, and that which is known secondarily is the act by which that object is known; and through the act the intellect itself is known, whose perfection is the act itself of understanding.[87]

The Intellect Understands the Act of the Will: "It would seem that the intellect does not understand the act of the will. For nothing is known by the intellect unless it be in some way present in the intellect. But the act of the will is not in the intellect, since the will and the intellect are distinct powers. Therefore, the act of the will is not known by the intellect."[88] St. Thomas proposes this difficulty in order to clarify the question as to whether the intellect understands the act of the will. His answer reaffirms the existential unity of the human supposit: intellect and will,

---

[86] This argument is concerned with the intellect as such. It must, therefore, be rightly applied to the different types of intellect: divine, angelic, and human. "For there is an intellect, namely, the divine, which is its own act of intellection. And so, in God, the understanding of His understanding and the understanding of His essence are one and the same act, because His essence is His act of understanding.

"But there is another intellect, namely, the angelic, which, as was previously stated, is not its own act of intellection, and yet the first object of this act is the angelic essence. Wherefore, although in an angel there is a logical distinction between his act of understanding and his understanding his essence, nevertheless, it is by one and the same act that he understands both." (*Loc. cit.*)

[87] *Loc. cit.* A much quoted parallel text is found in *De Veritate,* X, 9: "The power of any potency of the soul is determined to its object; hence, its action primarily and principally tends to that object. But it cannot do this with regard to those means by which it tends to the object except by a kind of reversion. . . . Hence, the action of our intellect first tends to the object which is apprehended by the phantasm, and then reflects upon that act in order to cognize it; and then, beyond that, reflects upon the species, the potencies, and the essence of the intellect itself." See also an excellent study of this article of the *De Veritate* by Father Charles Boyer, S.J., *"Le sens d'un texte de St. Thomas"* (*Gregorianum,* 1923).

[88] *S. Th.,* I, 87, 4, objection 1.

although distinct as potencies, are not distinct subjects. ". . . Since both are rooted in the same substance of the soul, and since one is in a way the principle of the other,[89] what is in the will is, consequently, in a way also in the intellect."[90] "Therefore, the act of the will is understood by the intellect, both inasmuch as one perceives that one wills, and inasmuch as one knows the nature of this act, and consequently the nature of the principle which is the habit or operative potency."[91]

ARTICLE IV: Knowledge of Immaterial Substances[92]

No Direct Knowledge of Immaterial Substances: ". . . Our intellect in the present state of life has a natural relation to the natures of material things; and, therefore, it can understand only by turning to the phantasms. . . . And thus it is manifest that immaterial substances, which do not fall under sense and imagination, cannot be known by us first and essentially (*primo et per se*) according to the mode of knowledge of which we have experience."[93] It should be plain from the explanation of human intellectual knowledge already presented that our possible intellect, in the present state of life, can be informed naturally only by likenesses abstracted from a phantasm; and, therefore, it directly knows only material things, since no phantasm can represent an immaterial object.

Moreover, it is impossible for our intellect to arrive at a perfect knowledge of immaterial substances by a series of abstractions from the phantasm. The reason is that ". . . immaterial substances differ altogether from the quiddity of material things, so that however much our intellect may abstract the quiddity of a material thing

---

[89] In the treatise on the will, we shall see that the intellect specifies the act of the will, and that at times the will moves the intellect to exercise its functions.

[90] *S. Th.,* I, 87, 4, ad 1^m.

[91] *Ibid.,* 87, 4, *c.*

[92] *Ibid.,* 88.

[93] *Ibid.,* 88, 1, *c.*

from matter, it could never arrive at anything like an immaterial substance. Therefore, we are unable to understand immaterial substances perfectly through material substances."[94]

Indirect Knowledge of Immaterial Substances: Nevertheless, ". . . from material things we can rise to some sort of knowledge of immaterial things, but not to a perfect knowledge; for there is no proper and adequate proportion between material and immaterial things; and the likenesses drawn from material things for the understanding of immaterial things are greatly at variance from them."[95] Under the circumstances, then, the best the human intellect can do is to understand these immaterial substances indirectly or by non-proper intellectual conceptions. These, it is true, are obtained by means of likenesses drawn from material things, but by way of *negation of their materiality,* so that we know "what these [immaterial] things are not rather than what they are."[96]

Yet, this knowledge is not purely negative. For, although these immaterial, limited substances are not in the same *natural* genus as material substances—since their forms have no relation to matter—yet they belong to the same *logical* genus, since they are in the predicament of substance (that to which is due a "to be" not in another). Because of this community of immaterial substances with material things, we can through the likeness derived from material things know something *positive* concerning immaterial things, "according to some common notion (*ratio*), though not according to their specific nature."[97]

Knowledge of God: "Since the human intellect in the present state of life cannot understand [perfectly, that is, by proper knowledge] immaterial created substances, much less can it understand [perfectly] the essence of the uncreated substance. Hence, it must

---

94 *Ibid.,* 88, 2, *c.*
95 *Ibid.,* 88, 2, ad 1^{m}.
96 *In IV Sent.,* dist. 49, 2, 7, ad 12^{m}.
97 *S. Th.,* I, 88, 2, ad 4^{m}.

be said absolutely that God is not the first object [proper object] of our knowledge. Rather, we know God through creatures [His effects]. . . ."[98] Unlike limited immaterial beings, however, "God has no community with (*non convenit cum*) material things, either in a natural genus or in a logical genus; because God is not in a genus at all. . . ."[99] Hence, God cannot be known positively by such knowledge. He does, however, have a community with creatures, not in the order of essence, but in the order of existence. He *is* Existence; creatures *participate* in existence according to the capacity of their essences. From a knowledge of creatures as existents we can rise to some *affirmative*[1] knowledge of God; but we must deny that in God essence is a limitation of existence; He *is* Existence.

Question IV

SPECIAL FUNCTIONS OF THE HUMAN INTELLECT

This question is divided into three articles in which we shall examine: (1) intellectual memory; (2) reasoning; (3) some other intellectual functions.

ARTICLE I: Intellectual Memory[2]

Intellectual memory can be defined as the faculty which retains intelligible species, so that by recalling them we may understand the same objects anew. It is the nature of the memory to preserve the species of those things which have been apprehended but which are not actually apprehended here and now. Experience teaches us that we possess such a faculty, for we are able to recall our former intellectual knowledge. Nevertheless, Avicenna, the great Arab philosopher and interpreter of Aristotle, argued that

[98] *S. Th.*, I, 88, 3, *c.*
[99] *Ibid.*, 2, ad 4^{m}.
[1] The problem of how we can have some *positive* knowledge of God will be treated at length in the *Philosophy of God.*
[2] *Ibid.*, 79, 6 and 7.

only sense memory is possible. A representative species, he held, can be preserved only in a corporeal organ. If it were retained in a faculty, the species would always be actuating the faculty, and, consequently, we would always actually know the same object. But the intellectual species are not in a corporeal organ. From this he concluded that the intelligible species cannot be retained.

Man Possesses Intellectual Memory: This opinion, however, is clearly erroneous. In the first place, there is no reason why a spiritual form (the intelligible species) which is received in a spiritual subject (the possible intellect) should corrupt. It must, therefore, continue to exist. Moreover, from the fact of sense memory, an *a fortiori* argument can be offered for intellectual memory.

> . . . The intellect is of a more stable nature, and is more immovable, than corporeal matter. If, therefore, corporeal matter holds the forms which it receives, not only while it actually does something through them, but also after ceasing to act through them, much more does the intellect receive the species unchangeably and enduringly. . . .[3]

As to the difficulty proposed by Avicenna, that the intellect would be reduced to act by the presence of the retained intelligible species, St. Thomas points out that the retained species holds the middle state between act and potency. It is a habit; and, like all habits, it should be considered as an *imperfect act,* which does not fully actuate the faculty, but merely facilitates such an actuation.

> The intelligible species is sometimes in the intellect only potentially, and then the intellect is said to be in potency. Sometimes the intelligible species is in the intellect according to the ultimate completion of the act, and then the intellect understands in act. And sometimes the intelligible species is in a *middle state* [italics added], between potency and act; and then we have habitual knowledge. In this last way, the intellect retains the species, even when it does not understand in act.[4]

[3] *Ibid.,* 79, 6, *c.* [4] *Ibid.,* ad 3^{m}.

Intellectual Memory Is Not Distinct From the Possible Intellect: We have seen that operations whose formal objects are specifically distinct cannot be reduced to one and the same operative potency, but require as immediate principles distinct faculties. Thus, for example, distinct operative potencies are required on the sensory level for the operations of seeing and hearing. No such diversification is necessary for the operations of seeing objects of different colors, for example, the green grass and the red flag, since green and red fall as individual differences under the common formal object of the visual sense, which is the object *as colored*. "Now the intellect is related to its object under the *common nature* [formal object] *of being,* since the possible intellect is that by which we become all things. Therefore, the possible intellect is not differentiated by any difference of being,"[5] including present and past. These differences are only accidental to the object of the intellect, and, consequently, the intellectual memory is not a power distinct from the possible intellect.

Furthermore, we must conclude that the possible intellect is the *sole* cognoscitive faculty in the intellectual order, precisely because it is related to its object under the common aspect of being. Any differences in being are accidental to its formal object and hence do not diversify the operative potency from which the various operations of knowing being proceed.

Although the possible intellect is the sole intellectual *cognoscitive* faculty, it is not the only intellectual *power* in man, for it is really distinct from the agent intellect. The reason is that ". . . as regards the same object, the active power [the agent intellect] which makes the object to be in act [as regards intelligibility] must be distinct from the passive power [possible intellect], which is moved by the object existing in act."[6]

Knowledge of the Past as Past: The intellectual memory, since

---

[5] *S. Th.,* I, 79, 7, *c.*
[6] *Loc. cit.*

it conserves species which have been abstracted from individual conditions, retains these without knowledge of time. The reason is that time is attributed to individual, not to universal natures, and consequently demands at least the conditions of matter. Man, however, knows the past as past in two ways:

a) As regards the *object* known, by means of sense memory which retains the conditions of matter, ". . . an animal remembers that he sensed before in the past, and that he sensed some past sensible thing."[7] For that reason, just as the intellect knows the singular by a return to the phantasm, so it may turn to the sense memory and know the past as past.

b) As regards the *act itself,* the intellect knows its acts in their succession, since these acts are individual. In this manner also it knows the past as past.

Use of Phantasm in Intellectual Memory: In recalling the intelligible species, which are retained in the possible intellect (intellectual memory) as habits, it is necessary for the intellect to "turn" to the phantasm. ". . . There is need for the act of the imagination and of the other powers in order that the intellect may understand actually, not only when it acquires new knowledge, but also when it uses knowledge already acquired."[8] This is evident from the fact that ". . . when the imagination is hindered by a lesion of the corporeal organ . . . we see that a man is hindered from understanding actually even those things of which he had a previous knowledge."[9]

The reason for this is that the operative potency must be proportioned to its proper object. Now the proper object of the human intellect is the nature (essence) of corporeal things. The corporeal individual, however, is apprehended by sense. Accordingly, sense as well as intellect must enter into the knowledge of man, whether the object be present or absent. In the latter case, since the object is not

[7] *S. Th.,* I, 79, 6, ad 2m.
[8] *Ibid.,* 84, 7, *c.*
[9] *Loc. cit.*

causing sense knowledge by its action, the intellect must "turn" to the phantasm of the imaginative sense, in which the object is *re*-presented. "If, however, the proper object of our intellect were a separate form, or if, as the Platonists say, the natures of sensible things subsisted apart from the individual, there would be no need for the intellect to turn to the phantasms whenever it understands."[10]

ARTICLE II: Reasoning[11]

Besides the knowledge of essences, the affirming of existence, and the preservation of that knowledge, we find in man another intellectual function, which is specifically human — the function of reasoning. "To understand is to apprehend intelligible truth absolutely. . . . To reason is to advance from one thing understood to another, so as to know intelligible truth."[12] To attain truth by reasoning is peculiar to man. A being whose nature is a pure form apprehends truth *absolutely;* for such a being, there is no need, therefore, to advance from one thing understood to another. The same, of course, is eminently true of God; since He is Pure Act, His intellect does not pass from potency to act as does the human intellect in the process of reasoning. It is because of the imperfection of man's intellect that he arrives *discursively* at the knowledge of intelligible truth by passing from the known to the unknown implicitly contained in the known — by reasoning.[13]

Analysis of Reasoning: "Reasoning . . . is compared to understanding as movement is to rest. . . ."[14] Now all movement proceeds from something immovable and ends in something at rest. The movement which we call reasoning is no exception.

---

[10] *S. Th.*, I, 84, 7, *c.*
[11] *Ibid.*, 79, 8.
[12] *Loc. cit.*
[13] Hence man is called the *rational* animal.
[14] *Loc. cit.*

a) In the *order of discovery* (*via inventionis*), reasoning proceeds from the first principles, which are absolutely immovable because self-evident, to conclusions which serve as principles for deriving further conclusions.

b) In the *order of judgment* (*via iudicii*), reasoning returns by analysis from conclusions to the first principles, in the light of which it examines what it has found, thereby achieving unity and certainty in knowledge.

Reason Is Not a Faculty Distinct From the Possible Intellect: Specifically distinct operations demand distinct faculties. But *rest* in the truth (understanding) and *movement* toward the truth (reasoning) are not specifically distinct operations, for both attain being. Moreover, even natural things are moved toward a certain place and rest in it because of the very same nature. Much more, therefore, does man understand and reason by the same power. It is clear, then, that in man intellect and reason are the same operative potency and that they are identified with the possible intellect.

ARTICLE III: Other Intellectual Functions

Conscience,[15] in spite of what is generally and erroneously believed, is neither a distinct faculty, nor a habit, but an action — a judgment. This is easily shown. Conscience implies the relation of a universal truth, that is, of a general principle of moral law, to some individual case. Now such an application requires an operation of intellect. Consequently, conscience is not a faculty distinct from the possible intellect. It is an action of the intellect, a judgment by which we apply a universal moral principle to a particular action that is being done, has been done in the past, or will be done in the future. Sometimes, however, the term *conscience* is used in a wider sense and is applied to the habit of

[15] *S. Th.*, I, 79, 13, *c*.

first moral principles—*synderesis.*[16] Discussion of this question, however, belongs to moral philosophy.

Speculative and Practical Intellect: The terms, *speculative* and *practical,* are applied to the intellect, not to denote two distinct cognoscitive intellects in man, but rather two functions of one and the same intellect. The *speculative* intellect " . . . directs what it apprehends not to operation but solely to the consideration of truth; while the practical intellect . . . directs what it apprehends to operation."[17] This distinction, however, is only accidental to the object of the intellect, namely, being. Now what is accidental to the nature of a formal object does not cause a diversity of operative potencies. Therefore, the speculative and practical intellects are not two distinct faculties; rather, they are two functions of the same faculty.

SUMMARY

Question I

NATURE OF THE HUMAN INTELLECT

Article I: *The Human Intellect Is Primarily a Passive Potency*

1. The human intellect is an *operative potency* of the soul; it is not the essence of the soul, "for then alone is the essence of that which operates the immediate principle of operation when operation itself is its 'to be' [existence]."

2. The human intellect is a *passive potency;* it has no innate knowledge. Its knowledge is acquired knowledge, derived from sense. At the beginning of its existence, the human intellect is like "a clean tablet (*tabula rasa*) on which nothing is written" (*possible* intellect).

3. The intellect is *spiritual.*

Article II: *Need of the Agent Intellect to Actuate the Possible Intellect*

1. *Problem:* How can material objects, or their sensory phantasms (which are partly material), move a spiritual operative potency, the intellect, from potency to act so that it can elicit the immanent operation of intellection?

2. *Positions:*

a) Innate ideas: the intellect somehow is already in act.

[16] *S. Th.,* I, 79, 12, *c.*

[17] *Ibid.,* 11, *c.*

b) Materialism: the material objects act upon a material intellect.

c) *Agent intellect:* a strictly immaterial power of the soul, always in act, through the instrumentality of the sensory phantasm actuates the possible intellect by producing in it an intelligible species of the object.

Article III: *The Process of Abstraction*

1. In the *formation of the intelligible species,* the agent intellect (a strictly immaterial power) is the principal cause; the phantasm (a likeness of the object) is the instrumental cause; the patient is the possible intellect; the effect is the eduction of the intelligible species.

2. The *intelligible species,* because it is educed from ("received in") a strictly immaterial faculty, is itself strictly immaterial; hence, it is intelligible in act. It is a form of the object without matter *and without* (abstracted from) the individuating conditions of matter; hence, it is a *universal* representation of the object.

3. The intelligible species is: (*a*) a strictly immaterial (*b*) representation of the object owing to the *joint causality of agent intellect and phantasm.* The agent intellect as *principal* cause contributes strict immateriality; the phantasm as *instrumental* cause contributes representativeness to the effect.

Question II

THE ACT (OPERATION) OF THE INTELLECT

Article I: *Need of the Mental "Word" (Verbum)*

1. The act of intellection (understanding) is an *immanent* operation. The eduction of the intelligible species merely places the possible intellect in act; it is not the act of understanding.

2. In the immanent action of understanding, the intellect *must form an intentional term,* which is the intellectual expression of the thing understood — an internal *"word,"* which is expressed by the external word. This term is needed because:

a) The intellect understands indifferently a thing absent or present;

b) The intellect understands things (corporeal beings) as separate from the material conditions without which they do not exist in reality.

3. There are *four distinct factors* in human intellectual knowledge: (*a*) the possible intellect — an operative potency; (*b*) the intelligible species — its actuation; (*c*) the operation of understanding — the act of a being in act; (*d*) the mental "word" — the term of this operation.

Article II: *Two Types of Mental "Word"*

1. *Definition:* in which the object is apprehended according to its essence.

2. *Composition* (or *division*): in which also the properties and accidents of the essence are understood.

Article III: *In the Forming of the Mental "Word" the Object Is Known First*

1. That which is understood *primarily is the object* of which the intelligible species is the likeness. The act of understanding, the intelligible species, the mental "word," and the intellect are known only by reflection and analysis.

2. The mental "word" is the *intelligible prolongation* of the object. It is the term of the action of an operative potency informed by a likeness (intelligible species) of the thing understood. Thus the intellect in act IS the thing understood in act.

Article IV: *The Truth of the Mental "Word"*

1. *Pseudo-Problem of Idealism:* How can the intellect prove that its knowledge is truly knowledge of the real? *Reply:* No "proof" is possible by using knowledge whose validity is already doubted. The realist explanation of knowledge — the intellect in act IS the thing understood in act — does away with this problem.

2. *Problem of Error:* Under what conditions can the intellect (which obviously does attain the real) be false?

a) Error *cannot* be had *per se* regarding the *proper* object of the human intellect (the essence of corporeal things), regarding immediately evident principles, and the conclusions that are seen to follow necessarily from them.

b) Error *can* be had *per se* in composition (or division) and *per accidens* as regards the knowledge of essences in as much as some composition or division accompanies this knowledge.

Question III

OBJECTS OF THE HUMAN INTELLECT

Article I: *Proper Object of the Human Intellect*

1. *Formal* object: being *as being*

2. *Material* object:

a) *Adequate* (extensive): all being — actual or possible, concrete or abstract, real or intentional, material or immaterial, substantial or accidental, limited or unlimited; in brief, any intelligible.

b) *Proper* (intensive): those beings to which the human intellect is connaturally proportioned — sensible (corporeal) being, for human intellectual knowledge is derived from sensory data.

Article II: *Knowledge of Corporeal Beings*

1. *Essences* of corporeal beings are known *directly* according to their absolute nature (without the individuating conditions of matter), e.g., man.

2. *Singular* corporeal beings are known indirectly by *"turning"* to the phantasm which represents the object according to its individual conditions, e.g., Socrates.

3. *Existing singular* corporeal beings are known by *prolongation* of the intellect's reflective act to the external sense species, which is being caused here and now by the action of the object, e.g., Socrates exists.

Article III: *The Intellect's Knowledge of Itself*

1. The human intellect knows *itself* in the very *act of understanding* something else. Since an intelligible species is needed to actuate the intellect, it does not know itself directly by its essence.

2. Intellectual *habits* (imperfect acts) are known through their operations.

3. The *first* thing *of the intellect* that is understood is its own act of understanding; through this act the intellect itself is known, whose perfection is the act (operation) of understanding.

Article IV: *Knowledge of Immaterial Substances*

1. The human intellect has *no direct* (*proper*) *knowledge* of immaterial substances, because its knowledge is naturally derived from phantasms, which cannot adequately represent immaterial substances.

2. Rather, the human intellect's knowledge of immaterial substances is *indirect* (*non-proper*) by means of likenesses drawn from material things, but by way of negation of their materiality.

3. Man's natural knowledge of God (the First Cause) is *through creatures,* which are effects, by way of causality, negation, and supereminence.

Question IV

SPECIAL FUNCTIONS OF THE HUMAN INTELLECT

Article I: *Intellectual Memory*

1. The intelligible species are retained *as habits* (imperfect acts) in the possible intellect.

2. Intellectual memory is *not* a power *distinct from* the possible intellect, which is related to its object under the common aspect of being (formal object) whether present or past.

3. In recalling the intelligible species, the intellect must *"turn" to the phantasm* of the imaginative sense, in which the object is *re*-presented.

Article II: *Reasoning*

1. To reason is to *advance* from one thing understood to another, from the known to the unknown implicitly contained in the known. Reasoning is compared to understanding as movement to rest.

2. *a*) In the order of *discovery,* reasoning proceeds from first principles, which are absolutely (immovably) understood, to conclusions. *b*) In the order of *judgment,* reasoning returns by analysis to first principles in the light of which it examines what it has found.

3. Reason is not a power distinct from the possible intellect, for rest in the truth (understanding) and movement toward the truth (reasoning) are not specifically distinct operations.

Article III: *Other Intellectual Functions*

1. *Conscience* is a judgment by which a universal moral principle is applied to a particular human act.

2. The *speculative* intellect contemplates truth (as an end); the *practical* intellect directs its knowledge (as a means) to action. They are two functions of the same faculty.

CHAPTER VII

THE SENSE APPETITES

PROLOGUE

All limited things seek that which is good; that is to say, in their actions they act to attain their end, to which they are in potency. Now the end, which is desired and sought, is desirable precisely because it is the good, the perfection of their nature. The inclination to the end, to the good, we call *appetite*.

These fundamental principles of finality were studied in *The Philosophy of Being*.[1] There it was established that the natural tendency (the natural appetite) of every limited being is to seek and, if possible, to attain its end. We know, therefore, that there is in man a constant and necessary inclination to a definite end. Just as the plant tends to grow and to produce its fruit, so man has a natural inclination to attain his last end. In the present chapter, however, we are not concerned with this primary tendency of human nature. Rather, we intend to show that, in common with the brute animals, man experiences successive inclinations toward and away from certain objects of sensory knowledge. In a subsequent chapter we shall demonstrate that man, because his intellectual soul is capable of knowing the true, is gifted with a higher appetite than that of the brute animals—the will. Moreover, this

[1] Cf. *The Philosophy of Being*, p. 144 *et seq.*

intellectual appetite, although ordered to the most sublime end, perfect happiness, is free, nevertheless, to choose the particular means to attain that end. In man, therefore, the sense appetites are related to the reason and the will, and should be subordinated to these higher powers.

Division: Our treatise on the sense appetites in man will be divided into two parts. In the first question, we shall consider the various types of appetites and show that there are two distinct appetitive potencies on the sensory level in man. In the second question, we shall discuss the passions (the operations of the sense appetites) and their relation to the reason and the will.

Question I

THE SENSORY APPETITIVE POTENCIES

This question is divided into two articles in which we shall consider: (1) the natural, sensory, and intellectual appetites; (2) the two distinct sensory appetites, the concupiscible and the irascible.

ARTICLE I: Natural, Sensory, and Intellectual Appetites[2]

While all creatures desire and seek the good, the manner of this desire for and search after the good differs vastly in the various kinds of beings. The reason is that different beings are ordered to distinct ends. Man, however, owing to the complexity of his nature, needs a wide range of tendencies and desires conducive to actions which will perfect his nature and bring it to its ultimate end, perfect happiness. We properly divide all the various types of appetites we find in man under three headings: natural, sensitive, and intellectual.

Natural Appetite: There are many beings which have no knowl-

---

[2] Cf. *De Ver.*, XXII, 1; *S. Th.*, I, 80, 1.

edge, and yet they tend to their appointed end by a natural inclination, which results from their substantial form; for ". . . some inclination follows every form."[3] These non-knowing natures need no distinct appetitive faculty to fulfill their natural inclination, a tendency to the end which is imprinted by the Author of nature, God, and which remains constant and uniform. We might say, moreover, that the definite inclination which every form — because it is the determining part of the nature — has for a definite end, is the law of the nature. All limited beings, whether material or immaterial, are subject to this law of their nature. Because their natures are specified by a definite form, there follows a natural inclination to an end proportioned to the form and to be achieved by action. A stone, for example, naturally falls to the ground and remains there; a tree naturally tends to grow and to produce fruit; an animal naturally is inclined to sense; man naturally strives to know the true and to love the good.

Sense Appetite: Besides the natural appetite, which results immediately from the substantial form, and which is the inclination of the being to its appointed end, we find that animals successively acquire new determinants which move their appetite.[4] These new determinants are the sensible forms acquired through sensory cognition. Knowledge of a sensible good results in a desire for that good. Now the sensory desire, which follows the knowledge of the sensible good, is from the animal itself (as knowing this or that particular good). The natural appetite, on the contrary, since it is a resultant from the substantial form, is from an extrinsic cause; it is a necessary determination to a particular course of action, "a kind of impression from God,"[5] directing the being to

---

[3] *S. Th.,* I, 80, 1, *c.* This statement, "an inclination follows upon every form," signifies that there is no form without its accompanying appetite. This is really a restatement of the principle of finality. A form is a nature (or the actual principle of the nature), and like all natures it is a principle of action toward an end. In order to act toward an end, it must be inclined toward it; it must possess an appetite.

[4] "*. . . in eis invenitur appetitus et movens appetitum.*" (*De Ver.,* XXII, 3.)

[5] Cf. *S. Th.,* I, 103, 1, *c.*

its end. Consequently, the natural appetite is constant and uniform. The sense appetite, on the other hand, is ever changing and never quite the same, because it is determined successively by new sense knowledge. Now, that which is ever changing must be really distinct from that which is ever constant. Consequently, the sense appetites must be distinct from the natural appetite. Moreover, if the substantial form were the immediate cause of the sensory appetitive operations, there would be no need of acquiring sense knowledge.

> . . . It is necessary to assign an appetitive potency to the soul. To make this evident, we must observe that some inclination follows every form; for example, fire by its form is inclined to rise and to generate its like. Now the form is found to have a more perfect existence in those things which participate in knowledge than in those things which lack knowledge. For in those which lack knowledge, the form is found to determine each thing only to one proper "to be" which is natural to each. Now this natural form is followed by a natural inclination which is called the natural appetite. But in those things which have knowledge, each one is determined to its proper "to be" by its natural form, but in such a manner that it is nevertheless receptive of the species of other things. . . .
>
> Therefore, just as in those things that have knowledge, forms exist in a higher manner and above the manner of natural forms, so there must be in them an inclination surpassing the natural inclination which is called the natural appetite. And this superior inclination belongs to the appetitive power of the soul, through which the animal is able to desire what it apprehends, and not only that to which it is inclined by its natural form. And so it is necessary to assign an appetitive [operative] potency to the soul.[6]

Intellectual Appetite: Besides sensory inclination to the good sensibly perceived, man has a higher inclination to the good consequent upon intellectual knowledge. This intellectual (rational) inclination to the good is the human will. That the will is distinct from the sense appetites is evident from the distinction between

[6] *S. Th.*, I, 80, 1, *c.*

the movers of these two appetites, which of themselves are passive operative potencies; for that which moves the appetites is the *apprehended* appetible. Now, since that which is apprehended by the intellect and what is apprehended by the senses are generically different, it follows that the will, the rational appetite, is distinct from the sensitive,[7] for the appetites must be proportioned to their (formal) motive principle.

ARTICLE II: The Concupiscible and Irascible Sense Appetites

We have shown that the sense appetite is really distinct from the natural appetite. The latter is unconscious and constant, while the former, since it follows successive new knowledge, is ever changing. The sense appetite, therefore, must be a distinct operative potency.

By comparing the dual tendency of the natural appetite with the inclinations of the sensible appetite, we shall discover the need of two distinct faculties of sensory appetition; for the sense appetite has some traits in common with the natural.

The natural appetite has a twofold tendency, a twofold activity. Owing to this appetite, every natural corruptible thing is inclined ". . . not only to the acquisition of what is suitable and to the avoiding of what is harmful, but also to resistance against corruptive and contrary forces which are a hindrance to the acquisition of what is suitable, and are productive of harm."[8] By its natural appetite, therefore, the corporeal being seeks two immediate ends — first, to receive what is profitable and favorable; second, to act, that is, to conquer all obstacles to the primary end.[9]

Two Distinct Formal Objects: In like manner, through its

---

[7] *Ibid.*, 2, *c.*
[8] *Ibid.*, 81, 2, *c.*
[9] In the sentient nature, to *receive* and to *act* must be reduced to diverse principles.

sense appetite an animal tends to two distinct types of appetible objects: sensible goods that are *easily* attained and those that are attained *with difficulty,* that is, only after some obstacles have been overcome. Since distinct formal objects diversify operative potencies, there must be two distinct sense appetites—the *concupiscible* and the *irascible.* Through the first, namely the concupiscible, ". . . the soul is inclined absolutely to seek what is suitable, according to the senses, and to fly from what is hurtful"; through the other, the irascible appetite, ". . . an animal resists the attacks that hinder what is suitable, and which inflict harm. . . ."[10] Hence, the proper object of the concupiscible is the pleasurable-sensible, while that of the irascible is the arduous-sensible. The operations of these appetites, since they are specifically distinct, cannot be reduced to one and the same operative potency.

Operations of One Diminish the Intensity of Operations of the Other: Another proof of the distinction between the two appetitive sense faculties may be found in the frequently experienced fact that the operations[11] of one diminish the intensity of the operations of the other.

> For sometimes the soul busies itself with unpleasant things, against the inclination of the concupiscible appetite, in order that, following the impulse of the irascible appetite, it may fight against obstacles. And so even the passions of the irascible appetite counteract the passions of the concupiscible appetite; since concupiscence, on being roused, diminishes anger, and anger, being roused, very often diminishes concupiscence.[12]

Finally, the concupiscible power is made to *receive,* that is, to acquire what is suitable to the animal nature, while the irascible is made to *react,* often violently, against obstacles. This fact is a sufficient reason for their distinction, for with regard to the

---

[10] *S. Th.,* I, 81, 2, *c.*
[11] We call these operations passions or emotions.
[12] *S. Th.,* I, 81, 2, *c.*

operative potencies of the soul, it is generally true that to receive and to act cannot be reduced to one and the same faculty. We have an excellent example of this fact in the distinction between the agent and possible intellects.[13]

Question II

OPERATIONS OF THE SENSE APPETITES

This question is divided into four articles: (1) the nature of the passions; (2) classification of the passions; (3) relations between passions and reason; (4) control of the passions.

ARTICLE I: Nature of the Passions

Various Meanings of the Term "Passion": The word *passion* in the writings of Aquinas has primarily a metaphysical meaning.[14] It often signifies a receiving, that is, a change; it indicates, therefore, that the subject is somewhat passive. Sometimes, however, together with the acquiring of form the term "passion" implies the loss of a form. Finally, at times it involves a change for the worse.

In this article, however, we are considering the passions, or emotions,[15] which are *the operations or acts of the sense appetites,* and we shall endeavor to discover what they are in themselves. Are they immaterial forms similar to sense species? Are they merely certain bodily changes which on occasion take place in the organism as consequents of external stimuli?

---

[13] "Generally we find that with regard to the potencies of the soul, to receive and to act pertain to diverse powers as is evident concerning the agent and possible intellect." (*De Ver.*, XXV, 2.)

[14] Cf. *ibid.*, XXVI, 1.

[15] In modern terminology, the word *passion* is usually reserved for signifying violent emotions, while mild emotions are referred to as "feelings." Essentially, however, passion, emotion, and feeling are the same, namely, the operations of the sense appetites.

Not an Act of Knowledge: At the outset, passion must be clearly distinguished from the sense knowledge from which its flows. ". . . The apprehensive potency is not drawn to a thing *as it is in itself,* but knows it by reason of an intention [the species] of the thing, which intention it has in itself, or *receives* in its own way [italics added]."[16] The appetitive potency, on the other hand, is drawn to a thing as it is *in itself*. This leaning or inclination toward a thing as it is in itself cannot be an act of knowledge, which is likened to rest. Rather, passion (emotion) signifies a movement toward an object or away from it.

> . . . The operation of the apprehensive potency is completed in the very fact that the thing apprehended is in the one that apprehends, while the operation of the appetitive power is completed in the fact that he who desires is borne toward the desirable thing. Hence, it is that the operation of the apprehensive power is likened to *rest;* whereas the operation of the appetitive potency is rather likened to movement [italics added].[17]

Not a Mere Bodily Change: A passion is not a purely physiological or organic phenomenon, as, for example, the secretion of an endocrine gland. It is true that some corporeal change is of the essence of a passion; it is the material element,[18] and may be the same for distinct passions. But formally a passion is psychic; that is to say, the motion which takes place in the sense appetite is formally immaterial.[19] The passion and the eduction of a sen-

Formal element - movement of appetitive power
Material element - bodily transmutation

---

[16] *S. Th.,* I–II, 22, 2, *c.*

[17] *Ibid.,* I, 81, 1, *c.*

[18] "It must be noted that in all the passions of the soul, the bodily transmutation, which is their material element, is in conformity with and in proportion to the appetitive movement which is the formal element. . . ." (*Ibid.,* I–II, 37, 4, *c.*) "In the passions of the soul, the formal element is the movement of the appetitive power, while the bodily transmutation is the material element. Both of these are mutually proportionate." (*Ibid.,* 44, 1, *c.*)

[19] Because a passion is a movement, the immaterial mutation which takes place does not terminate in a complete form. Passion is ". . . a certain motion of the soul." (*Ibid.,* 23, 2, *c.*)

sible species have this in common: both are accompanied by corporeal change.[20] This change, however, is only accidental (*per accidens*)[21] to the eduction of the sensible species; in the passion, on the contrary, the bodily change is essential (*per se*).[22] This organic mutation is the material element of the passion; the psychic inclination to a sensible good or away from a sensible evil is the formal element.

Genesis of a Passion: How are these movements of soul and body, which we call passions, originated? First, a sensible object is known. Because it appears good, it is loved and desired by the appetitive faculty.[23] This love and desire are movements of the soul, psychic inclinations, which result from sense knowledge—whether this knowledge be had from the external senses or from the imaginative sense as directed by the higher reason. How is the bodily change related to this psychic motion? The soul naturally moves the body because it is the act of the body, its essential actual principle. Hence, the immaterial movement of the soul is naturally the cause of the bodily mutation.[24]

The process of the passional act seems the reverse of the act of sensory apprehension. In sense knowledge, the bodily change, which is caused by the contact of the object with sense organ, is antecedent to the immaterial mutation in the operative potency. In the operation of the sense appetite, on the contrary, the corporeal change results from the immaterial movement of the soul.

Definition: The operations of the sense appetite, which are called passions, are *movements of the soul* (psychic motions)

[20] ". . . bodily change . . . is found in the acts of the sense appetite, not spiritual change alone. . . ." (*Ibid.*, 22, 3, *c.*) Cf. also: *S. Th.*, I–II, 22, 2, ad 3m.

[21] In sense knowledge, the corporeal transmutation does not enter *per se* but *per accidens* into the formation of the species, precisely because the species terminates the immaterial mutation.

[22] *S. Th.*, I–II, 22, 2, ad 3m.

[23] Sense knowledge specifies the operation of the sense appetite. In the order of exercise (of efficient causality), the sense appetite is moved immediately by the First Mover, God.

[24] Cf. *S. Th.*, I–II, 37, 4, ad 1m.

caused by the sensory knowledge[25] *of a particular good or evil object and accompanied by an organic mutation.*[26]

ARTICLE II: Classification of the Passions

A passion is primarily a psychic *motion*—either an inclination and urge toward a sensible good, or a turning away from a sensible evil. Thus the basic and initial passions are love and hate. Like all motions, a passion suggests a starting point, a term, and a possible series of stops in between. We shall discover in man eleven different passions. Of these, six are the operations of the concupiscible appetite: *love* and *hatred, desire* and *aversion, joy* and *sadness.* Five are the acts of the irascible appetite: *hope* and *despair, daring* and *fear,* and *anger.*[27]

Passions of the Concupiscible Appetite:[28] In the genesis of a passion, I must first perceive a sensible object; it attracts me; I love it. *Love*[29] is the first passion, the fundamental emotion. Another object may appear as a menacing evil; my first reaction, my first emotional response is dislike—*hatred.* These two basic emotions are the starting point of a series of passions. It should be noted, however, that love is the absolutely primary passion; for nothing is hated unless it is opposed to a good which one loves.

---

[25] Knowledge specifies appetite in the order of object (of formal and final cause).

[26] "Some bodily change . . . always accompanies an act of the sensitive appetite, and this change affects especially the heart, which is the first source of movement in animals. Therefore, acts of the sensitive appetite, inasmuch as they have annexed to them some bodily change, are called passions. . . ." (*S. Th.,* I, 20, 1, ad 1^{m}.) Such statements occur frequently throughout St. Thomas' treatise on the passions.

[27] Cf. *S. Th.,* I–II, questions 22–48.

[28] *Ibid.,* 23, 4, *c.*

[29] Love can be on two levels: sensory and intellectual. The term is here used to signify the inclination of the sense appetite to sensible good. "Love, desire, and the like can be understood in two ways. Sometimes they are taken as passions—arising, that is, with a certain commotion of spirit. And thus they are commonly understood, and in this sense they are only in the sensitive appetite. They may, however, be taken in another way, insofar as they are simple affections without passion or commotion of spirit, and thus they are acts of the will. And in this sense, too, they are attributed to the angels and to God. . . ." (*Ibid.,* I, 82, 5, ad 1^{m}.)

Let us now suppose that the pleasurable good perceived and loved is not possessed. My natural reaction is to desire to possess it. *Desire* (*concupiscentia*)[30] is the passion from which the faculty gets its name, "concupiscible." Should the object be evil and therefore hated, the consequent passion aroused will be *aversion.* This passion is a motion of the appetite turning away from an unpleasant object.

Finally, if I attain the good object which was desired, the soul is flooded with sensible delight, sensible *joy* (pleasure). On the other hand, if the evil from which I turned away overtakes me, it oppresses me and I am *sad.* Sensible *joy* and *sadness* are the passions which terminate the series of emotions of the concupiscible power, which has for its object the pleasurable good.

Passions of the Irascible Appetite:[31] The passions of the irascible appetite presuppose some initial passion in the concupiscible with regard to an *arduous* object, that is, with regard to a sensible good difficult to obtain, or a sensible evil difficult to avoid. In other words, we must love and desire, or hate and turn from an object, before we are able to *hope* or to *despair.* These passions of hope and despair arise precisely because of the difficulties which prevent us from attaining the object of our love or which prevent us from escaping the evil we hate.

Let us first consider these emotions in reference to an arduous sensible object that we *love* and desire to obtain. By looking at the sensible goodness (the pleasurableness) of the object, we may consider ourselves able to overcome the difficulties that hinder us; consequently, we are inclined to the object of our love and desire. For the pleasurable good which is difficult of attainment, when considered *as pleasurable,* produces a tendency to the object of our desire. This tendency is the passion of *hope.* Accordingly, hope

---

[30] St. Thomas generally uses the term *concupiscentia* for the passion of desire. This term should not be understood here in the theological sense of desire for unlawful carnal pleasure. Rather, it embraces desire for any pleasurable good.

[31] Cf. *S. Th.,* I–II, 25; *De Ver.,* XXVI, 4.

(the passion) is a psychic movement toward a particular sensible good that is essentially attractive. If, on the other hand, the difficulties that stand in the way seem insurmountable, so that we realize the futility of our efforts, there will be a turning away from the object of our desire. This turning away from the sensible good is the passion of *despair*. In this case, the sensible good is considered not precisely as pleasurable, but *as arduous,* as difficult of attainment, and hence in a certain sense evil.[32]

Let us now consider an object of *hatred* which could be averted by making a firm stand against it. Let us also suppose that we think ourselves capable of facing and of conquering the evil that is threatening us. This knowledge will excite in us the passion of *daring,* and we shall, as a consequence, withstand our adversary courageously. In such a case, the object, although evil, contains a motive for our movement toward it; for in order to avoid a greater evil — death, for example — we are willing to go toward a lesser evil. When, on the contrary, we consider the approaching evil precisely as evil, we judge that it has the aspect of something to be shunned. This estimation weakens our courage and dampens our spirits, and there arises a movement away from the evil. This psychic recoil is the passion of *fear.*

Finally, *anger* may arise from daring. It is a motion toward an evil not considered as such, that is, as evil; rather, the evil is considered the means of effecting revenge against one's adversary and this is regarded as a good. Now the passion of anger, no matter how violent, cannot endure indefinitely. Either the action resulting from anger will bring about revenge, and in our triumph we shall taste joy; or the anger will be futile, and then sadness and gloom will weigh heavily on the soul.

From this exposition of typical emotional sequences, we note that the passions of the concupiscible appetite must *begin* and *end* the cycle of emotions.

---

[32] *S. Th.,* I–II, 25, 3, *c.*

Accordingly, the passions of the irascible faculty stand between those concupiscible passions that denote movement toward good or evil, and those concupiscible passions that denote rest in good or evil. And it is therefore evident that the irascible passions both arise from and terminate in the passions of the concupiscible faculty.[33]

Terminative Passions: Because of the profound influence which they exert upon our psychological and moral life, we shall further examine these four passions: joy and sadness, hope and fear. They are called the *terminative* passions because they terminate the psychological series of emotions. Since they are the last in a passional sequence, their influence is often enduring. Consequently, they may have a greater effect on our psychological integration and moral life than the other passions, which are more fleeting in nature. Indeed, these terminative passions will be strong determinants in the formation of psychological personality, and their influence will be of utmost importance in the development of the moral personality, or character, as well. For that reason, it is of special importance that the terminal passions never be allowed to trespass beyond the rule of reason. They must always be subject to rational control.

a) *Joy and sadness:* Of the four terminative passions, sensory joy (pleasure) and sadness are *unqualifiedly* terminative. They are the operations of the concupiscible appetite which absolutely end any single series of passions. For that reason, all other factors being equal, their influence is more complete. Consequently, whenever these passions are inordinate, they may cause greater harm. For example, immoderate sadness, which is not checked, may ultimately bring about serious mental disturbance; even sensory

[33] *Ibid.,* 1, *c.* The following is a parallel passage: "This is clear also from the fact that the irascible is, as it were, the champion and defender of the concupiscible, when it rises against what inflicts harm from which the concupiscible flies. And for this reason all the passions of the irascible appetite rise from the passions of the concupiscible appetite and terminate in them. For instance, anger rises from sadness, and having wrought vengeance, terminates in joy. For this reason also the quarrels of animals are about things concupiscible — namely food and sex." (*Ibid.,* I, 81, 2, *c.*)

joy, when uncontrolled by reason, may lead to great disorder.

b) *Hope and fear:* Hope and fear are not terminative passions in the absolute sense. The reason is that they belong to the irascible appetite, whose operations are not a rest, but a motion toward a good or from an impending evil. We have noted that an emotion of the concupiscible appetite (love or hatred) must begin the appetitive process, and that another operation of the sense appetite (joy or sadness) must terminate the passional series. This termination is a "rest" of the appetite in the good or evil which is present. In a certain sense, hope is terminative as regards motion toward a good loved and desired; for the inclination will remain until the desired object is attained. In like manner, fear, which is a motion away from a hated evil, will endure until the danger no longer exists. Hope and fear, therefore, may be considered as "terminative" passions in the order of motion; joy and sadness as terminative in the order of rest. Hope and fear look to the future; joy and sadness are concerned with the present. Of all the sensory appetitive operations of man, these four passions are the most far-reaching in their influence, and, consequently, are aptly called the principal[34] passions.

ARTICLE III: Relations Between Passions and Reason

In brute animals, the operations of the sense appetites — the passions — terminate sense knowledge. The passions do not go beyond sense life. In man, however, the passions and emotions are closely connected with his intellectual life; for man is a strict unit of body and intellectual soul, and there is a constant interdependence between the lower and higher functions of his nature.[35]

---

[34] *S. Th.*, I–II, 25, 4, *c.*

[35] St. Thomas has several remarkable texts which might serve as a philosophical prologomenon to the science of experimental psychology. We quote one of the more important: "According to the order of nature, since the powers of the soul are bound together in one essence, and since soul and body are united by the 'to be' belonging to the composite, the superior and inferior powers and the body as well transmit to

Now, since man's intellectual operations imply a free will as the corresponding appetite, a full understanding of the passions in man will require a knowledge of the intimate relations between the passions and the will, and of their reciprocal influence. Furthermore, these relations and this mutual influence imply either a control or a lack of control of one over the other. Consequently, the discovery of the principles underlying such control will depend upon our understanding the nature of these relations.

Problem: The passions are powerful psychic forces capable of strong opposition to reason. The passions, we know from experience, are not the slaves of reason. Indeed, even while obeying and following intellectual direction, they retain such independence of pace that, unless constantly controlled and moderated, they can easily transgress the bounds set by right reason. This fact gives rise to the following problem: How can the reason (intellect and will) control the excesses of passion,[36] and even marshal their powerful forces for the development of the virtues?

Influence on the Act of the Will: Although many men allow their passions to run wild,[37] reason, nevertheless, can normally

---

each other whatever any one of them possesses to excess; this is why the body, due to the act of apprehension by the soul, is changed in the line of heat and coldness, sometimes even to the point where health and sickness are involved and to the point where death may be incurred: for it happens that men die from joy or sadness or love . . . and likewise, on the contrary, bodily change affects the soul. For the soul, since it is united to the body, imitates the body's dispositions in the line of madness or docility, and the like. . . . So also the superior powers affect the inferior; for passion in the sensitive appetite follows upon an intense act of the will, and the animal powers are withdrawn from or impeded in their acts due to intense contemplation; and, on the contrary, the inferior powers affect the superior; as when due to the vehemence of passion in the sensitive appetite the reason is so darkened that it judges to be absolutely good, as it were, something toward which the man is affected by passion." (*De Ver.*, XXVI, 10.)

[36] We do not ask, "*Can* reason control passion?" but, "*How* can it exercise this control?" The reason is obvious. If the passions were not controllable, man would be reduced to the status of brute animals. Let us recall the principle that in a perfect unit (*unum per se*) the less perfect is for the more perfect, and the lower for the higher — not *vice versa.*

[37] "Men for the most part follow the impetus of the passions . . . for it belongs only to the wise to moderate the passions by reason." (*C. G.*, III, 154, No. 5.) Cf. also *S. Th.*, I–II, 9, 5, ad 3[m].

control them. In other words, despite the fact that the will—whose acts are specified[38] by the intellectual judgment of the good—is sometimes profoundly influenced by the emotions, it generally remains free. Only in rare instances does a spontaneous passion so overwhelm and darken reason that the judgment of conscience cannot occur and animal instincts rule supreme. What kind of control, then, can reason exercise over the passions? This is a very delicate question, and is, of course, the pivotal point of the matter under discussion in the present and in the following article. In order to find a solution, it will be necessary to consider the three general situations[39] in which the passions may influence the will through the judgment of reason which specifies the will-act: (1) when the passion is spontaneous and *antecedent* to the act of the will; (2) when an intense will-act spontaneously stimulates *concomitant* passion; (3) when the passion is *consequent* to the act of the will.

1. Passion Is Antecedent to the Act of the Will: This situation is not infrequent. An object is apprehended by the senses and spontaneously desired (or hated) by the sense appetite. The influence of the passion upon the will is not direct, that is, in the line of efficient causality (order of exercise); rather, its influence is in the order of *object,* of specification. The passion biases or "colors" the phantasm which is the instrumental cause in the production of the intelligible species in the possible intellect. Informed by this species, the intellect makes its judgment concerning the suitability of an action. It is this judgment which may *specify,* that is, give the form to the will-act. Obviously, judgments of this kind are apt to be in error[40] concerning the

38 We will what we intellectually judge to be good in some way. In the next chapter we shall see how the intellect as a formal cause moves the will.

39 Cf. *S. Th.,* I–II, 24, 3, ad 1m.

40 "The passions . . . obscure the judgment of reason. . . ." (*Loc. cit.*) ". . . the passion of the sensitive appetite moves the will in so far as the will is moved by its object—namely, inasmuch as through being disposed in a certain way by a passion, a man judges something to be fitting and good, which he would not judge thus were it not for the passion." (*Ibid.,* 10, 3, *c.*)

objective goodness or evil of a proposed action; and the will which freely follows such a judgment will indirectly be affected by the emotional tone of the sensory experience from which the judgment takes its origin. Hence, what would not seem good under other circumstances appears fitting and suitable because of the disposition resulting from the passion.[41]

What will be the outcome of the influence of such a passion upon the reason and upon the free will of man? There are two possibilities:

> First, so that his *reason is wholly bound* [our italics], so that he has not the use of reason; as happens in those who through violent anger or desire (*concupiscentia*) become mad or insane, just as they may from some other bodily disorder, since such passions do not occur without some change in the body. And of such the same is to be said as of irrational animals, which follow, of necessity, the impulse of their passions; for in them there is neither movement of reason, nor, consequently, of will.
>
> Sometimes, however, the reason is not entirely engrossed by the passion, so that the judgment of reason retains, to a certain extent, its freedom; and thus *the movement of the will remains in a certain degree* [italics added]. Accordingly, in so far as the reason remains free and not subject to the passion, the will's movement, which also remains, does not tend of necessity to that whereto the passion inclines it. Consequently, either there is no movement of the will in that man, and the passion alone holds its sway; or if there be a movement of the will, it does not necessarily follow the passion.[42]

2. Intense Act of the Will Stimulates Concomitant Passion: It

[41] " . . . That which is apprehended as good and fitting moves the will by way of object. Now that a thing appear to be good and fitting happens from two causes: namely, from the condition either of the thing proposed or of the one to whom it is proposed . . . and hence it is that the taste, according as it is variously disposed, takes to a thing in various ways, as being fitting or unfitting. . . . Now it is evident that according to a passion of the sensitive appetite man is changed to a certain disposition (*ad aliquam dispositionem*). Wherefore, according as man is affected by a passion, something seems fitting to him which does not seem so when he is not so affected; thus that seems good to a man when angered which does not seem good when he is calm. And in this way, the sensitive appetite moves the will, on the part of the object." (*Ibid.*, 9, 2, *c.*)

[42] *Ibid.*, 10, 3, *c.*

is a fact of experience that not every act of the will necessarily excites an emotional reaction. The will ". . . can be moved to some particular good without any passion of the sensitive appetite. For we will and do many things without passion, and through choice alone; as is evident in those cases in which reason resists passion."[43] When, however, acts of the will are elicited with intensity, there is often a natural reaction in the lower faculties, and some passions are stimulated. For this reason, besides the moral virtues of temperance and fortitude, " . . . which are concerned with the passions as their proper matter, and hence cannot be without passions,"[44] even the other moral virtues such as justice — whose act is not about the object of the passions but about the rights of other men — will at times through the perfection of their operations give rise to accompanying passion.[45]

This stimulation of concomitant passion by way of *redundance* is possible because one and the same intellectual soul is the substantial form of the body, and, consequently, the soul is the first (essential) principle of *all* the operations of man, whether on the intellectual or sensitive level. Accordingly,

> . . . when the higher part of the soul is intensely moved to anything, the lower part also follows that movement; and thus the passion that results in consequence, in the sensitive appetite, is a sign of the intensity of the will, and so indicates greater moral goodness [or evil].[46]

Indeed, a lack of passion in such a case may manifest a lack of perfection in the act of the will. "Hence, the movement . . .

[43] *S. Th.,* I–II, 10, 3, ad 3m.
[44] *Ibid.,* 59, 5, *c.*
[45] "Those moral virtues, however, which are not concerned with the passions, but with operations, can be without passions. Such a virtue is justice; because it applies the will to its proper act, which is not a passion. Nevertheless, joy (*gaudium*) results from the act of justice, at least in the will, in which case it is not a passion. And if this joy be increased through the perfection of justice, it will overflow into the sensitive appetite, in so far as the lower powers follow the movement of the higher. . . . Wherefore, by reason of this kind of overflow (*redundantia*), the more perfect a virtue is, the more does it cause passion." (*Loc. cit.*)
[46] *Ibid.,* 24, 3, ad 1m.

in the sensitive appetite cannot be lacking altogether, unless the movement of the will be altogether lacking or weak. Consequently, lack of passion . . . is also a vice. . . ."[47]

3. The Will (Through Reason) Deliberately Incites Consequent Passion: Besides arising as the sensory concomitant of an act of intellectual appetite, the passions may arise ". . . by way of choice, when, to wit, a man by the judgment of his reason chooses to be affected by a passion in order to work more promptly with the cooperation of the sensitive appetite."[48] It is because the will and the universal reason—through which the will operates in exciting the passion—are the supreme operative potencies in man that they are able to move the sense appetites. This influence of the will and the reason can be the arousing of passional operation when man is in an emotionally quiescent state, or it may be the exciting of a contrary and opposed emotion for the purpose of moderating the excesses of a present passion. The latter instance is of greatest importance in the actual practice of emotional control.

ARTICLE IV: Control of the Passions[49]

Since the sense appetites are inferior to reason, their operations—the passions—should be controlled by the higher faculties of man. The nature, however, of this mastery of intellect and will over the passions is peculiar; it is not a direct, but an *indirect* control. The reason is that a passion is aroused through sense knowledge of a particular object, and not immediately and directly by the command of the reason made under the influence of the will. Accordingly, the control of the passions will be effected by proposing to the sense faculty of knowledge an object which will move the sense appetite in accordance with reason's command. There are

---

[47] *Ibid.*, II–II, 158, 8, *c.*
[48] *Ibid.*, I–II, 24, 3, *c.*
[49] *Ibid.*, I, 81, 3.

various ways[50] in which the reason may bring this about.

Role of Intellect: The will (as an efficient cause) can move the intellect to recall definite objects, definite considerations, that are concerned with the passional situation. Now, we have seen that the human intellect does not act without an accompanying phantasm. Consequently, whenever the intellect (ruled by the will) applies itself to a universal consideration, the accompanying phantasm is brought into consciousness and serves as the sensory knowledge that will specify another and, perhaps, opposed passion. Thus the passion of hate may be moderated by a consideration of the lovable qualities of the object which under another aspect arouses one's hatred. It should be noted that universal considerations alone will not suffice; rather, an application must be made by the particular reason, the cogitative sense, to a particular instance; for the passions are concerned with particular, sensible goods and evils, not with abstract, universal values.

> In two ways do the irascible and concupiscible powers obey the higher part, in which are the intellect (or reason) and the will: in one way as regards the reason; in another as regards the will. They obey the reason in their own acts, because in other animals the sensitive appetite is naturally moved by the estimative power. . . . In man [however] the estimative power . . . is replaced by the cogitative power, which is called by some the particular reason, because it compares individual intentions. Hence, in man the sensitive appetite is naturally moved by the particular reason. But this same particular reason is naturally guided and moved according to the universal reason; and that is why in syllogisms particular conclusions are drawn from universal propositions. Therefore, it is clear that the universal reason rules the sensitive appetite, which is divided into concupiscible and irascible, and that this appetite obeys it. But because to draw particular conclusions from universal principles is not the work of the intellect as such (*simplicis intellectus*), but of the reason (*rationis*), hence it is that the irascible and con-

[50] Ultimately, a change in the passion can be brought about only by a change in the sensory phantasm which specifies the passion. This may be effected by turning to other external or internal objects of experience.

cupiscible are said to obey the reason rather than to obey the intellect. Anyone can experience this in himself; for by applying certain universal considerations, anger or fear or the like many be lessened or increased.[51]

It will be seen that, ultimately, control of the emotions is effected by *control of the sense knowledge* which specifies the passion. This control can be brought about by applying universal considerations[52] to a particular passional situation, or by a change in external and internal sensations under the influence of the higher powers. In brief, to change the phantasm is to change the passion.

Role of the Will: The will, while having no direct influence in the actual production of the passions, has, nevertheless, as efficient cause, direct control as regards the *execution* of the external (and internal) operations which are consequent upon the passion. In regard to the external operations which follow upon the passions, there is a great difference between brute animals and men. For, in non-rational animals, execution immediately follows the psychic motion of the sense appetite.

> For example, the sheep, fearing the wolf, flies at once, because it has no superior counteracting appetite. On the contrary, man is not moved immediately according to the irascible and concupiscible appetites; but he awaits the command of the will, which is the superior appetite. For wherever there is order among a number of motive powers, the second moves only by virtue of the first; and so the lower appetite is not sufficient to cause movement, unless the higher appetite consents.[53]

A Political, Not a Despotic, Control: The control which the reason has over the passions—since it is only indirect—is not an absolute rule. The passions are not slaves; they possess means of

[51] *S. Th.*, I, 81, 3, *c.*

[52] The concrete, individual passional situation must be judged as suitable or harmful in some way. "The [mere] imagination of a form without an estimation . . . does not move the appetite." (*Ibid.*, I–II, 9, 1, ad 2m.)

[53] *Ibid.*, I, 81, 3, *c.*

resistance; they have to be circumvented. Consequently, they cannot be governed by what is called a *despotic* rule, but only by a *political* rule, somewhat as free men are ruled by a government which they can resist.

> . . . The sensitive appetite has something of its own, by virtue of which it can resist the commands of reason. For the sensitive appetite is naturally moved, not only by the . . . cogitative power, which the universal reason guides, but also by the *imagination and the sense* [italics added]. Whence it is that we experience that the irascible and concupiscible powers do resist reason, inasmuch as we sense or imagine something pleasant, which reason forbids, or unpleasant, which reason commands.[54]

We must, therefore, take means to anticipate and prevent those passions which are apt to rise against reason, by controlling our sensory knowledge and the external conditions which elicit that knowledge. When, however, they do arise, we must endeavor to control them in accordance with right reason. This we shall do by exciting the proper phantasms in the imaginative sense. For the internal sensitive powers, both the appetitive and apprehensive, " . . . are subject to the command of reason, which can not only incite or modify the affections of the appetitive power, but can also form the phantasms of the imagination."[55]

Control of Bodily Dispositions: Since in a passion the organic change is an essential factor related to the psychic movement as matter to form,[56] the passions will be dependent not only on the appetitive power, but also on the dispositions of the body.[57] Now ". . . the condition and disposition of the body is not subject to the command of reason, and, consequently, in this respect the movement of the sensitive appetite is hindered from being wholly subject to the command of reason."[58] We can, however, prepare

[54] *S. Th.*, I, 81, 3, ad 2m.
[55] *Ibid.*, ad 3m.
[56] Cf. *ibid.*, I–II, 37, 4.
[57] *Ibid.*, 17, 7, *c.*
[58] *Loc. cit.*

the body indirectly. St. Thomas himself suggests a number of bodily helps to this end. He wrote an entire article in which he proposes to overcome sadness by means of baths and sleep.[59]

Clearly, then, the reason enjoys only an indirect control over the dispositions and conditions of the body.[60] That is why persons of certain temperaments find it difficult to moderate passions whose material element is founded on heredity, environment, education, and the like.

Conclusions:

1. The passions are the movements of the sense appetites. Hence, they are not an evil; rather, they belong to the perfection of man's nature.

2. Since the sense appetites are inferior to reason, their operations (the passions) should be moderated and controlled by reason; for any inordinate movement of the sensitive appetite would be contrary to the perfection of man's nature.

3. This control of the passions is not of a despotic nature, but political, because of the peculiar relations between sense appetites and reason. It is a control not easily attained, since in the present state of man the tendency of the passions toward inordinate objects

[59] *S. Th.*, I–II, 38, 5.

[60] St. Thomas was well aware of the importance of the dispositions of the body, not only as regards the passions and talents (on the sensory plane), but also as regards the vigor and capacity of the individual intellect. He proposes certain inferences which flow necessarily from the fundamental truth that matter, the principle of individuation, limits the form, and that man is an *unum per se,* an existential unit. "It [virtue] is natural to man according to the individual nature, in so far as by reason of a disposition in the body, some are disposed either well or ill to certain virtues. This happens according as certain sensitive powers (*vires*) are acts of certain parts of the body, whose disposition helps or hinders these powers in the exercise of their acts, and in consequence, the rational powers also, which such sensitive powers assist. In this way, one man has a natural aptitude for science, another for fortitude, another for temperance." (*Ibid.*, 63, 1, *c.*)

"Although the intellect is not a power of the body, yet in us the operations of the intellect cannot be exercised without the operation of bodily powers, namely, the imagination, the memory, and the cogitative power. . . . For this reason, goodness of disposition in a man's body fits him to understand easily inasmuch as the aforesaid powers are strengthened by such disposition. . . . Thus, even physicians are able to judge of a man's intellect from his bodily temperament, as a proximate disposition thereto." (*C. G.*, III, 84.)

is frequently stronger than the tendency to the moral good. This is the basic reason why the development of good habits in the sense appetites is essential in the moral life of man.[61]

4. Nevertheless, the passions are capable of being ordered to the right end. When ordered in accordance with right reason, they will contribute to the perfection of our intellectual and moral life.[62]

SUMMARY

Question I

THE SENSORY APPETITIVE POTENCIES

Article I: *Natural, Sensory, and Intellectual Appetites*

1. *Natural* appetite: inclination to good consequent upon natural (substantial) form; is constant and uniform.

2. *Sense* appetite: inclination to sensible good consequent upon sensory (intentional) form; varies with sense knowledge.

3. *Intellectual* appetite (will): inclination to good (any good) consequent upon intellectually known form; it is the appetite proportioned to the intellect.

Article II: *The Concupiscible and Irascible Sense Appetites*

1. The *formal object* of the concupiscible appetite is sensible good *as pleasurable;* the formal object of the irascible appetite is sensible good *as arduous;* distinct formal objects manifest distinct operative potencies.

2. The operations of one appetite often *diminish the intensity* of the operations of the other, thus manifesting their real distinction.

Question II

OPERATIONS OF THE SENSE APPETITES

Article I: *Nature of the Passions*

1. A passion is *not an act of knowledge,* which is likened to rest.

[61] This problem will be studied in the chapter on habits.

[62] "Accordingly, just as it is better that man should both will good and do it in his external act, so also it belongs to the perfection of moral good that man should be moved unto good, not only according to his will, but also according to his sensitive appetite, according to that which is said in Psalm 83, 3: 'My heart and my flesh have rejoiced in the living God,' where by *heart* we are to understand the intellectual appetite, and by *flesh* the sensible appetite." (*S. Th.,* I–II, 24, 3, *c.*)

Rather, passion is a *motion* (inclination) toward a sensible object or away from it.

2. A passion is *not a mere bodily (organic) change,* which is the material element of a passion. Formally, passion is *psychic*—an immaterial motion toward a sensible good or away from a sensible object.

Article II: *Classification of the Passions*

1. Of the *concupiscible* appetite:	love (like) — desire hate (dislike) — aversion	— joy — sadness
2. Of the *irascible* appetite:	hope — daring — anger despair — fear	↑ (to joy / sadness)

N.B. *Terminative* passions are those which end the psychological series of emotions. Joy and sadness are unqualifiedly terminative; hope and fear are qualifiedly terminative.

Article III: *Relations Between Passions and Reason*

1. Passion *antecedent* to the act of the will biases or "colors" the phantasm from which is formed the intelligible species for the judgment of suitability of action. This judgment of reason specifies the will-act. Hence, the influence of the passion is indirect, that is, in the order of *object:*

a) Reason may be wholly bound; hence, no movement of the will occurs.

b) Reason may not be entirely engrossed by passion; hence, the movement of the will remains, but is impaired by the passion.

2. Intense act of the will incites *concomitant* passion by natural redundance, because the intellectual soul is the substantial form of the body.

3. The will (reason) excites (*consequent*) passion by way of choice.

Article IV: *Control of the Passions*

1. Role of *intellect:* The application of universal considerations is accompanied by phantasms which may specify another and perhaps opposed passion. In brief, to change the phantasm is to change the passion.

2. Role of the *will:* The *execution* of operation consequent upon passion awaits the command of the will, which is the superior appetite of man.

3. This control of the passions by reason is a *political, not a despotic,* control, for the passions are moved also by sense knowledge.

CHAPTER VIII

THE WILL

Man has freedom of judgment and choice (liberum arbitrium); *otherwise, counsels, exhortations, commands, prohibitions, rewards, and punishments would be in vain.*[1]

PROLOGUE

"Some inclination is consequent upon every form."[2] Now, since man through intellectual knowledge acquires the forms (species) of things, without matter and without the conditions of matter, there must be present within his nature an inclination *surpassing* the inclination of *the sense appetites,* which have for their object the sensible forms. This superior inclination we call the intellectual appetite, or will.

Moreover, from our own experience, we know that we desire some goods that are *in no way material,* such as honor, virtue, peace, happiness. We are able also to choose objects which are *universal,* for example, to be always kind to all. Then, too, even particular material goods can be loved precisely under the aspect *of good,* rather than under the restricted aspect of pleasurableness; we can, for example, desire to take an unpleasant medicine because we see in the unpleasant object a goodness with reference to an

[1] *S. Th.,* I, 83, 1, *c.*
[2] *Ibid.,* 80, 1, *c.*

end, health. We conclude that, since distinct formal objects diversify operative potencies, there must be a superior appetite in man, an appetite above the sensory level, proportioned to intellectual knowledge — the will.

We can arrive at a better understanding of the nature of the will by comparing its mode of action to that of other beings. It is evident that ". . . some things act *without* judgment, as a stone which moves downwards; and in like manner all things which lack knowledge. And some act from judgment, but *not* from a *free* judgment, as the brute animals. . . . But man acts from *free* judgment and has the power of being inclined to various things."[3]

Concerning the first type of beings, the world of inanimate bodies, we observe that their motions do not proceed from themselves but from an extrinsic cause; they do not move themselves, but are moved by external agents. More perfect is the motion of plants, which perfect themselves by their own action; but in no way do they judge the goodness, the suitability of their actions.

As we ascend higher in the consideration of reality, we find that the beings we call animals not only move themselves, but they possess from their estimative power a kind of "judgment" concerning what is to be done; they are able to discern what is suitable or unsuitable, friendly or inimical. Yet, they are not capable of judging concerning this judgment itself; that is, they are not able to deliberate about it, nor estimate its value. The reason for this is that this "judgment," this estimation, is predetermined and passes into act whenever the animal contacts certain specific objects of sensation. This necessary determination to judge in a specific way on the instance of a specific experience is imprinted in the nature by the Author of nature, and the operation of the sensitive appetite follows this non-free estimation or "judgment." Accordingly, since animals do not themselves determine this judgment, their act of "choice" is not free. Like

[3] *Ibid.*, 83, 1, *c*.

the plants and inanimate bodies, they in no way determine the finality of their actions; rather, they are necessitated to their end in every respect.

Man, on the contrary, is endowed with reason and is able to form a judgment that is not necessarily determined to one thing by an extrinsic agent. By a comparison of the various courses of action open to him, by discerning the good in them and their limitations, by a process of deliberation, he is able to judge *freely* what is to be done.[4] This he does because he knows the end as end, and the means as means, and the relations between means and end. Hence, man is able to move himself not only as regards the execution and specification of his actions, as do the brute animals, but even as to the particular finality of his actions. Only as regards his primary finality, his ultimate end, is man absolutely dependent on an extrinsic mover. As regards proximate or immediate ends, he ". . . enjoys liberty of judgment and of choice, that is, of judging freely of the things to be done and not to be done."[5]

Division: In the present treatise, we intend to show that man enjoys definite freedom, what this freedom is, and what it implies. Three fundamental points will be considered: (1) the necessity and the freedom of the will; (2) the interaction of intellect and will in the free act; (3) God and the human will.

Question I

NECESSITY AND FREEDOM OF THE WILL

This question is divided into four articles: (1) the will cannot

[4] "Only intellectual beings are free in judging, and this is to possess freedom of judgment and of choice (*liberum arbitrium*)." (*C. G.*, II, 48, 2.)

[5] *De Ver.*, XXIV, 1. We translate *liberum arbitrium* as "freedom of judgment and of choice," since the theory of St. Thomas implies — as we shall see — a definite control by the will over the practical judgment which specifies the will-act. *Liberum arbitrium* is not to be regarded as a distinct faculty. Rather, it is a common function of intellect and will: the judgment is formed by the intellect, and choice is from the will.

be coerced, that is, necessitated in the order of exercise; (2) the will is necessitated to absolute good in the order of specification; (3) the will is not necessitated (is free) as regards limited goods; (4) the three modes of freedom.

ARTICLE I: The Will Cannot Be Coerced (i.e., Necessitated in the Order of Exercise)

Freedom: It is obvious that freedom of any kind is opposed to necessity. Necessity implies a "must": a necessary being is one which *must* be, which cannot not-be; a necessary happening is one that cannot not-happen, since it is already determined. Freedom, on the contrary, implies the absence of necessity of some sort. If, therefore, a certain kind of freedom is affirmed of man, it will be essential to discover in what precise sense man's rational appetite is necessitated, and in what precise manner it is not necessitated, that is, free.

Order of Exercise and Specification: Now there are two general ways in which an appetite can be necessitated, or determined, in its operations. The first is had by a determination in the order of *efficient* causality, or, as it is sometimes called, the order of *exercise*. The second arises in the order of *formal* and *final* causality, the order of *specification,* and comes from the object. To clarify this distinction, let us bear in mind that we can consider any activity in two distinct ways. For example, ". . . the sight sometimes sees actually and sometimes sees not; and sometimes it sees white, and sometimes black."[6] If we consider that the seeing subject is placing an action rather than not, we are reflecting on the *exercise* of the action. If we consider that the subject sees *this* rather than *that,* we are viewing the *specification* or object of the action. As regards the human will-act, we must inquire both into the exercise of the act of willing and into the specification or form that this act takes.

---

[6] *S. Th.*, I–II, 9, 1, *c*.

ACT OR NOT ACT - ORDER OF EXER
ACT ON THIS OR THAT - ORDER OF SPEC.

We must ascertain whether the will is necessitated in either of these two orders, and in what precise sense it is free.

Twofold Actuation of the Human Will: The human will is an operative potency which needs to be actuated[7] both in the efficient and formal lines of causality; that is to say, it must be actuated to be able to exercise its act of willing, and this operation must be specified, determined by a definite willed object. The proof of this is that the will is not always operating; moreover, when it does act, it does not perform only one definite act. These are facts of experience about which there can be no doubt. The point now at issue is whether the will can receive a determination from an extrinsic cause necessitating its action in the order of exercise.[8]

No Necessity in the Order of Exercise: The necessary determination caused by an extrinsic agent so that a subject is not able to do the contrary is generally termed *coercion,* or constraint. Can the will be forced *to love* or *not-to-love* a particular object? No, that is impossible; and we must in our consideration of the acts of the will exclude all necessity arising from constraint or violence, for a coerced inclination of a nature is a contradiction.

> For we call violent that which is against the inclination of a thing. But the very movement of the will is an *inclination* to something. Therefore, just as a thing is called *natural* because it is according to the inclination of nature, so a thing is called *voluntary* because it is according to the inclination of the will. Therefore, just as it is

[7] "A thing requires to be moved by something in so far as it is in potency to several things. For that which is in potency needs to be reduced to act by something in act; and to do this is to move (*movere*). Now a power of the soul is found to be in potency to different things in two ways: first, with regard to acting and not acting; second, with regard to this or that action. Thus, the sight sometimes sees actually, and sometimes sees not; and sometimes it sees white, and sometimes black. It needs, therefore, a mover in two respects: viz., as to the exercise or use of the act, and as to the determination of the act. The first of these is on the part of the subject, which is sometimes acting, sometimes not acting; while the other is on the part of the object, by reason of which the act is specified." (*S. Th.,* I–II, 9, 1, *c.*)

[8] The second and third articles of this question will consider whether the will can be necessitated in the order of specification, and in what precise sense it is free in both orders.

> impossible for a thing to be at the same time violent and natural, so is it impossible for a thing to be absolutely coerced, or violent, and voluntary [italics added].[9]

It is possible, of course, for reason to be so bound by the passions[10] that the will, whose object is the intellectually *known* good, cannot function. But in such a case there is no voluntary action; the will simply does not act.

We also admit that the *commanded* acts — those operations of the other powers of the soul and of the members of the body which are under the control of the will — may be done under violence, so that the will in a certain sense may be said to ". . . suffer violence, in so far as violence can prevent the exterior members from executing the will's command. But as to the will's own proper act [elicited act],[11] violence cannot be done to the will."[12]

Accordingly, as regards the order of exercise, that is, the order of willing or not willing, we must affirm that no power, not even God,[13] can force the will to act.[14] Nor, for that matter, can the will constrain itself to act against its own inclination. That is impossible because it is a contradiction.[15] Hence, we must conclude that in the order of exercise the will is free from coercion and constraint.

---

[9] *S. Th.,* I, 82, 1, *c.*

[10] It should be noted that the influence of passion upon the will is indirect and in the order of the object (of specification), not in the order of efficient causality (of exercise).

[11] The internal acts make up the *elicited* acts as distinguished from the *commanded* act.

[12] *S. Th.,* I–II, 6, 4, *c.*

[13] No one, not even God, could ever coerce a natural appetite, for this appetite is the nature itself as related to its end. A corporeal nature, it is true, can be *destroyed* by violent action; it can be made to act externally contrary to its natural inclination. Nevertheless, the nature, as long as it remains what it is, cannot be changed as regards its radical tendency or finality to its end. For the nature is nothing but the essence viewed as a principle of action inclined necessarily to a definite end.

[14] "God cannot coerce the will." (*De Ver.,* XXII, 8.)

[15] "The will cannot coerce itself, for this implies a contradiction." (*Ibid.,* 9, ad 1^{m}.)

ARTICLE II: The Will Is Necessitated to Absolute Good (in the Order of Specification)

Problem: Is there any *object* which necessitates the will to act? In other words, is there any reality which, being known, determines the act of the will in the order of formal and final causality in such a manner that the will could not *not-will* this object? The solution to this problem cannot be approached without a thorough understanding of the formal object of the will.

Formal Object of the Will: Since the will has for its formal object the good (being) precisely *as good,* it is necessitated *under this aspect* to will whatever it wills. In order to clarify this important truth, it will be helpful to recall and explain the relation between the material and formal objects of a faculty. A restricted formal object implies a restricted material object. For example, the sense of sight, which attains its object under the aspect of *color,* can know colored things; it cannot, however, know objects which are color*less*. On the other hand, a cognoscitive faculty which has no restriction in its formal object can attain to all things regardless of their sensible differences; its material object is unlimited precisely because of the universal aspect under which the faculty attains its objects. Such a faculty is the intellect, a power ordered to know being *as being,* and hence to know all beings.

Now the will is the rational appetite — the appetite proportioned to the human intellect. Since the intellect has for its formal object being (the true) precisely as such, it follows that the will — which is the inclination consequent upon intellectual knowledge — must have for its formal object being (the good) precisely as good. Consequently, there can be no extensive limitation in the material object of the will. In other words, the will can tend to all beings, in so far as they are good; it can embrace *all* goods, whether material or immaterial, limited or unlimited; only non-good cannot be its object.

Only Absolute (Universal) Good Can Necessitate the Will: The question now arises whether any of the various goods presented to the will through intellectual knowledge can, in the order of specification (of object), necessitate the will to action. Again, the answer lies in a reflection on the nature of the will's formal object, being (the good) viewed *as good*. By its very nature, the will can be inclined to any object in so far as it is good. That object, therefore, which is good universally, whose perfection is absolute, so that its every aspect is desirable, cannot be rejected by the will, if the will is to act at all. Those goods, however, which are particular (limited), and which consequently present an aspect of non-desirability, cannot necessitate the will to accept them.

> The will is moved in two ways: first, as to the exercise of its act; second, as to the specification of its act, derived from the object. . . . As to the second manner of motion, the will is moved *by one object necessarily* [italics added]. . . . For in the movement of an [operative] potency by its object, we must consider under what aspect (*ratio*) the object moves the potency. For the visible moves the sight under the aspect of color actually visible. . . . If the sight were confronted with something not in all respects colored actually, but only in some respects, and in other respects not, the sight would not of necessity see such an object: for it might look at that part of the object which is not actually colored, and thus would not see it. Now just as the actually colored is the object of sight, so good is the object of the will. Therefore, if the will be offered an object which is good universally (*universaliter*) and from every point of view (*consideratio*), the will tends to it of necessity, if it will anything at all, since it cannot will the opposite. If, on the other hand, the will is offered an object that is not good from every point of view, it will not tend to it of necessity. And since the lack (*defectus*) of any good whatever has the aspect (*ratio*) of non-good, consequently, that good alone which is perfect and lacking in nothing is such a good that the will cannot not-will it. . . .[16]

[16] *S. Th.,* I–II, 10, 2, *c.* Happiness is the possession of the good. Perfect happiness is the possession of the universal good. Man cannot *not-will* happiness. In point of fact, all his voluntary acts result precisely from the fact that the will must seek the

Natural Necessity of Will to the Last End (Perfect Happiness):[17] A nature, we have seen, is a principle of operation necessitated to a definite end. This end is the good of the nature and is necessarily sought. The nature of every limited being is subject to this necessary seeking, for this is the law of finality. The will, of course, is no exception to this law; it too in a certain manner is a definite limited nature necessarily ordered to its supreme end by the author of nature. What, then, is the end of the will? What is that to which the will is primarily and immutably inclined, though admittedly it has successive changing inclinations to every type of suitable good? To this question St. Thomas answers as follows:

> . . . Natural necessity is not repugnant to the will. Indeed, just as the intellect of necessity adheres to first principles, so the will must of necessity adhere to the last end, which is *happiness;* for the end is in practical matters what the principle is in speculative matters. . . . For what befits a thing naturally and immovably must be the root and principle of all else pertaining thereto, since the nature of a thing is the *first* in everything, and every movement arises from something *immovable* [all italics added].[18]

In other words, the last end—perfect happiness—to which

---

absolute good. This momentous truth, that the will: (*a*) cannot *not-will,* desire, and seek the absolute good, (*b*) that it does so implicitly and fundamentally in every willful act, is—as we shall show—the very reason why the will is necessarily free in willing any means, any particular good.

[17] ". . . the will itself is a sort of nature. . . . Now it belongs to every created nature that it be ordered by God to the good so that it naturally desires the good. Hence, there is in the will a certain natural appetite to the good suitable to it; and besides this it has inclinations to objects according to its own determination, not from necessity; and this belongs to it in as much at it is a will. . . .Just as nature is the foundation of the will, so the appetible object which is naturally desired is the principle and foundation of other appetibles. Now among appetibles the end is the foundation and principle of the means to the end, since those things which are on account of the end are not desired except by reason of the end. Consequently, that which the will necessarily wills (to which it is determined by a natural inclination, as it were) is the last end. . . ." (*De Ver.,* XXII, 5.)

[18] *S. Th.,* I, 82, 1, *c.* The following is a parallel passage: ". . . every movable is reduced to the immovable, and the indeterminate to the determinate, as to their principle; hence that to which the will is determined is properly the principle of desiring those things to which it is not determined; and this is the last end. . . ." (*De Ver.,* XXII, 5.)

the will tends naturally, ". . . stands in the same relation to things appetible as the first principles of demonstration to things intelligible. . . ."[19] Just as the first principles are necessarily known, and just as the intellect knows secondary principles and conclusions demonstrably in the light of first principles, so is the last end necessarily and primarily sought; so too, whatever else besides the last end is sought by the will is sought secondarily, that is, as a means to the last end. For this end, although the last in attainment, is the first in intention; and the primary and constant natural tendency of the will to this end is the first principle or starting point of all human operations concerned with the attainment of immediate (proximate) ends; for these are but means to the last end, which is primarily and necessarily sought whenever the will acts.[20]

Moreover, it is by virtue of this primary and necessary volition of the last end, which is the first principle of human operation, that the will is able freely *to move itself* as regards the means, which are proximate ends. For ". . . the end is in the order of appetibles what a principle is in the order of intelligibles. But it is evident that the intellect, through its knowledge of a principle, reduces itself from potency to act as to its knowledge of conclusions; and thus it moves itself. And, in like manner, the will, because it [necessarily] wills the [last] end, moves itself [freely] to will the means."[21]

In summary: the will is a nature necessarily inclined to the good absolutely; consequently, it can be necessitated in the order of object only by a good which is itself absolute, unqualified, unlimited; the possession of this good is man's last end—perfect happiness; this end is sought primarily and implicitly in man's free acts.

[19] *S. Th.*, I–II, 10, 1, *c.*

[20] In the philosophy of morality, we shall see that the existential dependence of a human-act-placed-for-a-proximate-end on this primary and natural tendency of the will to the possession of absolute good is the foundation for the moral order.

[21] *Ibid.*, 9, 3, *c.*

ARTICLE III: The Will Is Not Necessitated (Is Free) as Regards Particular Good

Indetermination to Means: We now propose to show the indetermination, or freedom, of the will in the order of specification as regards proximate ends (means)[22] from the fact of its natural determination to the last end. In other words, we maintain that the foundation for the freedom of the human will regarding particular (limited or qualified) good is the fact of its necessary determination to absolute good. Man has freedom as regards qualified, limited good because he is not free, that is, because he is necessitated, as regards the unqualified, absolute good. No individual good less perfect than that which is universally good can necessitate his will in the order of specification. Although man's will can be inclined to any object which the intellect can apprehend as good, still the will need not be inclined to such an object if the intellect can discern in it some lack of good, some limitation. It follows that the will is not necessitated, is free, to accept or reject limited goods. Hence, although man is necessitated to his last end, the possession of absolute good, he can choose the means which are the immediate (proximate) ends of action.

> Man does not choose of necessity. . . . The reason for this is to be found in the very power of the reason. For the will can tend to whatever the reason can apprehend as good. . . . In all particular goods, the reason can consider the nature of some good, and the lack of some good, which has the nature of an evil; and in this way, it can apprehend any single one of such goods as to be chosen or to be avoided. The perfect good alone, which is happiness, cannot be apprehended by the reason as an evil, or as lacking in any way. Consequently, man wills happiness of necessity, nor can he will not

---

[22] Although ". . . choice is an act of the will already fixed on something to be done by the chooser" (*S. Th.,* I–II, 10, 4, *c.*), that is, of a will fixed on an end, nevertheless, ". . . that which is the end in one operation may be ordained to something as an end, and in this way it is a matter of choice. . . . But the last end in no way is a matter of choice." (*Ibid.,* 13, 4, *c.*)

to be happy, or to be unhappy. Now since choice is not of the end, but of the means . . . it is not of the perfect good, which is happiness, but of other and particular goods. Therefore, man chooses, not of necessity, but freely.[23]

No Necessitation to Particular Goods Necessarily Connected With Happiness: Besides the last end (perfect happiness), which man must necessarily will, there are certain particular goods ". . . which have a necessary connection with happiness, namely, those by means of which man adheres to God, in whom alone true happiness consists."[24] But the connection between these particular goods and the attainment of happiness is not realized with absolute certitude in this life.[25] Consequently, ". . . until through the certitude produced by the vision of God the necessity of such a connection be shown, the will does not adhere to God of necessity, nor to those things which are of God."[26] As regards those particular goods which do *not* have a necessary connection with happiness, it is obvious that man is in no way necessitated to will them, for he can be happy without them.

We conclude that since the will can be necessitated in the order of specification only by universal (unqualified or absolute) good, it is free as regards any particular (qualified or limited) good. This argument we may express in greater detail in the following syllogistic form:

Major: Whatever is necessitated to the possession of absolute (universal, unqualified) good as its last end cannot be necessitated to the possession of particular (limited, qualified) good. For that nature which is fully actuated by a certain perfection cannot be completely actuated by a lesser perfection. By way of example, we

[23] *Ibid.*, 6, *c.*

[24] *Ibid.*, I, 82, 2, *c.*

[25] The problem as to whether those saints who were confirmed in grace saw this connection during their earthly life is transmitted to theology.

[26] *S. Th.*, I, 82, 2, *c.* Although God is the absolute good, and although we know that He is the absolute good, the will, nevertheless, is not necessitated to love Him in this life precisely because the knowledge we have of God is non-proper and analogous.

may observe that if a certain mass of iron requires a magnet of a definite attractive power to draw it, a lesser magnet will not move it.

Minor: But the will is necessitated to the possession of absolute good. For the will has for its formal object the good (being) precisely *as good,* without limitation or qualification; it is the rational appetite proportioned to the intellect. Now the intellect has for its object being (the true) *as being,* and hence can know all beings, all truth, without qualification — including unlimited being. Since being, the true, and the good are convertible, the will also must have an absolute object, which is the absolute good.

Conclusion: Therefore, the will is not necessitated to particular (limited, qualified) good; that is to say, it is free as regards the means to the last end.

Other Arguments for Freedom: The argument for freedom proposed in this article is undoubtedly the most conclusive, for it is founded upon the absolute truth of metaphysical principles. Besides this demonstration, other proofs — from experience and moral obligation — are often advanced. These, however, are absolutely true only in so far as they can be reduced to metaphysical principles.

a) *Argument from experience:* All men who have the use of reason are aware that their internal act of willing is free from any necessary determination. *Before* the act of choice, we know that we are not determined to a single action or to a single course of action; rather, we are able to deliberate concerning various proposed acts. *In* the act of choice, we are aware that we determine ourselves to one alternative though we could choose the other or others. *After* the act of choice, we realize that we could have determined otherwise. These are facts of experience which directly manifest the existence of a free motive power which we call the will.

b) *Moral argument:* No morality, no moral order, is conceivable unless the will is free. The reason is that moral principles suppose moral obligation, which in turn postulates freedom. For moral obligation is a peculiar type of necessity based on intellectual knowledge of a nexus between means and the attainment of the last end; it is a necessity that we can resist; the placing of the means is within our own power. Furthermore, we hold others responsible for not placing such means to the end precisely because it is in their power to place these means. These facts are unintelligible unless man has the power to determine himself to those means which are necessarily linked with the attainment of his end.

> Man has freedom of judgment and choice (*liberum arbitrium*); otherwise counsels, exhortations, commands, prohibitions, rewards, and punishments would be in vain.[27]

ARTICLE IV: The Three Modes of Freedom[28]

We have seen that the will is a nature determined to a last end — happiness. This end to which the will is determined is the principle for desiring that to which the will is not determined. Since we find a threefold indetermination of the will — in regard to the *object,* to the *act,* and to the *relation* of the means (particular good) to the last end — we conclude that man enjoys three types of freedom.

1. Freedom of Specification: As regards the *object* of the will, we have proved that the will is not determined to those things which are means. The reason is that there are diverse means for reaching the end.[29] Hence, the will cannot be determined to one means, whereas natural things are determined not only to their end but also to the means, in as much as for them the means is

[27] *S. Th.,* I, 83, 1, *c.*

[28] Cf. *De Ver.,* XXII, 6.

[29] Sometimes there is only one means for the attainment of a particular end. In such a case, if we have freely willed the particular end (which really is a means to the last end), the sole means is willed necessarily by *necessity of end* (which has been already willed). Cf. *S. Th.,* I, 82, 1, *c.*

identical with their last end. For the end of a material supposit is to be just what it is at every moment of its existence; this end, of course, is actually attained at every moment by every material being. The human will, on the contrary, necessarily desires the last end, but not the immediate (proximate) ends, which are only means to the last end. Consequently, regarding particular goods, the human will has the power to seek this or that. This is called the freedom of *specification.*

2. **Freedom of Exercise:** Regarding its own *act,* the will is not necessarily determined, since where a particular object is concerned, it can act or not act, as it will. This, obviously, is not the case with inanimate beings, for such beings do not move themselves. The will, however, can move itself to will or not-to-will. This is the freedom of *exercise.*

3. **Freedom of Contrariety:** Regarding the *relation* to the *last end,* which is perfect happiness, the will is not necessitated in as much as it can desire: (*a*) that which disposes man's nature to his last end, or (*b*) on the contrary, that which causes an aversion from his true end, even though such an object is desired under the aspect of good. This third mode of indetermination results from two things: first, from the indetermination regarding the object, that is, regarding the means available; second, from the indetermination of the knowledge, which can be right (*recta*) or wrong (*non recta*). Consequently, the will is not determined as regards moral good and moral evil. Man, even though he necessarily desires his last end (perfect happiness), is capable of freely choosing and freely performing a morally evil action because of the pleasure entailed, or on account of the temporal gain obtained. Since, as we shall see in moral philosophy, moral good and moral evil are opposed as contraries,[30] this mode of indetermination is aptly called freedom of *contrariety.*

This last mode of freedom implies a lack of perfect freedom, in

---

[30] *S. Th.,* I–II, 18, 5.

so far as it supposes some form of willful error.[31] It is, therefore, better to say that to will evil is not true freedom, nor a part of freedom, although it can be a manifestation of freedom.

Question II

INTERACTION OF INTELLECT AND WILL IN THE FREE ACT

This question is divided into three articles: (1) the causality of intellect and will in the free act; (2) an analysis of the various will-acts; (3) self-determination of the will through the intellectual judgment.

ARTICLE I: Causality of Intellect and Will in the Free Act

Problem: Man enjoys freedom because his will is not determined to any particular good. In placing a will-act, however, a determination is required, since all actions are definite. This fact gives rise to the question of the origin of this determination. Does the will determine itself; that is to say, does it, by its own power, go from potency to act? That, of course, is impossible, since nothing can be reduced from potency to act except by a being in act. What, then, are the causes of this determination of the will? At this point, it should be noted that we are not questioning the fact of the freedom of man. That has been established in the preceding question. The problem now is: *How* does a free act occur? Or, what is the metaphysical structure of the act of choice?

The will is not the sole source of man's freedom. It is true that the foundation of this freedom is the indetermination of the will as regards the means to the last end. It is also true, as we shall see,

[31] God and the blessed in heaven cannot will evil, cannot sin, because there is no possibility of error in their apprehending and comparing. Cf. *ibid.*, I, 62, 8, *c.*

that the free act of choice belongs to the will as its efficient cause. But the will of man is an appetite which requires and somehow follows *intellectual knowledge* in order that it may act. What is the influence of this knowledge upon the formation of this act? In other words, what part does the intellect play in determining the will-act? St. Thomas Aquinas, when speaking of the liberty of man, constantly uses the term *liberum arbitrium*—freedom of judgment and of choice—thereby implying that the role of the intellect is an important one.

Active Indetermination of the Will: The indetermination of the will is not comparable to that of the possible intellect. The possible intellect, of itself, is passive both in the order of exercise and of specification. It is actuated in the order of efficient causality (order of exercise) by the action of the agent intellect and phantasm acting conjointly as principal and instrumental efficient causes. In the order of specification it is ultimately determined by the object as represented by the phantasm. This indetermination of the possible intellect in two orders is aptly called *passive* indetermination.

The indetermination of the will, on the contrary, is an *active* indetermination, an *active indifference;* this means that the will, being actuated by the Supreme Mover in the order of exercise, is free to will or not will any object as means to the last end.[32] Unlike the possible intellect, it is not necessarily determined in the order of specification by the object which may be presented through in-

[32] When the will produces the immanent act of willing a limited good, its object is willed under the very aspect of good. Underlying the free inclination to this participated good is the necessary inclination of the will as a nature to unparticipated good. Consequently, when the non-necessitating, participated or limited good is presented by the practical intellect, the will must determine itself, that is, exercise its freedom, if this good is to be embraced. Because this limited *good* participates in goodness, it *can* be an object to which the will moves itself; because this object is a *limited* good, the will need not incline itself by the immanent operation of willing. Only unparticipated good adequately presented in intellectual knowledge (and those goods known with absolute certainty to have a necessary connection with the last end) can necessitate the will to incline itself naturally. For that is its nature—to be necessarily inclined to the unparticipated good, the possession of which is man's last end.

tellectual knowledge; rather, the will freely determines the object willed, through its control of the intellect. As regards the order of exercise, we must bear in mind that God's motion of the will[33] does not move the will to one determined particular object; rather, this motion to the universal good makes possible the free act of the will. Indeed, it is by virtue of this actuation of the will in the order of exercise that the will is able to determine itself. ". . . The will is an active principle that is not determined to one thing, but having an indifferent relation to many things. . . ."[34]

Intellect Moves the Will: The question now arises as to whether this active indeterminate principle, the will, can without any knowledge from the intellect determine itself to this or to that operation. This, of course, is impossible, for the will is an appetite, not a cognoscitive faculty; as such, it can love only the *known* good. In order to determine itself to this or that object, to will or not to will, to will what is morally good or evil, knowledge is required. This knowledge is proffered by the intellect, and gives the form, the direction to the will-act. The intellect, therefore, moves the will not in the order of efficient causality, but of specification and finality. The will does not receive a "push" from the intellect; rather, it is enticed, attracted, drawn by what the intellect proposes. To be more exact, we should say that *man* by his practical[35] intellect freely judges that to be good which he loves and desires by his will. Furthermore, there is no priority except that of nature between the act of the intellect and that of the will; their causality is mutual and simultaneous. Man wills what he *freely judges* to be good.

---

[33] "God moves man's will, as the Universal Mover, to the universal object of the will, which is the good. And without this universal motion man cannot will anything. But man determines himself by his reason to will this or that, which is a true or apparent good." (*S. Th.*, I–II, 9, 6, ad 3^{m}.)

[34] *Ibid.*, 10, 4, *c.*

[35] "Just as the imagination of a form without estimation of fitness or harmfulness does not move the sensitive appetite, so neither does the apprehension of the true without the aspect of goodness and desirability. Hence, it is not the speculative intellect that moves, but the practical intellect." (*Ibid.*, 9, 1, ad 2^{m}.)

Will Moves the Intellect: The will, in turn, is capable of a definite control over the intellect. In the formation of the judgment of the good, the will is able to direct the intellect to consider this object rather than another, to see the good rather than the limitation in a given object, and thus to influence the judgment which will specify the act of choice. Why is the will capable of exercising such an influence on the intellectual faculty? This is a very delicate problem and its solution will be found in an analysis of the interaction between intellect and will.

Interaction Between Intellect and Will: While the intellect moves the will in the order of *specification,* the will, as the highest appetite of man, can move the intellect to the *exercise* of its act. The reason for this is that the good in general (*bonum in communi*), universal good, is the object of the will; included in this object as a particular good is the true, which is the object of the intellect. Consequently, the will as an efficient cause is able to move the intellect as well as the other powers of the soul to their good—operation. For the ends and perfections of every faculty are included under the object of the will as particular goods, and the particular goods are contained in the universal, or general, good.[36]

> A thing is said to move in two ways: First, as an end, as when we say that the end moves the agent. In this way the intellect moves the will, because the understood good is the object of the will, and moves it as an end. Secondly, a thing is said to move as an agent, as what alters moves what is altered, and what impels moves what is impelled. In this way the will moves the intellect and all the powers of the soul. The reason is that, wherever we have an order among a number of active potencies, that potency which is related to the universal end moves the potencies which refer to particular ends. . . . Now the object of the will is the good and the end in general (*in communi*), whereas each power is directed to some suitable good proper to it, as sight is directed

[36] Cf. *S. Th.,* I–II, 9, 1, *c.*

to the perception of color, and the intellect to the knowledge of truth (*verum*). Therefore, the will as an agent moves all the powers of the soul to their respective acts, except the natural powers of the vegetative part, which are not subject to our choice (*arbitrio*).[37]

Will Moves Intellect to Consider the Good or Lack of Good: Since the object about which the will is to be determined is a particular good, the will is not necessitated to any particular action. For every limited good may be viewed by the reason (moved by the will) not only as a good, but also as non-good, since it lacks perfection; consequently, reasons may be found for willing and for not willing such a good.

> . . . The will can tend to whatever the reason can apprehend as good. . . . [Now] in all particular goods, the reason can consider the nature of some good and the lack of some good, which has the nature of an evil; and in this way, it can apprehend any single one of such goods as to be chosen or to be avoided. The perfect good alone, which is happiness, cannot be apprehended by the reason as evil, or as lacking in any way.[38]

We see, therefore, that the intellect moved by the will must consider either the good or the evil of the object. The outcome of this is that the practical judgment which results from such willful consideration determines the will to act or not to act, to will this or that in accordance with the direction given to the intellect by the will. Accordingly, both intellect and will play an important role in the free act.

ARTICLE II: Analysis of the Various Will-Acts

Unity of Human Acts: In the analytical study which we are about to make of the various intellectual and volitional acts of man, we should not lose sight of the fact that the ultimate principle of these operations is not the intellect, nor the will; rather, it is the existential unit, the rational supposit, that acts; for "actions

[37] *Ibid.*, I, 82, 4, *c.*
[38] *Ibid.*, I–II, 13, 6, *c.*

belong to supposits." Not the intellect, not the will, but *man* acts. (However, viewed as a rational being, precisely as rational, man acts by means of intellect and will.) In like manner, the intellectual analysis, the dissecting of the psychological process into distinct parts, which we are about to make, should not cause us to forget the unity of human action. I have knowledge of a certain object; I love it; I want it; I choose what appears to be the most apt means to attain it; I proceed to get the object; I reach it; I enjoy its possession. The operations of intellect and will in such a process are obviously successive and distinct, yet they make up one human act. The psychological structure of such actions has a real unity owing to the intention of the will, which directs and integrates all the resulting operations of intellect and will by its efficient dynamism. The human act, although it comprises a complex psychological sequence, has real unity. It is the unity of intention of the will to an end through freely chosen means.

Three Psychological Stages: In the interrelated series of intellectual and volitional operations that make up a human act, we can discover three psychological stages in which the will is concerned: (*a*) with the (proximate) end, (*b*) with the means, and (*c*) with the execution of the means. In each of these stages we shall find various operations of the intellect and will moving each other formally and efficiently. The intellect moves the will in the order of specification by presenting the good to be loved; the will moves the intellect in the order of exercise by directing it to focus upon this or that object, or on this or that aspect of the same object, its goodness or its limitation of goodness. The free act resulting from this mutual and simultaneous causality is ". . . materially the act of the will and formally the act of the intellect."[39] The free act, therefore, is in the will as in a subject, but the formal specification is from the intellect as efficiently directed by a previous or accompanying act of the will.

[39] *S. Th.,* I–II, 13, 1, *c.*

A. Order of the End:[40] The first operation is always an operation of the intellect. For the will can be inclined only to the *known* good.[41] The intellect first *apprehends* the good and presents it to the will. This good, a particular good (and only a means to the last end), is the object of the will-act, its proximate end. The act of the will, *volition,* which follows the apprehension of this limited good and is specified by it, is a free act.[42] The reason is that the "apprehension" of the intellect is really a judging of values, an estimation of the goodness of the object. Now the will can never be necessitated to a particular good, which is only a means to the last end and in which the intellect can discern limitation.[43] Consequently, this will-act is not necessarily determined; that is to say, it is not specified by this end which has been examined and judged in the intellectual apprehension. This free act is the first moment of the psychological process; it is the act of ***volition*** (*velle*).[44]

---

[40] In this analysis, we are not concerned with man's last end. The end referred to here is the proximate or immediate end of the human act, e.g., I kill a man in order to rob him, or to take revenge, or to defend my life. These immediate ends are objects of the will-act of volition. They are not the last end. Consequently, they are freely chosen *as means* to the last end.

[41] There is no question here of purely speculative knowledge, which is concerned with the true, but of the practical knowledge of the good. Only under the formality of the good can the intellect move the will to action. "The knowledge of the true does not move the appetite unless viewed as good and desirable." (*S. Th.,* I–II, 9, 1, ad 2m.)

[42] The will cannot be necessitated to the particular good. The proximate end is only a means to the last end and is therefore a limited good. Hence, the act of volition willing this proximate end is a free action. The spontaneous acts of the sense appetites, on the other hand, are necessary acts and may in their first moments escape rational control. They should not, however, be confused with the acts of the intellectual appetite, the will.

[43] ". . . under the good which is common (*sub bono communi*), there are contained many particular goods to none of which is the will determined." (*S. Th.,* I–II, 10, 1, ad 3m.) The will, however, can sometimes be necessitated to a particular good by "necessity of the end." This merely signifies that when an end has been freely willed, if there is only one possible means by which we can attain that end, the means must be accepted, that is, willed necessarily (*ex necessitate finis*); otherwise, the end is not efficaciously willed. Cf. *ibid.,* I, 82, 1.

[44] Scholastic writers speak of certain necessary motions of the appetite (*motus primo primi*) which sometimes precede a human act and may even influence its moral goodness or evil. These are the spontaneous motions of the sense appetites, the passions or emotions. They are caused directly by sense knowledge and gen-

Following the act of volition, the intellect, under the efficacious influence of the will, considers this good as attainable or not attainable.[45] The intellect then forms a judgment in which it proposes to the will the *end as attainable.*[46] Thereupon follows the act of the will called *intention,* by which we tend to the end and implicitly will the means. This operation, which is specified by the knowledge of the end as attainable, is of course a free act. Should there be only one possible means, the process of the elicited human act is terminated. The reason is that in willing the end, the will necessarily wills this means (*ex necessitate finis*), at least implicitly. The intention in such a case is identical with the act of choice, and the order of execution immediately follows.

We should note that while volition is an inclination of the will to the (proximate) end absolutely, intention is a motion of the will to the end according as this (proximate) end is the term of means.[47] "For when we speak of intending to have health, we mean not only that we will to have it [volition], but that we will to reach it by means of something else [intention]."[48] What this "something else" may be has not yet been determined. Hence, the intellect must now make an inquiry into the means by which the end may be attained.

B. Order of the Means: Let us suppose that there are various means by which the good intended (proximate end) may be

---

erally precede intellectual apprehension. Such spontaneous reactions are not free, since the necessitating object of the sense appetite is the particular, sensible good. Hence, they are not moral acts, but they often affect the morality of the will-act by emotionally "coloring" the phantasm from which the intellectual apprehension, the judgment of reason, is obtained.

45 The will may also direct the intellect (in the order of exercise) to remain in the contemplation of this particular object. This, we shall see in moral philosophy, is a moral act of thought.

46 Should the end be proposed as not attainable, the psychological process is terminated; for we do not intend unattainable goods.

47 "Intention is an act of the will in relation to the end." (*S. Th.,* I–II, 12, 1, ad 4^{m}.) In the intention, in willing the end as attainable, we implicitly will the means. "The intention of the end, and the willing of the means, are one and the same motion." (*Ibid.,* 4, *sed contra.*)

48 *Ibid.,* 1, ad 4^{m}.

attained. In this case, a consideration or deliberation as to what may be the most apt means must follow. Moved by the intention, the intellect in an operation called *counsel* envisages the various means. Concomitant to this operation, which may require a number of distinct correlated acts of intellect and will, is the will-act of *consent*. This is an inclination of the will to the end as the term of any one of a number of means (*in globo*) now under actual consideration. By reason of this act of the will and under its efficient direction, the intellect considers the good discovered in this or that particular means or series of means. As yet, however, there has been no selection of one definite means to be preferred to others. The intellect's deliberation, which is a process of reasoning, terminates in a *practical judgment* or decision (*sententia*), which looks to action. This judgment, which was freely evolved under the influence of the will (in the order of exercise), determines, that is, specifies, the free act of *choice* (*electio*) which follows immediately. We choose what we intellectually *judge* to be the most apt means. Choice, then, is the free act par excellence.[49] It completes what is known as the *elicited* human act.

C. Order of Execution. We have now reached the stage of the *commanded* act, that is, the placing of action by other faculties or by the members of the body under the control of reason. Moved efficiently by the will, which has chosen the means, the intellect issues a *command* ordering the will to direct to action the various faculties and bodily members whose operations are needed for the attainment of the end. This command (*imperium*)[50] of the intellect determines (in the order of specification) the will, which is the supreme mover in man, to move the various powers and members

---

[49] We do not mean to deny that volition and intention, as well as consent, are free. The point we wish to make is that the act of choice manifests more completely to us the nature of freedom.

[50] Note that command is an act of the intellect, a rational directive to action. Failure to understand this important point is one of the root reasons for the prevalent voluntaristic positions regarding law and authority.

to action. The consequent act of the will, which moves the other faculties and bodily members to operation, is called *use*.[51]

Finally, once we have attained the good desired, the intellect understands this fact and presents to the will the knowledge of the possession of the good. This knowledge is an intentional possession[52] of the end originally intended. This *judgment of possession* determines the will specifically to the act of *fruition,*[53] which is intellectual delight, or joy. It is the "rest"[54] of the will in the good possessed.

Diagram of the Will-Acts: The diagram on page 253 may help us to visualize the psychological unity of the various intellectual and volitional operations that comprise a human act.

Variations in Psychological Sequence: Obviously, the analytic order given above is not adhered to rigidly in all our human acts. It may happen that the psychological sequence does not go beyond the consideration and *acceptance of a thought,* without any intention of employing means to attain the object proposed as good. In such a case, in the act of volition the will freely moves the intellect to a continued contemplation of the object viewed as good. In this instance, there is a consent concomitant to volition, that is, an acceptance of the goodness found in the contemplation

---

[51] The act called *use* is found not only in the order of execution but throughout the various psychological moments of the elicited act; for the will moves the intellect and this motion may be considered *use.*

[52] The possession of a limited good when subordinated to the last end is a true happiness, but only *imperfect* and incomplete. When such possession is not properly related to the last end, it is a *false* happiness.

[53] Fruition in the will is the property of the intellectual knowledge of the possession of the end; fruition *necessarily* results from this knowledge. It should be noted also that some delight, some imperfect fruition, may be had at every stage of a human act, even when the act is immediately concerned with the means, and not with the end. The reason is that any action of life, because it is a reality, is a good. Moreover, because a vital action is immanent, it is an ontological perfection of the agent, and therefore is possessed by the agent. Finally, some delight, some imperfect fruition, may accompany the knowledge of the possession of the good even when this possession is imperfect or only in hope (*non in re sed in spe*).

[54] The "rest" of the will is its purest activity; it should not be considered as a cessation from action. Moreover, it is only relatively a "rest" if the good possessed is a limited (particular) good and therefore only a proximate end or means.

Toward bonum - so will is dominant cause.

Order of the End

Intellect: specification; formal causality.

Will: exercise; efficient causality.

1. *Knowledge* of the good; a judging of objective value.

2. *Volition* of the good. Either (*a*) man wills to remain in contemplation of the good, or (*b*) the will moves the intellect to form a judgment of the good as attainable.

3. *Judgment* of the good as attainable.

4. *Intention:* motion of the will to end as the term of means.

Order of Means

5. *Counsel:* a consideration of the various means.

6. A general *consent:* motion of the will to the end as the term of any one of a number of means (*in globo*) now being considered.

7. *Practical judgment:* the decision in which a definite means is proposed as more suitable.

8. *Choice:* the selection of a definite means (or series of means) to the end. This completes the elicited act.

Order of Execution

9. *Command* (*imperium*): an intellectual directive to the will to move the proper faculties or members of the body to action.

10. *Use:* Motion of the powers and members to action by the will.

11. *Judgment* of actual *possession* of the good.

12. *Fruition:*[55] intellectual delight; rest of the appetite in the good possessed.

[55] Note that the act called *fruition* is not a commanded act, but results as a property from knowledge of the possession of the good.

of the object without the will's intending the good as attainable.[56] The imperfect fruition which may accompany and follow this consent terminates the series necessary for a complete human act.

An act of *desire* is had when the operation does not go beyond the act of the will called choice. An act of imperfect desire presupposes an intention which is inefficacious as regards placing the external act. A perfect act of desire is had when the commanded act is not placed solely because of impeding extrinsic causes and not because of a lack of perfection in the intention.

The intention, as we have already indicated, is sometimes identical with the act of choice — when there is only one possible means. The classic example is that of the person who intends to cross the sea and, therefore, necessarily intends to take a ship.

Furthermore, the interrelated operations of intellect and will in the deliberative process that precedes choice may be indefinitely multiplied according to the number of means and series of means that may be available and acceptable. In spite of the various complications, the unity of the psychological process remains undisturbed by virtue of the intention, which in its reaching out to the end unites all the successive psychological moments. Should this intention be withdrawn at any stage of the process, the series of intellectual and volitional acts concerned with the attainment of the particular good in question would be terminated.

ARTICLE III: Self-Determination of the Will Through the Intellectual Judgment

The exercise of freedom in man, we have seen, requires related operations of intellect and will in the order of end, means, and execution. Although the underlying principles of interaction be-

[56] ". . . since the acts of the will reflect on themselves, in each act of the will we can find consent and choice and use; so that we may say that the will consents to choose, and consents to consent, and uses itself in consenting and choosing." (*S. Th.*, I–II, 16, 4, ad 3m.)

tween intellect and will are the same in all three orders, they are made more manifest to us in those acts which are directly concerned with the means. Consequently, in our analysis it will be sufficient to examine the exact causal relationship of intellect and will in the acts immediately concerned with the free act of choice.

Mutual, Simultaneous Causality: According to St. Thomas, the causality of intellect and will is mutual; they act upon each other simultaneously. For this reason their causality may be compared to that of matter and form. Like matter and form, intellect and will have a reciprocal influence in producing the free act. There is, however, this important difference: matter and form are intrinsic causes, whereas the intellect has its influence on the will as an *extrinsic* formal cause.[57] Moreover, the will itself (in consenting) acts in the order of efficient causality upon the intellect as it forms the practical judgment; hence, the will (as well as the intellect) must be an extrinsic cause.

> When the acts of two powers are ordered to one another, in each of them there is something belonging to the other power; and consequently each act can be denominated from either power. Now it is evident that the act of the reason giving direction as to the means, and the act of the will tending to these means according to the reason's direction, are ordered to one another. Consequently, there is to be found something of the reason, viz. order, in the act of the will which is choice; and in counsel, which is an act of reason, something is found of the will, both as matter (since counsel is of what man wills to do), and as motive (because it is from willing the end that man is moved to take counsel regarding the means). And, therefore . . . the Philosopher says that choice is intellect influenced by appetite, thus pointing out that both concur in the act of choice. . . .[58]

[57] The object of the will which specifies the act is really its end. For the good is the end, and the object of the will is viewed as good. Hence, the object which specifies the will-act is the final cause which is an extrinsic cause. Its effect in determining (specifying) the act of the will is had from without by being desired. The will being determined by the object acts in this way, that is, according to the object. We may call this formal-final causality extrinsic.

[58] *S. Th.,* I–II, 14, 1, ad 1^{m}.

Will Determines Itself in the Act of Choice: What is the result of this reciprocal influence? On the one hand, the will acting upon the intellect causes it to consider the good that is in this object rather the good in another.[59] Consequently, the last practical judgment (decision) will affirm that *this* means is to be embraced in preference to all other means. On the other hand, the intellect, by presenting this means to the will as the best, will specify the act of the will, the act of choice. The outcome of this mutual causality is what we call the choosing, the free act of choice. It is free because *its determination* both in the order of specification and in the order of exercise *has been caused by the will itself*. For the will directs the intellect which specifies; and the will, the agent, elicits the act of choice in the order of exercise. Thus, ". . . the act of choice is produced by one faculty [the will] in so far as it is related to the other [the intellect]. Hence, the Philosopher explains that choice is the act of the intellectual appetite or of the appetitive intellect."[60]

The Free Act Is Formally an Act of the Intellect, Materially an Act of the Will: Where, then, is the free act? In both faculties, but in a different manner in each.[61] The act of choice is *materially* an act of the will, but *formally* an act of the intellect. For

> . . . in a sense, reason precedes the will and directs its act, namely, in so far as the will tends to its object according to the order of reason; for the apprehensive power presents to the appetite its object. Accordingly, that act whereby the will tends to something proposed to it as being good, through being ordained to the end by the reason, is materially an act of the will, but formally an act of the reason. Now in such matters, the substance of the act is as the matter in comparison to the order [form] imposed by the higher

---

[59] Even if ". . . two things are proposed as equal under one aspect, nothing hinders us from considering in one of them some particular point of superiority, so that the will is turned toward that one rather than toward the other." (*S. Th.*, I–II, 13, 6, ad 3^m.)

[60] *De Ver.*, XXIV, 4.

[61] *". . . liberum arbitrium esse dicitur facultas voluntatis et rationis."* (*S. Th.*, I–II, 1, 1, *c.*)

> power [reason]. Therefore, choice is substantially, not an act of the reason, but of the will; for choice is accomplished in a certain movement of the soul toward the good which is chosen.[62]

Some philosophers find this doctrine difficult to understand because of an initial confusion of formal and efficient causality. Consequently, they fail to grasp the true meaning of the mutual and simultaneous causality of intellect and will in the act of free choice. For this reason, they insist that the will does not need a practical judgment showing that this object, this act, is better or more suitable here and now. They would have the will—which is an appetite, not a cognoscitive faculty—operate as if it were a complete intellectual supposit capable of holding out against the conclusions of practical reason in the last practical judgment which terminates counsel. This, of course, is contrary to our own experience and fails to explain the specification of the will-act.

The will is free to choose this or that, to act or not to act, to choose moral good or moral evil. But, we insist, the will chooses this definite act precisely because the determination which comes from the last practical judgment has been caused *by its own influence upon the intellect* in the formation of that judgment.[63] For this reason, ". . . the judgment about a particular thing to be done here and now can never be contrary to the appetite."[64] The choice, therefore, is necessarily connected with the practical judgment which gives its specific determination.[65]

Conclusions: (1) The indetermination of the will is an *active* indetermination; that is to say, the will—being actuated (in the order of exercise) by the motion of the First Mover to its last end—is in act to act; this signifies that the will, being determined

---

[62] *Ibid.,* 13, 1, *c.*

[63] ". . . the will in a certain sense moves the reason by commanding its act, and the reason moves the will by proposing to it its object. . . . Hence, it is that both potencies can in some way be informed by each other." (*De Ver.,* XXIV, 6, ad 5^m.)

[64] *Ibid.,* art. 2.

[65] ". . . choice follows the decision (*sententia*) or judgment, which is, as it were, the conclusion of a practical syllogism." (*S. Th.,* I–II, 13, 3, *c.*)

to the last end, is free — in the same operation — to choose the means (particular goods). (2) The intellect, which determines the will in the order of specification (of object), does so by the practical judgment which moves (formally and as an end) the will to perform this definite act. (3) In the formation of the practical judgment, the intellect depends upon the direction given to it by the will in the order of exercise. (4) The free act, accordingly, is materially an act of the will, but formally an act of the intellect.

Question III

GOD AND THE WILL

This question is divided into two articles: (1) the human will is moved by God; (2) the divine motion does not necessitate the will to a particular good.

ARTICLE I: The Human Will Is Moved by God

Problem: The question of God's moving the will has been the source of acrid and endless controversy. Many have feared that a divine motion of the will would mean the destruction of human freedom; they forgot that God always moves according to the nature of the moved instrument, and, moreover, that coercion of the will is an impossibility. Others have held a predetermination of the will to one that is certainly not consonant with the active indetermination of that faculty. The complete solution of this thorny problem we shall leave to the philosophy of God. In the present article, however, we shall endeavor to show that the human will needs to be moved by another (in the order of exercise), and that this other can only be the First Mover, God. In the following article, we shall see that the divine motion does not necessitate the will to a particular limited good.

Necessity of Motion: In accordance with the principle of efficient causality, which states that whatever is moved must be moved by another, it is obvious that the human will must be moved in the order of exercise, that is, of efficient causality. For the will is neither a pure act nor a limited nature always in act to operation; rather, it is an operative potency, and does not act at all times. Hence, it must be put in act as regards operation.

> For everything that is at one time an agent in act and at another time an agent in potency must be moved by a mover. Now it is evident that the will begins to will something, which previously it did not will. Therefore, it must, of necessity, be moved by something to will it. And, indeed, it moves itself . . . in so far as through willing the end it reduces itself to the act of willing the means. . . . And if the will moved itself to will this [end], it must, of necessity, have done this with the aid of counsel following some previous volition. But this process could not go on to infinity. Therefore, we must, of necessity, suppose that the will advances to its first movement by the instigation (*instinctu*) of some exterior mover. . . .[66]

This Mover Is Not the Intellect: It does not suffice to say that the will is moved by the intellect, which knows and proposes the good *as the object* of the will. The reason is that the motion of the intellect is in the line of formal and final causality. It specifies the act of the will; that is, it gives it its form, or direction, but it does not put the will in act to operation. "In this way [as an end] the intellect moves the will, because the understood good is the object of the will, and moves it as an end."[67]

Nor the Sense Appetites: Nor can the sense appetites, either the concupiscible or the irascible, move the will in the order of exercise, that is, as efficient causes. At best, we might say that ". . . according as a man is affected by a passion [of the sensitive appetites], something seems fitting to him, which does not seem so when he

[66] *S. Th.*, I–II, 9, 4, *c*.
[67] *Ibid.*, I, 82, 4, *c*.

is not so affected; and thus that seems good to a man when angered, which does not seem good to him when he is calm. It is in this way that the sensitive appetite moves the will, on the part of the object,"[68] that is, in the order of specification and not in the order of exercise.

Nor a Corporeal Being: It is fairly obvious that no corporeal being can move the will efficiently. For the will is "in the reason"; that is to say, it is the rational appetite. "Now the reason is an [operative] potency of the soul not bound to a bodily organ, and so it follows that the will is a potency absolutely incorporeal and immaterial. But it is evident that no body can act on what is incorporeal, but rather the reverse. . . . Therefore, it is impossible for a . . . body to act directly on the intellect or the will."[69]

God Alone Moves the Will in the Order of Exercise: It follows from all this that no being, no matter how powerful, can move the human will in the order of exercise except the First Mover, God. The reason for this is that ". . . although it is possible for something to move a natural thing, without being the cause of the nature of the thing moved, yet *that alone which is in some way the cause of a thing's nature can cause a natural movement in that thing* [italics added]."[70] In other words, any motion in the order of exercise given to a being by an extrinsic cause which is not God, the author of nature, cannot be a natural motion; it is necessarily violent, that is, not caused by the nature. For example, a man may throw a stone upward, but this motion is not natural to the stone. The natural motion of the stone, on the contrary, is that caused by its nature, that is, by a form which has been imprinted in it by God, the author of nature. Now the motion of the will, to be natural, must be voluntary, not coerced. Therefore, no other being beside God can move the will in the order of

---

68 *S. Th.*, I–II, 9, 2, *c.*

69 *Ibid.*, 5, *c.* This article is directed primarily against the pseudo-science of astrology.

70 *Ibid.*, 6, *c.*

exercise, since such motion would not be natural and, consequently, not voluntary.

Only God Can Be the Cause of the Nature of the Will: That the cause of the nature of the will is none other than God is evident for two reasons: (1) The will is an operative potency of a spiritual subject, the soul. Since the soul cannot be educed from matter, it must be created by God together with its potencies. Creation, however, is an operation of God alone. (2) The will is naturally inclined to the universal good. But only God, who is the universal good, can cause a universal inclination. Accordingly, God alone can be the cause of the nature of the will.[71]

We see, then, that God, who moves all things according to their natures, moves the will in the order of exercise according to the nature of the will,[72] so that the will may be able to determine the free act of choice by influencing the intellect in the formation of the practical judgment.

The Will Determines Itself: The determination of the will, therefore, comes about in this wise: The will is moved by God necessarily to universal good, and, consequently, it is able freely to move and direct the intellect. The intellect, in turn, by its judgment, is able to specify the act of the will, that is, to determine the will in the line of formal and final causality. Hence, it can be said that the will determines its own free act — not immediately, but through the medium of the intellectual judgment. In a true sense, the will *moves itself* (*voluntas movetur a seipsa*). It does so mediately by moving the intellect; it does so immediately in the act of choice in the order of exercise. For, being moved to act (operate) by the divine motion, and having received from the intellect the determination needed in the order of specification, it wills freely to act or not to act, to do this or to do that. This is the *act of a perfect being* (*actus perfecti*), that is, of a subject which, being in act, acts immanently.

---

[71] *Loc. cit.*

[72] *De Malo,* VI, art. unic.

ARTICLE II: The Divine Motion Does Not Necessitate the Will to the Particular Good

No Coercion of the Will: The divine motion is necessitating in as much as the will, being moved by God, necessarily tends to the last end. This necessitation of the will to the universal good is not a coercion. Rather, it is the most perfect, the most *natural* motion of the will. The question here is whether the divine motion could ever necessitate the will to a limited (particular) good. Such a necessitation would be a coercion; that is to say, it would be against the nature of the will, which is free as regards the particular good because it is necessitated to the absolute (universal) good. A divine motion, therefore, could not necessitate the will to a particular good since such an action would be contrary to the will's nature. In brief: the act of the will is an *inclination* to the good; a coerced inclination, however, involves a contradiction, and hence is impossible.

God Moves in Accordance With the Nature of the Moved: Now God always moves an instrument in accordance with the nature of the being which is being moved. But it is the nature of the will to act freely regarding the good that is particular and limited. Therefore, the motion from God can in no way constrain the will against its inclination. Such a constraint would imply the *annihilation* of a free nature. Rather, God's motion naturally and necessarily inclining the will to the universal good *establishes* the freedom of the will as regards particular good. The will, therefore, is not coerced to the particular good. The passages in the writings of St. Thomas which express this notion are common. The following are a few of the more important:

> God, as the Universal Mover, moves man's will to the *universal object of the will,* which is the good. And without this universal motion man cannot will anything. But man *determines himself* by

his reason to will this or that, which is a true or apparent good [italics added].[73]

God operates in every agent according to the nature of that agent. . . . Whence it follows that although God operates as a cause in the hearts of men, this does not prevent human souls themselves from being the causes of their motions.[74]

That is commonly called an instrument which is a mover moved by another, whether a principle of motion be present in it or not. And, therefore, the aspect of liberty should not be denied to an instrument entirely; because a thing can move itself, even though moved by another. And such is the case with the human soul.[75]

The will is said to have control of its act . . . because *the first cause does not act on the will in such a way as to determine it necessarily to one thing,* as it determines a nature; and therefore the determination of the act remains in the power of the reason and of the will [italics added].[76]

Since the will can incline to either of two things as it pleases, it is determined to one of them by something, namely, by the counsel of reason, and not by some extrinsic agent.[77]

Since God moves all things according to their nature . . . He moves the will also according to its condition, not necessitating it, but leaving it disposed *indeterminately to many.* And hence it is clear that if the motion of the will be considered as regards the exercise of its act, it is not moved necessarily [italics added].[78]

God operates in natural things as one supplying the power of acting; and at the same time determines the nature to such and such an action; but He acts on the faculty having the freedom of choice in such a way that when He supplies the power of acting, the will itself acts while He is operating; the determination of the action and the end is firmly established in the power of the faculty

---

[73] *S. Th.,* I–II, 9, 6, ad 3m.
[74] *De Ver.,* XXIV, 1, ad 3m.
[75] *Ibid.,* ad 5m.
[76] *De Pot.,* III, 7, ad 13.
[77] *De Malo,* III, 3.
[78] *Ibid.,* VI, art. unic.

having freedom of choice, however. And, therefore, it retains control of its act.[79]

Conclusions: (1) In the order of exercise, the will is moved only by God. This motion, which is not specified to a limited (particular) object, implies no determination, except of course to the universal good. Consequently, the divine motion does not coerce; that is to say, it does not necessitate the will to the particular good. (2) The will is moved, but not necessitated, in the order of specification by the object (the proximate end) through the intellect. (3) The will being actuated in the order of exercise by the divine motion can move all powers, even itself. (4) Therefore, it controls and directs the intellect regarding the required specification for its act of choice. (5) Being actuated in the order of exercise by a divine motion, and in the order of specification by the intellect, the will places its free act, the act of a perfect being (*actus perfecti*).

SUMMARY

Question I

NECESSITY AND FREEDOM OF THE WILL

Article I: *The Will Cannot Be Coerced* (*i.e., Necessitated in the Order of Exercise*)

1. Freedom implies the *absence* of *necessity* of some sort.
2. The human will is an operative potency which *needs* to be *actuated* in:

a) The order of *exercise,* for the will is not always acting;

b) The order of *specification,* for the will does not always will the same.

3. The will cannot be necessitated in the order of exercise (*coerced*) because the will-act is an inclination to the good; a *coerced inclination* is a contradiction.

Article II: *The Will Is Necessitated to Absolute Good* (*in the Order of Specification*)

1. The will is the rational appetite — the appetite proportioned to the intellect; it has for its *formal object* the good *as good* (absolutely).

[79] *In II Sent.,* dist. 25, q. un., art. 3.

2. Consequently, that object which is good *universally,* whose perfection is absolute, so that its every aspect is desirable, cannot be rejected by the will, if the will is to act at all; i.e., the will is necessitated to absolute good.

3. The will is a *nature* necessarily inclined to the last end, perfect happiness. Just as the first principles are necessarily known (by the intellect), so is the last *end* (perfect happiness) *necessarily* and *primarily* sought (by the will); it is free, however, as regards the means (particular goods) to the end.

Article III: *The Will Is Not Necessitated (Is Free) as Regards Particular Good*

1. *Metaphysical* argument: That which is necessitated to absolute (universal, unqualified) good cannot be necessitated by any lesser (particular, qualified, limited) good, which is but a means to the last end. (For in all particular goods the reason can consider the lack of some good.) But the will is necessitated to absolute good as its last end. Therefore, it is free as regards particular good.

2. We *experience* that the act of willing is free from any necessary determination BEFORE, IN, and AFTER the free act.

3. The moral *order* and moral *obligation* postulate freedom.

Article IV: *The Three Modes of Freedom*

1. Of *specification* — to will this or that.
2. Of *exercise* — to will or not to will.
3. Of *contrariety* — to will moral good or moral evil.

Question II

INTERACTION OF INTELLECT AND WILL IN THE FREE ACT

Article I: *Causality of Intellect and Will in the Free Act*

1. The intellect moves the will in the order of *specification,* of object (of formal and final cause) by proposing the intellectually known good.

2. The will moves the intellect in the order of *exercise* (of efficient cause) to consider this object rather than that, its good or its limitation.

Article II: *Analysis of the Various Will-Acts*

Order of End

1. *Knowledge* of the good.	2. *Volition:* motion of will to good absolutely.
3. *Judgment* of the good as attainable.	4. *Intention:* motion of will to end as the term of means.

Order of Means

5. *Counsel:* a consideration of the various means.
6. *Consent:* motion of will to end as term of any one of a number of means (*in globo*) now under consideration.
7. *Practical judgment:* the decision in which a definite means is proposed as more suitable.
8. *Choice:* the selection of a definite means (or series of means) to the end.

Order of Execution

9. *Command:* an intellectual directive to move the proper faculties or members of the body to action.
10. *Use:* motion of the powers and members of body to action by the will.
11. *Judgment* of actual *possession* of the good.
12. *Fruition:* intellectual delight; rest of the appetite in the good possessed.

Article III: *Self-Determination of the Will Through the Intellectual Judgment*

1. The causality of intellect and will in the free act is *mutual* and *reciprocal.* The reason gives direction as to the means and the will tends to these means according to the reason. It is from willing the end that man is moved to deliberate (take counsel) concerning the means.

2. The will *determines itself* in the act of choice by moving the intellect to form the practical judgment which specifies its own (the will's) act of choice.

3. The free act is *formally* an act of the intellect, *materially* an act of the will.

Question III

GOD AND THE WILL

Article I: *The Human Will Is Moved by God*

1. *Necessity* of motion: The will is an operative potency not always in act (in the order of exercise); hence it must be placed in act.

2. This mover is *not:* (*a*) the *intellect,* whose motion is in the order of specification, (*b*) nor the *sense appetites,* which may affect the judgment of the intellect, (*c*) nor any *corporeal being,* which could not act on an immaterial power.

3. *God alone* moves the will in the order of exercise; for that alone

which is the cause of the *nature* of a thing can cause a *natural* movement in that thing. Other beings can cause only a violent motion.

4. Only God can be the *cause of the nature* of the will, for: (*a*) the will is an operative potency of a spiritual subject, the soul, which comes into existence by creation; (*b*) the will is naturally inclined to the universal good. But God alone who is the universal good can cause a universal inclination.

Article II: *The Divine Motion Does Not Necessitate the Will to the Particular Good*

1. A necessary motion to a particular good would be a *coercion,* that is, contrary to the will's nature, whose act is an *inclination* to the good.

2. God moves in accordance with the nature of the moved. By inclining the will necessarily and naturally to the universal good, he *establishes* the freedom of the will as regards particular good.

3. Moved necessarily to the universal good, the will moves itself *freely* through the judgment of reason to the particular good.

CHAPTER IX

THE HABITS

PROLOGUE

Man is capable of a vast range of operations. The subject from which these operations ultimately proceed is the existential unit, the human supposit; *that which* (*principium quod*) acts is the person. The proximate and immediate principles *by which* (*principia quibus*) the rational supposit acts are the operative potencies. The faculties, however, are not able to perform the actions needed for man's development and perfection *constantly, easily,* and *with pleasure* unless they are informed and determined by acquired dispositions which prepare them for action. These dispositions, which are formed by repeated actions, incline the operative potency in which they inhere to activity of a definite type. Such inclinations to actions of a determinate species we call *habits,* and — more specifically — operational habits.

Existence of Habits: That man possesses habits of operation in the order of knowledge is obvious from the fact that our knowledge is not always in act nor merely in potency. There is, for example, a difference between one who has acquired the science of geometry and one to whom this realm of knowledge is still a closed field. As regards the latter, his intellect is still purely in potency with respect to this branch of human knowledge. As regards the former, a teacher of geometry, let us say, it is obvious that his intellect possesses some actuation which the intellects of his prospective students do not have. Though his intellect is not always in act (second act, operation) as regards this knowledge, still he is intellectually different from his students in that his intellect is disposed and inclined to pass into act as regards the knowledge of geometry with a certain facility, accuracy, and even pleasure. In brief, the science of geometry is present in his intellect, not always actually, nor merely potentially, but *as a habit.*

Justice and injustice are habits of the will. Although this faculty naturally tends to its own good, nevertheless, by repeated choices it can develop the disposition or inclination to will to others the good due to them and thus to act in accordance with the rights of others. It is evident that in our dealings with others we carefully discriminate between the just and the unjust, that is, between those who possess the virtue (the good habit) of justice and those who have formed the vice (the evil habit) of injustice. We distinguish, too, between the temperate and the intemperate, between the brave and the cowardly, that is, between those who actually possess good habits in the sense appetites facilitating the political control of the passions by reason, and those who lack such dispositions and hence are subject to the contrary and opposed vices. Accordingly, that man acquires and possesses habits of operation, both good and bad, is beyond dispute.

Psychological and Moral Aspects of Habits: The question of habits can be studied from two points of view: the psychological and the moral. In the philosophy of man we inquire into the metaphysical causes of habits to arrive at a knowledge of their intimate nature; such an inquiry considers the psychological aspect. The moral aspect of habits, however, will be considered in the science of ethics, which views good and bad habits, virtues and vices, as related to man's nature and to his ultimate end. These two considerations are so intimately connected that the science of morals — which in its detailed application is largely a study of the various habits of man — would be relegated to the task of solving practical cases if it did not depend upon and constantly use the data secured by the psychological study of the habits. Indeed, were this dependence lost sight of, ethics would be dislodged from the high status of a philosophical science and reduced to a mere art — the art of casuistry. Hence, the psychological study of the habits, and of the operative potencies in which they inhere, is an immediate and necessary prolegomenon if we are to have a true science of moral philosophy, and not a series of ethical postulates that appear neither intelligible nor certain.

Division: This treatise on habits will be divided into six articles: (1) the nature of habits; (2) the need for habits; (3) the subjects of habits; (4) the cause of formation of habits; (5) the growth and decrease of habits; and (6) classification of habits.

ARTICLE I: Nature of Habits[1]

Definition: "The word *habit* is taken from 'to have' (*habere*). Now habit is derived from this word in two ways: in one way, inasmuch as man, or any other thing, is said to have something; in another way, inasmuch as a thing is disposed in some way either in regard to itself (*habet se*), or in regard to something else."[2] It is in this second sense that habit signifies, as Aristotle states, *a quality whereby a thing is disposed well or ill, either in itself or in relation to something else.*[3] Thus health is a quality by which the body is disposed well in itself; the virtue of justice, on the other hand, is a quality whereby man is disposed well to actions that are concerned with the rights of others.

Quality: Quality, in turn, is defined as *a determination of the substance in itself, regarding its accidental being, according to a*

[1] *S. Th.,* I–II, 49.
[2] *Ibid.,* 1, *c.*
[3] Aristotle, *Metaphysics,* V, text 20. "Disposition is the order of that which has parts either as to place, or as to potentiality, or as to species." (*Ibid.,* text 19.)

certain measure.[4] This definition must be explained. Quality determines a *substance;* it is a modification of a subject already constituted in being. Hence, it is a determination of the subject as regards its *accidental* or secondary being ("to be") as opposed to its primary or existential perfection. What (specific) essence is to being considered simply and primarily, quality is to the secondary actuation or development of being. Quality is a determination of the substance *in itself;* it is not a relation, which signifies merely "to another." The phrase *according to a certain measure* indicates the reason for the different types of quality; for qualities are distinguished according to the four modes in which they may determine the subject with relation to its accidental perfection. We may, accordingly, distinguish four types of qualities consequent upon the measure of the accidental dispositions: (1) in regard to the very nature of the subject—habits; (2) in regard to action—the operative potencies; (3) in regard to being acted upon—passive quality; (4) in regard to quantity—external form (figure) or shape. We see, then, that habits belong to the first type of qualities; they are modes or determinations of a subject as regards the very nature of the thing and its operations.

Entitative and Operational Habits: With Aristotle, we have defined habit as "a quality whereby a thing is disposed well or ill, either in itself or in relation to something else." The last phrase, *either in itself or in relation to something else,* suggests the further distinction between two species of habits. One species embraces the *entitative* habits, which are in general the dispositions of the body, such as health, beauty, and the like. The other includes the *operational* habits, which dispose the soul through its operative potencies to action. In this treatise, we are not concerned with the entitative dispositions of the body, but with the operational habits whereby man is disposed to perform certain actions. The operational habits are defined by St. Thomas as ". . . *qualities or*

[4] Cf. *S. Th.,* I–II, 49, 2, *c.*

forms inhering in an [operative] potency and inclining that potency to actions of a determinate species."[5] We should note that these habits do not determine, that is, necessitate, the operative potency to a definite act; rather, they *dispose* it to perform more easily a certain operation or series of operations.

Habits Imply Order to Action: The operational habits are forms — accidental forms — which inhere in an operative potency and dispose it to perform definite actions with ease, constancy, and pleasure. These habits, ". . . even on the part of the subject (operative potencies) in which they are, imply primarily and principally relation to an act."[6] They do not actuate fully the operative potency whose operation they modify. The reason is, of course, that the nature of an operative potency consists in a relation, an order to a *complete* act, namely, operation; habits, however, are but dispositions, inclinations to operation along a definite line.

Habits Are Incomplete Acts: Although an operational habit is a form and hence an act, it is not a complete act. These habits, explains St. Thomas, are not perfect acts, nor are they mere potency; rather they are ". . . midway between pure potency and perfect act."[7] "Habit is an act, in so far as it is a quality; and in this respect it can be a principle of operation. It is, however, in a state of potency in respect to operation. Wherefore, habit is called first act, and operation, second act. . . ."[8]

The operational habits, then, manifest a twofold relation. As regards the operation, they are in potency; as regards the faculty in which they inhere, they are acts, for they determine, that is, incline, the potency to this or that action.[9] Since they do not fully

[5] *S. Th.,* I–II, 54, 1, *c.*

[6] *Ibid.,* 49, 3, *c.*

[7] *Ibid.,* 50, 4, ad 2^{m}.

[8] *Ibid.,* 49, 3, ad 1^{m}.

[9] "For a habit is compared to a power of the soul as act to potency, since a power of itself is indeterminate and by means of the habit is determined to this or that." (*De Virt. in Com.,* III.) Much of what was explained about the operative potencies can be applied to habits.

actuate the operative potency, but merely prepare it for the complete act, which is operation, habits, somewhat like motion, are imperfect acts.

ARTICLE II: Need for Habits[10]

Three Necessary Conditions for Formation of Habits: St. Thomas proposes three conditions which must exist in order that a habit may be formed. What he really wishes to show is why habits are extremely necessary for the full development of man.

"The first condition is that what is disposed should be distinct from that to which it is disposed; and so, that it should be related to it as potentiality to act."[11] This statement, of course, implies the most fundamental reason why we need habits. Unlike God, we are not pure act; rather, we are imperfect beings seeking perfection. The partial actuation of the good habit brings us closer to the goal of our existence.

"The second condition is that what is in potency in regard to something else should be capable of determination in several ways and to various things."[12] This suggests the immediate and the essential reason for our need of habits. Our specifically human faculties, which of themselves are indeterminate, can be actuated in various ways, and some of these actuations are not suitable to our nature. Good habits (virtues) will make it relatively easy for us to perform those actions which will perfect our nature, and to avoid those actions which would injure and frustrate our nature as regards its ultimate end. We should note, therefore, that strictly speaking there are no habits (*habitus*) in animals, for they cannot determine the end of their actions.

"The third condition is that in disposing the subject to one of those things to which it is in potency, several things should concur,

---

[10] *S. Th.*, I–II, 49, 4, *c.*

[11] *Loc. cit.*

[12] *Loc. cit.*

capable of being adjusted in various ways, so as to dispose the subject well or ill to its form or to its operation."[13] In other words, the various factors which enter into the placing of an act need to be adjusted properly, else the proper measure and direction of the action may not be in proportion to our nature and end. Here again, habits — especially the habit of prudence — are needed to direct us to the proper means and, as a result, to the true end.

Good Habits, the Complement of the Faculty: Operative potencies look to action, which is their sole *raison d'être*. These potencies, or faculties — as they are often called — are *capacities* for action; they do not, however, necessarily give a *facility* for action. For, those operative potencies which are the subject of habits are of themselves *indeterminate* as regards all actions that fall within their range. In order that they may be inclined to actions of a definite type with a certain ease, constancy, and pleasure, these potencies must be perfected, complemented, by dispositions to actions that will complete the nature. Such dispositions to actions which will perfect nature are the good habits, the *virtues*.

As regards man's *human* acts — the moral acts, over which he has the power of self-determination — it is necessary that he acquire good habits to complement those operative potencies from which the moral act proceeds or which may have an influence on the moral act. The will, for example, needs to be complemented by the habit of justice, inclining it to will to others the good that is due to them. Prudence is needed in the practical intellect so that man will judge rightly concerning the means to his last end. Since the sense appetites are able, by the violence of the passions, to obscure the judgments of reason which specify the will-act, it will be necessary for the perfection of man to develop good habits moderating the passions in accordance with the norm of right reason.

It is true that even if there were no habits residing in these

[13] *S. Th.*, I–II, 49, 4, *c.*

lower faculties (the concupiscible and irascible appetites) the will and reason, since they are superior powers, could circumvent them and by a quasi-violence oblige them to obey. But in such a case, as St. Thomas remarks with profound psychological insight, a certain sadness would follow because of the lack of integration and order among the faculties. Consequently, if habits were not gradually developed to facilitate the political control of the passions, reason might in the end give up its attempt to "force," as it were, the lower appetites to obey. This is clearly manifested in the case of those who have strong sensory desires which, after a few feeble attempts to control, they allow to overcome reason.

Hence, we can readily see why we should form good habits, or virtues,[14] in the sense appetites from early youth, in order to enable us to meet difficulties and temptations bravely when they arise in our life. Courage and fortitude, for example, will help us to meet reverses and obstacles with equanimity; humaneness (*mansuetudo*) and gentleness will alleviate anger; chastity will preserve us from inordinate venereal pleasures; sobriety and abstinence will keep us from losing self-control in the enjoyment of food and drink.[15] Thus the passions, instead of becoming tyrannical masters, will play the role of useful servants and will be an aid to the moral perfection of man.

---

[14] The psychology of bad habits, or vices, is identical with that of the good habits. They are formed and developed by repeated actions elicited under the control of reason.

[15] It might appear from this that the passions are opposed to the good habits, and therefore are against reason and bad in themselves. This is not true. Passions, as was explained earlier, are the acts of the sense appetites. They are, therefore, good in themselves and extremely helpful in the complete development of man. It is because they are apt to go beyond the proper measure required by the nature of man that they can become harmful. Hence, good habits, or virtues, must be acquired in order that the passions may be *controlled* by the higher part of the soul, not that they may be destroyed.

It should be noted, however, that the revolt of the sense appetites against reason is due fundamentally to original sin. Hence, this inordinateness cannot be removed entirely by the implanting and developing of virtues, but it is largely diminished by them. Still, the passions retain their proper motions and at times may rise against reason; in such cases, they will have to be curbed. (Cf. *De Virt. in Com.*, IV.)

ARTICLE III: Subject of Habits[16]

A Body Is Not the Subject of Operational Habits: As we have seen in the preceding article, the operative potencies which are the subject of habits are *determinable* in diverse ways. Consequently, neither such faculties nor their inherent habits can be found in bodies. Moreover, the natural forces in inanimate beings and plants cannot possess habits, for they are determined to one mode of action.

> An [operative] potency sometimes has a relation to many things; and then it needs to be determined by something else. But if a potency has not a relation to many things, it does not need a habit to determine it. . . . For this reason the natural forces do not perform their operations by means of habits: because they are of themselves determined to one mode of operation.[17]

The same may be said of the judgment of the estimative power in animals. Hence, brute animals are incapable of forming and developing habits in the strict sense. Man alone can be the subject of operational habits in the precise meaning of the term.

Nor can operational habits inhere principally in the *human* body, though its act is the spiritual soul. The reason is that these habits are dispositions to operation. Now the soul, and not the body (of which it is the act), is the primary principle of action. Consequently, habits — since they are determinants of action — are principally modifications of the soul, not of the body. We may add that since the soul is not its "to be," it can operate only through its operative potencies. The operative habits, accordingly, do not inhere immediately in the essence of the soul, but in the faculties.

A Body Can Be the Subject of Entitative Habit: "If, however, we speak of the disposition of the subject to form, thus a habitual

---

[16] *S. Th.*, I–II, 50.
[17] *Ibid.*, 49, 4, ad 2m.

disposition can be in the body, which is related to the soul as a subject is to its form. And in this way health and beauty and such like are called habitual dispositions."[18]

Not Every Potency Is the Subject of Habits: Not every potency can be the subject of operational habits, but only those potencies which are both *agent* and *acted upon.* There are powers, such as the agent intellect, which are always in act. These obviously do not need to be further determined by habits, since they are in act to act. There are other operative potencies which act only in so far as they are being moved. Such, for example, are the external senses. They are in act, and they act, because the sensed object here and now acts upon them. For that reason the species which is educed from the potency is more like a passion or a motion than like a form. Consequently, in view of the fact that a habit is a form which remains in the faculty, there can be no habit in the external senses, since a passion or change cannot be permanent. Hence, only those operative potencies which are both agent and acted upon and which, moreover, are acted upon in such a way that they are not determined to one definite operation, can be the subject of habits.[19] Since such faculties retain a certain freedom of action, they can be made more complete for action by something superadded; not, however, by a mere passion which does not endure, but by a form which remains and is not easily removed. In this way, without being determined to one action, a faculty of this kind can be made more complete and inclined to action of a definite type. Let us now see which of the operative potencies of man can be complemented by habits.

Habits in the Internal Senses: From what we have previously noted, we must infer that the internal senses can acquire habits in so far as those senses act in accordance with the judgment (command) of reason, but not when their actions result from merely

---

[18] *Ibid.,* 50, 1, *c.* One entative habit is found in the soul, namely sanctifying grace.
[19] Cf. *De Virt. in Com.,* I.

natural instinct. "According as they act from natural instinct, they are ordained to one thing, even as nature is; but according as they act at the command of reason, they can be ordained to various things. And thus there can be habits in them. . . ."[20] It is only because of this dependence upon reason that the senses are not determined to one operation, but may be directed by the higher powers to various possible actions.

The Intellect Is the Subject of Habits: In the first place, the *possible* intellect is a subject of habits. For that which is in potency to many is an apt subject of habits. But the possible intellect is in potency to all knowledge; therefore, it is an apt subject of habits.

Now the habits in the possible intellect will consist in the intelligible species. These, however, are said to be habits not in so far as they actuate the intellect, but in so far as they remain in the intellectual memory. Consequently, though the intellect is not being actuated here and now—and therefore is not actually considering this knowledge—it is able to recall and to consider at will, and with a facility which it did not possess before. In order to acquire the habitual species, the intellect had to discover and learn. Now it needs only to recall.

As regards intellectual memory, the Arab philosopher Avicenna proposes this difficulty: a species which is retained in the intellect actuates the operative potency. Consequently, if the intellect were informed by even *one* habitual species, it would never be able to stop thinking about that one object, and could think of none other. The answer to this difficulty, of course, lies in the fact that an intelligible species which is retained as a habit is not a perfect act, but an imperfect one. Therefore, it does not actuate the operative potency, the possible intellect, but merely prepares for that actuation.

The intelligible species is sometimes in the intellect only in potentiality, and then the intellect is said to be in potentiality. Some-

[20] *S. Th.*, I–II, 50, 3, *c.*

> times the intelligible species is in the intellect as regards the ultimate completion of the act, and then it understands in act. And sometimes the intelligible species is in a middle state, between potentiality and act: and then we have habitual knowledge. In this way the intellect retains the species, even when it does not understand in act.[21]

The Will and the Sense Appetites Are Subjects of Habits: It is true that regarding the universal good, which is its end, the will is sufficiently inclined by its very nature and needs no habit to complete it. Regarding the means, however, which are particular goods, the will is free and needs good habits. For

> . . . since it is necessary for the end of human life, that the appetitive power be inclined to something fixed, to which it is not inclined by the nature of the power, which has a relation to many and various things, therefore it is necessary that in the will and in the other appetitive powers, there be certain qualities to incline them, and these are called habits.[22]

A general argument to show that all appetitive faculties of man, namely, the will as well as the sense appetites, are in need of habits and can be the subject of them, may be proposed thus: Every power which may be variously directed to act needs a habit whereby it is well disposed to act. But the will, because it is a rational power, may be variously directed to act; and the sense appetites—inasmuch as they act at the command of reason and not from natural instinct—can be ordered to various things. Therefore, both will and sense appetites are the subjects of habits.[23]

ARTICLE IV: The Cause of Habits[24]

It might be asked whether the nature[25] of a being can of itself be the efficient cause of habits. We do not deny that nature is the

[21] *Ibid.*, I, 79, 6, ad 3^m^.
[22] *Ibid.*, I–II, 50, 5, ad 1^m^.
[23] Cf. *ibid.*, 50, 5, *c.*
[24] Cf. *ibid.*, 51.
[25] By *nature* we understand the substance of a being considered as the first principle of operation.

cause of the entitative dispositions such as health and beauty, which are in the body, but if we restrict our question to the operational habits, the answer is that nature cannot cause the habit itself, although it may prepare for its production and development.

To begin with, we may state that what is from nature are the various *inclinations* and *aptitudes* to habits, not the habits themselves. These must be formed by the operations of the faculties. Aptitudes and inclinations to habits arise both from specific and from individual nature. Obviously, those which flow from the specific nature are common to all men, while those which are due to the individual nature are individual characteristics.

Specific Nature: There are in the specific nature, and therefore in every man, an active and a passive principle which make possible the formation and the development of the natural inclinations of the individual, as well as of all other habits. These two elements are sometimes called habits in their inception, or inchoative habits. We shall consider the diverse faculties which are the seats of habits—namely the intellect, the will, and the two sense appetites—and indicate in each the active and passive elements which make for the specific inchoation of habits.[26]

a) *Intellect:* The possible intellect is in potency to all intelligible things. It is the passive element for all intellectual habits. Now intellectual habits consist in the retained species, and, consequently, they suppose the actual previous knowledge of these intelligible beings. This knowledge is caused by the agent intellect, the active element, which by its light actuates the objects that were only intelligible in potency. Now some of the intelligibles become known without study; they result immediately from any knowledge by a quasi-intuition. These are the first principles in the speculative as well as the practical order. The habitual knowledge of these is called the *habit of principles*. Obviously, there is in every man a natural tendency to know these first principles. We may say, therefore,

[26] *De Virt. in Com.*, VIII.

that the habit of principles is caused by the specific nature, and hence is common to all men. And, let us add, these first principles are the foundation for all the habits of science which can be acquired by study.[27]

b) *The will:* The active principle in the will is its natural inclination to its end — the good. The passive principle is the very indetermination of the will regarding a particular good. Because of these two principles, habits may be developed not only in the will, but also in the other faculties in so far as they depend on the will and are under its control. From the consideration of the nature of the appetitive faculties, it is clear that we can find no specific determination to any particular habit. "The reason for this is that the inclination to its proper objects, which seems to be the beginning of a habit, does not belong to the habit, but rather to the very nature of the operative potencies."[28]

c) *The irascible and concupiscible appetites* can be controlled by reason. Hence, they are capable of receiving habits (passive element). These habits are made more perfect according as the faculties are disposed (active element) to seek the good of reason.

All the dispositions to habits mentioned above flow from or are caused by the specific nature. Hence, these natural dispositions — inchoative habits — are found in all men.

Individual Nature:

a) *Intellect:* It is a matter of common knowledge that certain men have greater intellectual gifts, greater talents, for some particular science or art. Foremost among the various factors which could be mentioned as cause for these natural dispositions are the conditions of the internal sense organs — the brain cells. These may be better disposed to acquire the sense knowledge required for this or that science. "In respect of the individual nature, a habit of knowledge is natural as to its beginning, in so far as one man,

---

[27] Cf. *S. Th.*, I–II, 51, 1, *c*.
[28] *Loc. cit.*

from the disposition of his organs of sense, is more apt than another to understand well, since we need the sensitive powers for the operation of the intellect."[29]

b) *Will:* There can be no individual determination of the will, since the will is a spiritual inclination which depends on another spiritual faculty for its specific determination to act.

c) *The sense appetites:* On the other hand, the sense appetites depend upon the individual nature, and, therefore, the organs of the body are often the fundamental reason for certain inclinations to definite habits. "On the part of the body, in respect of the individual nature, there are some appetitive habits by way of natural beginnings. For some are disposed from their own bodily temperament to chastity or meekness or the like."[30]

There is, therefore, a certain beginning (*inchoatio*) of good habits or virtues, which follows the nature of each individual according to his natural temperament; and this is due to the disposition of his body, or again, says St. Thomas, it could be caused by a direct divine impression. Such an impression or such a temperament is not a virtue but the natural aptitude for a virtue. To acquire a complete habit, we need action.[31]

Nature, therefore, is not the cause of the complete habit. Indeed, unless we perform constant actions, the inchoation which happens to be in an individual will never be developed into a real habit.[32] Actions — frequent intense actions — are necessary for such development.

---

[29] *S. Th.*, I–II, 51, 1, *c*.

[30] *Loc. cit.*

[31] We are prescinding here from the fact that in the order of grace, the supernatural order, God can and does infuse the theological virtues in the intellect and will without any action on the part of the unconscious infant. In philosophy the objects of our search are only the habits that are proportioned to man's nature. And while we do not deny that God did infuse such natural habits in certain cases, we are inquiring here into the ordinary way in which virtues may be acquired.

[32] A point of interest regarding self-analysis and self-direction is mentioned by St. Thomas. The natural inclination which one has to one virtue will generally be accompanied by a natural inclination to a parallel vice. For example, one who is naturally brave is apt to be harsh and cruel to others; at least he is less disposed

Formation of Habits: Actions Are the Cause of the Complete Habits: We have explained that a *natural aptitude,* or, as it is sometimes called, an inchoative habit, may be found in individual men. As regards their specific nature, these aptitudes are equally present in all men. If, however, we consider the individual nature, since the passive principle, matter, is never disposed in exactly the same way in two different individuals, we must conclude that these natural aptitudes vary considerably.[33]

The problem we must now solve is: How are we going to develop these inchoative habits, these obscure seeds of latent talents and virtues into complete habits which will dispose the faculties for action? *Habits are caused by actions.* The point is that these actions must somehow be caused by the faculty in which the habit is to be developed. If the faculty, therefore, were merely passive, no habit could be educed. If it were merely active, as for example the agent intellect, there would be no need of habit. "But there is an agent in which there is both the *active* and the *passive* principle of its act, as we see in human acts."[34] We have already indicated the active and passive elements of the various faculties which can be the subjects of these habits. It will be well now to consider the various faculties and point out how they move themselves and move each other in such a way that the active element will be the principle of the act, and the passive element will allow for the production of habit.

In General: The possible intellect is primarily *passive;* it must therefore be actuated by the agent intellect. Being in act, it conceives the object and reasons about conclusions; it also moves the will in the order of the end, for the good moves the appetite.

---

naturally to humaneness and kindness. Now men are ordered to the perfect good as to their end; to attain this end, therefore, it is necessary for them to develop inclinations to all the virtues. Since, however, the various virtues are not all natural even in their inception in the same individual, it is necessary to cultivate the virtues we lack by practicing their acts. (Cf. *De Virt. in Com.,* VIII, ad 10.)

[33] For this reason it is essential, in developing talents of children, to make a study of each individual's temperament in order to discover along what lines he may be better educated.

[34] *S. Th.,* I–II, 51, 2, *c.*

The will in its turn is able to move the sense appetite. Clearly, then, man by his own action can reduce himself to act precisely because he has both active and passive principles. "Therefore by such actions habits can be caused in their agents, not indeed with regard to the first active principle, but with regard to that principle of the act which is a moved mover."[35] The repeated action partly actuates what is passive in the faculty, and in time the habit is formed. "For everything that is passive and moved by another is *disposed* by the action of the agent. And, therefore, if the acts be multiplied, a certain quality is formed in the operative potency which is passive and moved, and this quality is called a habit."[36]

Let us now try to understand in particular how these habits are formed in the various faculties. It is obvious, of course, that they are formed differently in the apprehensive and appetitive faculties.

In the Apprehensive Faculties: Regarding the intellect and the internal sense faculties, the action consists in being assimilated to the object of knowledge. A habit, therefore, is formed in the intellect in as much as, through the operation of the agent intellect, the understood species remains habitually as an imperfect act, and can later help to actuate the faculty fully when the will so chooses. Such a habit could be, for example, a principle that is immediately evident, as *the whole is greater than the part*. As to the formation of the habits of science, they are caused in the intellect in as much as the intellect is moved by the first principles.

In the Appetitive Faculties: The action of the appetitive faculty consists in a certain inclination to that which is desirable. In order, therefore, that a habit be formed in an appetitive faculty, that faculty must be inclined to a determined object.

Now in inanimate beings of nature, inclination follows form (the natural form); and this inclination is to one determined object, to one determined end. Hence, there is no need of habits

---

[35] *S. Th.*, I–II, 51, 2, *c.*
[36] *Loc. cit.*

in such beings; they must necessarily act as they do. A stone must fall to the ground; smoke must rise.

Rational beings, however, since they are not determined to one act, but can incline themselves to various contraries, obviously do not have a form which inclines them to this rather than to that act or object. They must be determined by their mover, that is, by themselves, to this or that. And by virtue of the fact that they so determine themselves to one action, they become somewhat disposed toward such an action.

Now when these acts are multiplied in the same direction, with the same determination, the inclination or disposition is made firm and strengthened; and, in time, the superimposed disposition (*dispositio superinducta*) becomes a quasi-form (*per modum naturae*) which tends to one definite operation and object.[37]

As we have learned, the will determines itself through the intellect. Hence the will, using reason as a guide, forms its own habits. This fact is nicely exemplified in the formation of the habit of justice. As for the lower appetites, by being subject to the higher appetite and to reason, and by thus acting in accord with reason, they form good habits which strengthen the political control of reason over the passions. We might say that a good habit in these lower faculties is a disposition to obey reason, a disposition which has been sealed and impressed by reason.

Actions, therefore, do cause habits, especially actions that are multiplied and intensified. "Habit is caused by action, in so far as a passive potency is moved by an active principle."[38] But what of a single act?

Is One Act Sufficient to Form a Habit? The answer is "yes," with regard to the *intellect*. "It is possible for a certain active principle to overcome entirely, by one act, the power of its passive principle. Thus one self-evident proposition convinces the intellect, so that it gives a firm assent to the conclusion."[39]

---

[37] Cf. *De Virt. in Com.*, IX. [38] *Loc. cit.* [39] *Loc. cit.*

"With regard to the *lower apprehensive potencies,* however, the same act needs to be repeated many times to be firmly impressed on the memory."[40]

The same holds true for the *appetitive powers* — one act will not suffice to form a habit. St. Thomas explains:

> It is clear that the active principle, which is reason, cannot entirely overcome the appetitive faculty in one act. For the appetitive power is inclined variously, and to many things, while the reason judges, in a single act, what should be willed in the light of various conditions and circumstances. Therefore, the appetitive power is not entirely overcome, so as to be inclined naturally to the same thing in the majority of cases, which inclination belongs to the habit of [moral] virtue. Therefore, a habit of virtue cannot be caused by one act, but only by many.[41]

ARTICLE V: Growth and Decrease of Habits[42]

The question of the growth and decrease of habits is both difficult and important. It is important, of course, because we want to know how we can develop our good habits and destroy, if possible, those which are evil. It is difficult, however, to understand how a spiritual or quasi-spiritual accidental form can increase or decrease and yet remain the same kind of form or habit.

In things extended, to be sure, increase is easily understood; it is but a quantitative addition. A body becomes larger and heavier by acquiring more extension and more weight. In regard to qualities, however, the question is quite different. The form specifies; it gives a perfection which allows no growth or decrease. A species is like a number, and one cannot add to a number without changing it. Hence, whatever departs from a specific perfection, whether by addition or subtraction, changes the species.

---

[40] *De Virt. in Com.,* IX.
[41] *Loc. cit.*
[42] *S. Th.,* I–II, 52 and 53.

The problem, therefore, is this: since habits are forms, will an increase or a diminution of their perfection cause a complete change of species, so that the habit will completely change? Or, can a habit grow or diminish and still remain the same kind of habit?

Now there are two ways in which some forms may receive a change and still remain in the same species: (1) the form or habit itself can increase; (2) the participation by the subject can be more or less perfect.

1. There are forms which receive their species from something to which they are related. Such forms can increase or decrease without changing species. This is due to the oneness of that to which they are related, and from which they received their species. The habit of the science of geometry, for example, which receives its species from the subject matter, may increase or decrease according as we learn new geometrical propositions. This increase does not change the fact that this habit is the science of geometry. It is clear that many habits can increase in this manner, since their objects are capable of extending to more or fewer things. True, this cannot be said of all habits.

2. All habits, however, can grow and diminish according to the participation by the subject; that is, the subject can be more or less actuated regarding the perfection of the habit.[43]

It we ask why one subject should be more perfectly actuated than another regarding the perfection of a particular habit, St. Thomas replies that one man may be better disposed than another either because he has prepared himself by more intense actions, or because of a better natural disposition or a more discerning judgment of reason.[44]

---

[43] *"Intenduntur et remittuntur in quantum subjectum reducitur magis in actum ipsarum per actionem agentis causantis eas. Unde virtutes acquisitae augentur ex actibus per quos causantur."* (*De Virt. in Com.*, XI.)

[44] In the supernatural order, the reason would be "a greater gift of grace, which is given to each one according to the measure of the giving of Christ." (*S. Th.*, I–II, 66, 1.)

And the same must be said of the moral virtues which reside in the appetitive potencies; for these habits are formed by the actions of the appetitive faculties, in so far as those faculties are directed by reason. "Therefore a habit, either of virtue or of vice, may be corrupted by a judgment of reason, whenever its motion is contrary to such vice or virtue, whether through ignorance, passion, or deliberate choice."[50]

A Habit Is Destroyed or at Least Diminished Through Mere Cessation From Action: This assertion follows naturally from all that has been said about actions as the cause of habits. Once we cease exercising the acts of a habit, we stop putting obstacles to the opposite acts, and consequently to the formation of the contrary habit. For the acts of a certain habit overcome the causes that might destroy that habit. It is evident, for example, that a moral virtue may enable one to moderate his passions; whenever, therefore, a man fails to control the excesses of passion by virtuous action, these passions grow inordinate because of the attractiveness of the apparent good, and in time they will give rise to actions that are of the contrary vice. Therefore, moral habit or virtue is destroyed by the mere cessation from action.

This is also true of the intellectual habits.[51] For once a man stops using them properly in his process of reasoning, strange fancies will arise in his imagination and dispose the intellect to false conclusions. In this way the intellectual good habits will be diminished and even destroyed.[52]

ARTICLE VI: Division of Habits[53]

To begin with, we should distinguish between the *good* and the *bad* habits. The good habits are those which perfect the nature of

[50] *S. Th.,* I–II, 53, 1, *c.*
[51] Excepting, of course, the habit of principles.
[52] Cf. *S. Th.,* I–II, 53, 3.
[53] *Ibid.,* 54. Cf. also *De Virt. in Com.,* XII.

their subjects by preparing them to elicit actions which perfect their nature; they are called *virtues*. The bad habits, on the contrary, do not perfect but go against the nature of their subjects; they are called *vices*. "In this way a good habit is specifically distinct from a bad habit, since a good habit is one which disposes to an act suitable to the agent's nature, while an evil habit is one which disposes to an act unsuitable to nature."[54]

Virtues:[55] We are, naturally, principally interested in the good habits — the virtues — since they are all-important means for the development and the perfection of the individual. Undoubtedly, the first distinction between virtues which suggests itself to a philosopher is that which arises from the difference in species. Species are distinguished according to that which is formal in the being. The formal aspect of a species is, as we know from logic, the ultimate difference which completes a definition, for it is the ultimate difference which constitutes a species. Consequently, a being which differs from another in its definition differs according to species.

Now, that which completes the definition of virtue and is therefore its formal aspect is *the good*. For virtue is *that which makes a man good and renders his action good* (*quae bonum facit habentem, et opus eius bonum reddit*). Consequently, the diverse classes or species of virtues will be due to the diversity of the good which is in them.

Man, the subject of virtues, is what he is because he is rational; hence, the good of man is a rational good. Here let us note what has previously been shown — namely, that the rational part of man comprises intellect and intellectual appetite. And let us further note that besides the will, which is proportioned to the intellect and hence belongs to the rational part, the sense appetites also must pertain to that same part. This is so because not only do

[54] *S. Th.,* I–II, 54, 3, *c.*
[55] See diagram of the virtues on the following page.

DIAGRAM OF VIRTUES

Virtues are *good* habits. They dispose man to actions that are suitable to his nature. Now the perfection of the nature of man is to be rational. A rational nature, however, is in potency to know all beings, to attain all truth, and to love the good. Hence the good of man is the absolute good. The actions of man which are suitable to his nature will dispose him to attain his end, that is, to know the true and love the good. These actions, therefore, will need to be ordered to understanding the true and to loving the good. The following habits will enable man to place such actions with relative ease, constancy, and delight.

					Virtue	
UNDERSTANDING THE TRUE	Intellect	*Speculative* (contemplation of truth)	Principles that are immediately evident		*Habit of Principles*	INTELLECTUAL VIRTUES
			Principles which result from reasoning regarding	a) Highest truths	*Wisdom*	
				b) Lower truths	*Science*	
		Practical (looks to action, tends to specify the act of the will according to the good presented by the intellect)	True knowledge of things to be made		*Art*	
			True knowledge of things to be done		*Prudence*	
LOVING THE GOOD	Will — Looks to the good due to others				*Justice*	MORAL VIRTUES
	Sense Appetites	Concupiscible	Tempers inordinate desires in accordance with the good of reason		*Temperance*	
		Irascible	Strengthens courage, controls fear, enables us to place difficult acts for the good of reason		*Fortitude*	

1. In the intellect there are three speculative virtues: Habit of Principles, Wisdom, and Science.
2. In the intellect there are two practical virtues: Art and Prudence.
3. In the appetites there are three moral virtues: Justice (in the will), Temperance, and Fortitude (in the sense appetites).

these inferior appetites obey the rational part of man, but they are at times a necessary stimulus and help to the human acts. Consequently, by being subservient to the higher faculties, they participate in the perfection of the rational part of man.

Division of the Good: The good of man, the rational being, is both the good of knowing and the good of loving. But the good is not attributed to these two perfections in the same manner. The good is said of the appetite *formally,* since the *good,* which has the nature of end, is the object of the appetite. But the object of the intellect is the *true*. Consequently, the *good* is attributed to knowledge only materially. To know the true is a good of the cognitive faculty; but in so far as it is a good, it is related not to the cognitive, but to the appetitive potency. For the cognition of the true—because it is a good—is something desirable.

From all this we can readily understand why the virtues which perfect the intellect are of a different species from those which perfect the appetite. Hence, we must distinguish between *the intellectual* and *the moral virtues*. The intellectual virtues perfect the intellect in the order of knowing the true; the moral virtues perfect the various appetites to love the good.

Intellectual Virtues: If we consider the intellectual nature of man in its relation to the knowledge of the true, we find that his means for knowing—namely, the acts of the intellect—differ according to the various objects which comprise the true. In the first place, the knowledge of necessary truths pertains to the *speculative* rather than to the practical intellect, whereas contingent truths are the object of the practical intellect.[56] Now, regarding the necessary truths, the intellect may know:

1. The principles that are immediately evident. This is the *habit of principles*.

2. The conclusions which result from reasoning. There are two classes of such truths:

[56] The speculative and practical intellect are not two distinct faculties, but two functions of the same intellect.

a) Conclusions which are about the highest realities—the ultimate causes—and this knowledge comprises the *habit of wisdom.*

b) Conclusions which manifest truths that are of a lower order. These are the *habits of science.*

There are, therefore, three intellectual virtues in the speculative intellect: the habit of principles, which St. Thomas often calls *intellect,* the habit of wisdom, and the habit of science.

But what of the contingent truths which are attained by the *practical* intellect? Here, again, we must distinguish between the true knowledge of things to be done by man as man (*recta ratio agibilium*), *i.e.,* the true knowledge of human acts, and the true knowledge of the things to be made, constructed, or fabricated (*recta ratio factibilium*). The first knowledge gives rise to the virtue of *prudence,* the second to the habit of *art.*

The virtue of *prudence* is a mode of knowing (*ratio cognoscendi*) and of rightly judging the free acts of man. This virtue is of the greatest importance in view of the fact that inordinate passions may easily lead one into grave error regarding what is to be done. There is need, therefore, of a directive norm—the virtue of prudence—in order that the intellect may rightly judge each thing concerning the good of man according to his nature and end. This virtue perfects the practical intellect and enables it to govern the other moral virtues which are in the appetitive parts. Indeed, it must be asserted that prudence is the source of all moral virtues, not as an efficient cause actually producing the virtues, but in the sense that no moral virtue can flourish—in fact, none is really possible—unless prudence be its true norm and directrix. For, since acts of the various virtues—such as temperance, fortitude, or justice—must vary constantly according to time, object, place, and the like, there is need of a *new prudential judgment* before each moral action. Without such a judgment, no virtue could function properly.

Now, regarding the things to be made, we need the virtue of *art.* This virtue, St. Thomas explains, is necessary for man because his actions must be so varied in doing the different things which civilized life requires. Such a habit could not be acquired by brute beasts. In evidence of this, we need only compare, for example, the art of building, the various architectures developed by man's ingenuity, to the uniform manner in which birds make their nests. Man, therefore, needs an intellectual habit, the habit of art, to enable him to make things in the best possible manner known to him.

There are, then, five *intellectual* virtues. Three are *speculative:* the habit of principles, wisdom, and science. The other two are *practical:* prudence and art.

Moral Virtues: When we speak of *moral virtues,* we must consider that the good is not attributed to all things human in the same manner. As a matter of fact, we find a threefold distinction of the good in human acts:

1. Regarding our actions which deal with external things that fall to our use, for example, such operations as buying and selling, we should consider not only the good of the subject, but the good of other men as well. In these external transactions with other men, the good of reason demands that everyone receive what is his due. In other words, the proper proportion required for the maintenance and development of human life must be insured. In order, therefore, that our actions may be placed according to the rights of all, we need the virtue of *justice.* This is a moral virtue, since its objects are the human acts. Justice resides in the will.

The second and third distinctions deal with the passions of the concupiscible and irascible appetites. The good of man in the midst of passion must be kept in view; in spite of the ardor and impetus of his passions, a man must not fail to follow the judgment of reason, the prudential judgment. There are two possible cases in which a virtue will prove necessary to restrain passions which might otherwise overcome the judgment of reason.

2. The passions of the concupiscible appetite are sometimes an obstacle to the good of reason because they allure and entice us to do what is not in keeping with the dictates of reason. There is need of a good habit, the virtue of *temperance,* to control the desires and concupiscences of man and to make it not only possible, but even easy and delightful for him to follow the law of nature and of God.

3. When, on the other hand, the passions impede the good of reason not by alluring, but by withdrawing us and causing us to run away from that which is our duty according to the good of reason, a virtue is needed in the irascible appetite. This virtue, which strengthens our courage and enables us to bear hardships and difficulties with perseverance and equanimity, is the virtue of *fortitude.*

There are, then, three *moral* virtues: justice in the will, temperance in the concupiscible appetite, and fortitude in the irascible appetite. These three virtues (the moral virtues) together with prudence are called the *cardinal* virtues. They are so called because all the other virtues are subordinated to and depend upon these major virtues.[57]

Sensory-Motor "Habits": The question may be asked: Should the neuromuscular development which results from constant exercise and which facilitates the operations of the external members

---

[57] To understand the place of the *theological* (supernatural) virtues in the study of the virtues, we must recall a fact which we know from revelation and which, therefore, does not pertain to philosophy — namely, the elevation of man to a supernatural end which is the vision of God. To attain this end, man must be able to perform supernatural actions which are in the order of this end. To perform such actions, he must have the three *theological virtues* — faith, hope, and charity — which enable him to know God, to expect to attain to the possession of Him, and to love Him. These virtues, being supernatural, cannot be acquired by human endeavor; they must be infused by God Himself. Faith is in the intellect, and hope and charity are in the will.

of the body be called a habit? Let us give some examples: a boy learns to play baseball by frequent practice, or to play the piano, or to typewrite. Are these really habits, or mere mechanical reflexes?

Let us recall that two factors are required for the formation of habits: repeated actions and the control of the will. Now it is obvious that both factors are essential in the acquisition of the dispositions which will make future sensory-motor actions more easy. Consequently, such dispositions must, broadly speaking, be called habits rather than entitative dispositions. It is true that these actions may become at times quasi-automatic. Once, for example, the habit of playing the piano is acquired, the pianist no longer adverts to the motion of each finger. But it must be said that these dispositions, which enable him to play with such ease were produced in the beginning by the will moving his fingers to strike a key, and that even now, at least in the initial moment, some act of the will is required to release the series of motions which must follow with ease, grace, and delight.

While we must admit the importance of the organic entitative dispositions needed in the body, which are produced by dint of repetition, it would seem that these dispositions to action are primarily in the soul;[58] for it is the soul which moves the body.

SUMMARY

Article I: *Nature of Habits*

1. A habit, *in general,* is a quality whereby a thing is disposed well or ill, either in itself or in relation to something else.

2. An *operational* habit is a quality or form inhering in an operative potency and inclining that potency to actions of a determinate species.

---

[58] "As to the operations which proceed from the soul through the body, they belong principally to the soul, and secondarily to the body. Now habits are proportioned to their operations. Whence by like acts like habits are formed. Therefore, the dispositions to such operations are principally in the soul. But they can be secondarily in the body, namely, in so far as the body is disposed and enabled with promptness to help in the operations of the soul." (*S. Th.,* I–II, 50, 1, *c.*)

3. In themselves, habits are *imperfect acts;* they do not fully actuate the operative potency but dispose it for the complete act (operation).

Article II: *Need for Habits*

1. Our specifically human faculties of themselves are *indeterminate* and can be actuated in various ways; some of these actuations are not suitable to our nature.

2. Good habits are needed to give a facility in performing those actions which will perfect our nature, and in avoiding those actions which would harm our nature.

Article III: *Subject of Habits*

1. Those operative potencies which are *determinable* in various ways.

2. Those faculties which place the human act — the intellect and will.

3. The sense appetites in as much as they act at the command of reason.

Article IV: *The Cause of Habits*

1. *Specific* nature gives the aptitude or inclination to form habits, e.g., the habit of principles in the possible intellect.

2. *Individual* nature gives the aptitude or bodily disposition to form habits along certain lines, but cannot cause the formed habit.

3. *Actions,* especially intense repeated actions, are the cause of the complete habit.

Article V: *Growth and Decrease of Habits*

1. Habits may *grow* by: (*a*) extension to more things, (*b*) greater participation by the subject.

2. Not every action can increase an existing habit, but only those whose intensity is proportioned to the perfection of the habit.

3. A habit can be *diminished* by contrary actions, and is *destroyed* by the production of the contrary habit.

Article VI: *Division of Habits*

1. A *good* habit (virtue) is one which disposes to action that perfects nature.

2. Five *intellectual* virtues: understanding, wisdom, science, art, prudence.

3. Three *moral* virtues: justice, temperance, fortitude.

EPILOGUE

THE LAST END OF MAN

In the closing pages of THE PHILOSOPHY OF MAN we should like to point out a truth which naturally results from all our findings, and which is of the greatest importance. This truth establishes a firm foundation for a philosophy of morality, that is, for a sound science of ethics. It is this: *the last end of man is happiness in the possession of God*. Let us explain this statement.

Last End and Nature: A limited being is ordered to an end distinct from its nature. It attains its end by action. Indeed, the achievement of the end, the completion and perfection of the being, is the *raison d'être* of action in any limited subject. Now the limits, the boundaries, of action are determined by some principle within the being. Thus a vegetable will not tend to attain its end by the same operations as will an animal. The basic and radical principle within the limited being that determines its action is called nature; it is the essence viewed as the first principle of action necessarily tending to a definite end—and, more precisely, to a definite last end.[1] (This tendency, this inclination, of nature to its ultimate end is through its highest appetite—in the case of man, through the rational appetite, the will.) Now the last end is desired first and is the rule and measure of all that is ordered to the end.[2] It is that good whose possession will fully actuate, fully satisfy, this primary inclination or tendency of

[1] The last end of a non-rational being is attained in every action. This is not true of the last end of man. The human acts merely *dispose* the nature toward or away from the last end. This point is discussed at length in *The Philosophy of Morality*. It should be noted too that a proximate or intermediate end of human action is only relatively an end, for it is but a means to the last end.

[2] "Every beginning of perfection is ordered to complete perfection which is achieved through the last end." (*S. Th.,* I–II, 1, 6, *c.*) ". . . the first good is the last end. . . ." (*Ibid.,* 4, ad 1^{m}.)

nature. We see, then, that the last end and nature are closely related. No nature is understood fully unless we understand also its last end; on the other hand, the last end of a being is understood by understanding its nature. The possession of the supreme good of nature is the completion and full actuation of the nature; it is the last end of nature. In the case of man, we call the possession of this good *happiness.*

Our Knowledge of Natures and Their Ends: How do we rise to a knowledge of a nature and, consequently, to a knowledge of its last end? We have seen that we know what things are by what they do; operations manifest what a thing is, that is to say, they give us a knowledge of the nature of the being from which they proceed. We will recall, too, that limited beings must operate through distinct operative potencies that are ordered to actions perfective of nature, and that these powers are diversified by specifically distinct operations. We have seen that these operations, in turn, are specified by their formal objects.[3] This, then, in the order of discovery, is the sequence of our knowledge: formal object — operation — operative potency — nature — last end.

Last End of Human Nature: Accordingly, in order to rise to a philosophical knowledge of human nature and, consequently, to a knowledge of man's last end, we have instituted a careful formal-object analysis of the operations of man, particularly of the operations proceeding from man as man, that is, from his highest operative potencies — the intellect and the will. The formal object of the intellect, we noted, is being *as being,* without qualification; not under a restricted aspect, as are the formal objects of the various senses, which, consequently, are limited in their material objects as well. Accordingly, the intellect is capable of knowing all being, all truth, including God, who is Pure Being, Absolute Truth, Intelligibility Itself. Moreover, an operative potency of

---

[3] ". . . the perfection of any power is known by the nature of its object. . . ." (*S. Th.*, I–II, 3, 8.) ". . . the final perfection of each power is to attain that in which is found the fulness of its formal object." (*Ibid.*, 3, 7, ad 3^{m}.)

knowledge ordered to absolute truth demands a proportionate appetite ordered to the absolute good. This appetite, the highest appetite in man, is the will, whose formal object is the good *as good* and which, therefore, is in potency to all good, including the absolute good. After recalling these fundamental principles, which were established in the course of our study of man, we are now able to show that the last end of man is the possession of the absolute, the unlimited good — God; and this is happiness.

Argument: Major: The last end of a nature is the attainment, the possession of that good which is the necessitating object of the nature's highest appetite; for such an object when attained will necessarily actuate the most radical and primary potency of that nature.

Minor: Now human nature by its highest appetite, the will, is ordered to the possession of absolute good. This we have discovered by a formal-object analysis of the operation of the will, which is the rational appetite proportioned to the intellect.

Conclusion: Therefore, the last end of human nature, the ultimate end of man, is the possession of the absolute good. Since God alone is the absolute good, man is ordered to God as his last end. The possession of God, therefore, is man's happiness.

No Created Good Can Be Man's Last End: The possession of God is the perfect happiness of man. Nothing else can give man this perfect happiness — whether it be the goods of fortune (wealth, fame, power), the goods of the body (health, beauty, pleasure), or the goods of the soul (wisdom, science, virtue). The reason is that these are imperfect, limited goods. Happiness, however, is the possession of perfect good.

> . . . The object of the will, which is the human appetite, is the universal good; just as the object of the intellect is the universal true. Hence, it is evident that naught can satisfy (*quietare*) man's will, save the universal good. This is to be found, not in anything created, but in God alone, because every creature has goodness by

participation. Wherefore God alone can satisfy (*implere*) the will of man. . . . Therefore in God alone does man's happiness consist.[4]

Perfect Happiness Not in This Life: Perfect happiness excludes every evil. "But in this life every evil cannot be excluded. For this present life is subject to many unavoidable evils; to ignorance on the part of the intellect; to inordinate affection on the part of the appetite, and to many penalties on the part of the body."[5] Furthermore, perfect happiness is the fulfillment of every desire. But ". . . the desire for good cannot be satiated in this life. For man naturally desires the good which he has to be abiding. Now the goods of the present life pass away. . . ."[6]

Imperfect Happiness: Nevertheless, a certain participation of happiness may be had in this life. For men can participate in the Supreme Good by knowing and loving God, though only imperfectly and interruptedly. Hence, men can enjoy happiness, albeit imperfect happiness, in this life.

> . . . Perfect happiness signifies the highest (*ultimam*) perfection. . . . In men, however, according to their present state of life, the highest perfection is had by means of an operation which unites man to God; but this operation neither can be continuous, nor, consequently, is it one only, because operation is multiplied by being discontinued. And for this reason in the present state of life, perfect happiness cannot be attained by man. . . . In so far, therefore, as we fall short of the unity of that operation, so do we fall short of perfect happiness. Nevertheless, there is a participation of happiness and so much the greater, as the operation can be more continuous and more one. Consequently, the active life, which is busy with many things, has less of happiness than the contemplative life, which is busied with one thing — the contemplation of truth.[7]

Happiness Is an Operation: It should be noted that the last end

---

[4] *S. Th.*, I–II, 2, 8, *c*.
[5] *Ibid.*, 5, 3, *c*.
[6] *Loc. cit.*
[7] *S. Th.*, I–II, 3, 2, ad 4^m^.

can be distinguished in a twofold manner: first, the thing itself which we desire to attain — in this case, God Himself; and second, the actual attainment or possession of God, that is to say, happiness. The first is the Uncreated Good, the second is created; it is an operation of man.

> In so far as man's happiness is something created, existing in him, we must say that it is an operation. For happiness is man's supreme (*ultima*) perfection. Now every nature inclined to a distinct end (*intentum*) is perfect in so far as it is in act; since potency without act is imperfect. Consequently, happiness must consist in man's last act. But it is evident that operation is the last act of the operator. . . . Therefore, man's happiness must of necessity consist in an operation.[8]

Moreover, this operation is one of *contemplation,* an operation of the *speculative* rather than of the practical intellect. For ". . . if man's happiness is an operation, it must be man's highest operation. Now man's highest operation is that of his highest power in respect of its highest object. But his highest power is the intellect, whose highest object is the Divine Good, which is the object, not of the practical, but of the speculative intellect. Therefore, happiness consists principally in such an operation, that is, in the contemplation of Divine things."[9]

Essence of Happiness: If we were to ask what is the *essence* of this operation by which we attain the last end, St. Thomas replies: ". . . the essence of happiness consists in an act of the intellect; but the delight that results from happiness pertains to the will."[10] The reason is that while "love ranks above knowledge as a motive power . . . knowledge precedes love in attaining; for nothing is loved save what is known. . . . Consequently, we first attain an intelligible by an act of the intellect. . . ."[11] The delight

---

[8] *Ibid.,* 2, *c.*
[9] *Ibid.,* 5, *c.*
[10] *Ibid.,* 4, *c.*
[11] *Ibid.,* 4, ad 4^m^.

in the will is related to the intellectual possession of the good as a *property;* this delight is necessary for happiness, not as constituting its essence, but as a property.

Man's Threefold Knowledge of God: By way of conclusion, we must say that the perfection of man, even in this life, consists in the knowledge of God and in the love which results from that knowledge. It must, therefore, be possible for man to obtain this knowledge necessary for his perfection. "Since man's perfect good consists in his knowing God in some way, lest so noble a creature should seem to be utterly void of purpose through being unable to obtain its own end, man has been given means of rising to the knowledge of God."[12] Now, during this life there are two ways by which we can come to the knowledge of God.

In the first, ". . . man begins from the lowest things and rising by degrees advances to the knowledge of God."[13] This is the *way of nature,* the way of philosophy, and it is within the power of every rational being. This knowledge, however, is very limited because of the weakness of the human intellect and the perfection of the object of knowledge, God, who is the most perfect being. For this reason, "since it was but a meager knowledge of God that man was able to obtain [by himself] . . . God in His overflowing goodness, in order that man's knowledge of Him might have greater stability, revealed to man certain things about Himself which surpass human intelligence."[14] This is the second way, the way of revelation, the *way of faith.* Because of this revealed knowledge, man is able to reach greater perfection in this life, and to prepare himself for the highest knowledge and love, which is the perfect happiness of the possession of God.

"Hence, man's knowledge of divine things is threefold. The first is when man, by the natural light of reason, rises through creatures to the knowledge of God. The second is when divine

[12] *C. G.,* IV, *Proemium.*
[13] *Loc. cit.*
[14] *Loc. cit.*

truth which surpasses the human intellect comes down to man by revelation, yet as not shown to him that he may see it, but expressed in words so that he may hear it. The third is when the human mind is raised to the perfect intuition of things revealed."[15] Then *man shall see Him as He is.*[16]

---

[15] *Loc. cit.*

[16] Perfect happiness is attained only in the next life. It consists in an immediate intellectual vision of the divine essence. Such a supernatural union is beyond man's natural power. Only through a special elevation of the soul by what theologians call the light of glory can the beatific vision be consummated.

INDEX